BTEC Tech Award

Sport

Student Book

Katie Jones
Katy Parker
Katherine Howard

Published by Pearson Education Limited, 80 Strand, London, WC2R 0RL.

www.pearsonschoolsandfecolleges.co.uk

Copies of official specifications for all Pearson qualifications may be found on the website: qualifications.pearson.com

Text © Pearson Education Limited 2022
Editorial by QBS Learning
Typeset by QBS Learning
Original illustrations © Pearson Education Limited 2022

First published 2022

26 25 24 23 22
10 9 8 7 6 5 4 3 2 1

British Library Cataloguing in Publication Data
A catalogue record for this book is available from the British Library

ISBN 978 1 292 44458 1

Acknowledgements
The publisher would like to thank the following for their kind permission to reproduce copyright material.

Text
Component 1: World Health Organisation: p. 8, Call for authors, Special issue: Interventions for the treatment of persons with obesity, © 2022, World Health Organisation; **The English Federation of Disability Sport**: p. 14, Rankin, Mary-Anne, Understanding the barriers to participation in sport; 2012, EFDS; **Headway:** p. 23, Concussion in sport; © Headway; Active Nation: p. 24, Disability sport; © 2019, Active Nation; **Guardian News & Media Limited:** p. 33, The big bike helmet debate: 'You don't make it safe by forcing cyclists to dress for urban warfare' by Peter Walker, © 2022 Guardian News & Media Limited, 21 Mar 2017; **National Health Service:** p. 54, Moderate intensity and Vigorous intensity , 2022 © Crown copyright, Contains public sector information licensed under the Open Government Licence v3.0.

Tables
Component 3: BMJ Publishing Group Ltd: p. 155, Han, T., Leer, E., Seidell, J. and Lean, M. (1995) *Waist circumference action levels in the identification of cardiovascular risk factors: prevalence study in a random sample.* BMJ (Clinical research ed.), 311. 1401-5. 10.1136/bmj.311.7017.1401; **BrianMac Sports Coach:** p. 162, Mackenzie, B. (2004) *Ruler Drop Test.* Available from: https://www.brianmac.co.uk/rulerdrop.htm [Accessed 29/6/2022]; **Harcourt Publishers:** p. 148, 152 and 156, Davis, B. et al. (2000) *Physical fitness and fitness testing.* In Davis, B. et al. Physical Education and the Study of Sport. 4th ed. London: Harcourt Publishers, p. 123 and p. 129; **Harper Collins Publishers Limited:** p. 143, Bizley, K. et al. (2010) *BTEC First Sport Level 2,* London, Harper Collins Publishers Limited, p. 303, Figure 3; **Lippincott Williams & Wilkins:** p. 153, McArdle, W. et al. (2000) *Essentials of Exercise Physiology,* 2nd ed. Philadelphia: Lippincott Williams & Wilkins, p. 394; **M. Evans and Company, Inc**.: p. 145, Cooper, K. H. (1982) *The Aerobics Program for Total Well-Being.* New York: M. Evans and Company, Inc.; **The National Archives**: p. 154, Contains public sector information licensed under the Open Government Licence v3.0; **National Register of Personal Trainers**: p. 149, © 2000-2022 National Register of Personal Trainers; **Nelson Thornes:** p. 144 and p. 160, Beashel, P., Sibson, A., Taylor, J. (2001) *The World of Sport Examined.* United Kingdom: Nelson Thornes; **Oxford University Press:** p. 165, Hede, C. et al (2011) *PE Senior Physical Education for Queensland*. UK: Oxford University Press, pp. 178–179; **Topend Sports**: p. 145, Wood, R. (2012) *Cooper Fitness Test Norms.* Topend Sports Website, https://www.topendsports.com/testing/norms/cooper-12minute.htm [Accessed 20 June 2022], p. 146, Wood, R. (2008) *push-up test: Home fitness tests.* Topend Sports Website, https://www.topendsports.com/testing/tests/home-pushup.htm, [Accessed 20 June 2022] and p. 157, Wood, R. (2008) *T-Test of Agility.* Topend Sports Website, https://www.topendsports.com/testing/tests/t-test.htm, [Accessed 16 June 2022]; **Wiley:** p. 161, Corbin, C.B. and Lindsey, R. (1994) *Concepts of Fitness & Wellness* as cited in Jacaranda Outcomes 1 PDHPE Preliminary Course 5th Edition (published by Wiley), Chapter 5: Physical Fitness Training and Movement Efficiency; **YMCA:** p. 147, Sinning, W.E., Golding, L.A. and Myers, C.R. (1989) *Y's Way to Physical Fitness: The Complete Guide to Fitness Testing and Instruction.* United States: YMCA of the USA.

Photographs
The publisher would like to thank the following for their kind permission to reproduce their photographs.

(Key: b-bottom; c-centre; l-left; r-right; t-top)

Component 1: 123RF: Stockbroker p. 6, Nosonjai p. 10(b), Olga Yastremska p. 12, Petr Joura p. 21(t), Veronastudio p. 38, Leonello calvetti p. 47(tl); **Alamy Stock Photo:** Kevin Britland p. 10(t), SD p. 15(b), Mark Pain p. 26, Andrey Baturin p. 32, Barrington Coombs/PA Images p. 40; **Shutterstock**: Ericsmandes p. 3, Master1305 p. 4, Matimix p. 15(t), Olena Yakobchuk p. 17, Jim David p. 20(l), Luiserossa p. 20(c), Veniamin Kraskov p. 20(r), Ahmad.faizal p. 21(c), Flashon Studio p. 21(b), Ljupco Smokovski p. 22, Fotogrin p. 23, 101akarca p. 24, Marco Ciccolella p. 25, Torwaistudio p. 28, Wavebreakmedia p. 30, Mike Flippo p. 31, Michael Woodruff p. 33(l), Maridav p. 33(r), Iurii Racenkov p. 34, Wavebreakmedia p. 35(t), Marino Bocelli p. 35(b), La vector p. 36, Leonard Zhukovsky p. 37, Caimacanul p. 44(l), Wayhome studio p. 44(r), Shot4Sell p. 46, Mybox p. 47(cr), Sport08 p. 47(tr), Avilika p. 48, Nicholas Piccillo p. 52(t), Pazargic Liviu p. 52(b), Nick Stubbs p. 57, Dmity Trush p. 60, Dragon Images p. 61.

Component 2: Alamy Stock Photo: John Fryer p. 69, Juergen Hasenkopf 75(t), REUTERS p. 75(b), Julian Eales p. 76, Yew! Images/Cultura Creative RF p. 78(bl), Sport In Pictures p. 83(tr), Xinhua p. 83(c), Frank Sorge/Agencja Fotograficzna Caro p. 84, Mike Egerton/PA Images p. 88, Cal Sport Media p. 92, David Collingwood p. 93, Robert Hoetink p. 95, Michael Weber/imageBROKER p. 96(l); Orange Pictures/Orange Pics BV p. 96(c), Carl Recine/Reuters p. 96(r), Dean Williams p. 97, Nigel French/PA Images p. 99, Juergen Hasenkopf p. 102, Mark Pain p. 106, Juergen Schwarz p. 107, Eric Audras/PhotoAlto p. 114, Afripics p. 121; **Getty Images:** Jamie Grill/Tetra Images p. 65, Vm/E+ p. 110, SolStock/E+ p. 112, Kali9/E+ p. 116, Richard Newstead/Moment, p. 118; **Shutterstock:** Ifong p. 66(l), Vecton p. 67 (Figure 2.2), Diego Barbieri p. 68, Yin Bogu p. 71(t), Ulrik Pedersen/CSM p. 71(c), Celso Pupo p. 71(b), PeopleImages.com - Yuri A p. 85, Jacob Lund p. 86, NotarYES p. 87.

Component 3: 123RF: Dotshock p. 174, Matimix, p. 184 and 191, Anton Gvozdikov p. 189, Scott Griessel p. 207, Diego Vito cervo p. 209(cr), Mark Bowden p. 221; **Pearson Education:** Q2A Media Services Inc. p. 133 and 177(t), Helen Cross p. 144(c), PDQ Digital Media Solutions Ltd p. 154(bc), 173, 179, 186 (figure 3.14) and 203(c), Oxford Designers & Illustrators Ltd p. 170 and 204(b), Jon Barlow p. 198, Pearson Education Ltd p 200, HL Studios p. 211(b); **Shutterstock:** Pressmaster p. 127 and 154(bl), Andrey Burmakin p. 128, Sheliakin Maksim p .132, Shutterstock p. 135, Nicholas Piccillo p. 146(t&b) and 153, Tom Wang p. 147, Microgen p. 148(t), 162 and 169(b), Jacob Lund p. 150, Watchares Hansawek p. 152 and 169(t), File404 p. 163, Dirima p. 176, wavebreakmedia p. 177(bl), Skydive Erick p. 178, aaltair p. 180, Peter Bernik p. vi(cl) and p. 182(c), WoodysPhotos p. vi(bl) and p. 182(bl), Rawpixel.com p. vi(br) and p. 183, Jiang Dao Hua p. 188, Capifrutta p. 192, Matimix p. 199, Alila Medical Media p. 202, Juice Flair p. 203(t), Blamb p. 204(t), Artur Didyk p. 205, Teguh Mujiono p. 206, Martan p. 208, GraphicsRF.com p. 209(l), Sportoakimirka p. 209(tr), Taka1022 p. 211(t), Maridav p. 219, Sportoakimirka p. 223 and 225.

Answers: Shutterstock: Vazzen p. 234.

Cover images: Drazen/Getty Images

All other images © Pearson Education with thanks to David Spencer.

Websites
Pearson Education Limited is not responsible for the content of any external internet sites. It is essential for teachers to preview each website before using it in class so as to ensure that the URL is still accurate, relevant and appropriate. We suggest that teachers bookmark useful websites and consider enabling learners to access them through the school/college intranet.

Notes from the publisher
Pearson has robust editorial processes, including answer and fact checks, to ensure the accuracy of the content in this publication, and every effort is made to ensure this publication is free of errors. We are, however, only human, and occasionally errors do occur. Pearson is not liable for any misunderstandings that arise as a result of errors in this publication, but it is our priority to ensure that the content is accurate. If you spot an error, please do contact us at resourcescorrections@pearson.com so we can make sure it is corrected.

Contents

CONTENTS

About this book

This book is designed to support you when you are taking a BTEC Tech Award in Sport.

About your BTEC Tech Award

Congratulations on choosing a BTEC Tech Award in Sport. This exciting and challenging course will introduce you to the sport, activity and fitness sector. By studying for your Award you will gain the important knowledge, understanding and skills that are the foundations for working in this area. To prepare you for working in this sector you will learn about the different types and providers of sport and physical activity, as well as the different types of participant and their needs. You will also learn about the different fitness tests, methods of training, and supporting equipment and technology that can be used. You will also have the opportunity to apply your learning by planning and implementing your own session plans for different groups of people.

How you will be assessed

You will be assessed in two different ways. Components 1 and 2 are assessed through internal assessment. This means that your teacher will give you a Pearson-set assignment and indicate to you the deadline for completing it. The assignment will cover what you have been learning about and will be an opportunity to apply your knowledge and skills. You teacher will mark your assignment and award you with a grade. Your assessment for Component 3 will be an external assessment. This will be an external assessment that is set and marked by Pearson. You will have a set time in which to complete this external assessment. The external assessment will be an opportunity to bring together what you have learned in Components 1, 2 and 3.

About the authors

Katie Jones

Katie is a current practitioner in sport- and health-related vocational education. She has over 25 years' experience in this field and a wealth of experience in writing assessor, student and teaching materials as well as specifications and assessments. Katie also holds a senior standards verifier position and has had a number of quality standards roles.

Katy Parker

Katy has over 10 years' experience of teaching across a range of vocational subjects at FE and HE level. She has contributed to a number of Pearson qualifications, and is passionate about encouraging young people to get outdoors and be active.

Katherine Howard

Katherine has over 20 years' experience as a sports practitioner working in schools and colleges in the UK and overseas. She is an experienced author and has written textbooks, teaching materials and online resources. Katherine also works as a subject expert, curriculum developer, content writer and assessor, and holds a number of senior assessment roles. She has enjoyed working with awarding bodies for different sport and PE qualifications.

How to use this book

The book has been designed in a way that will help you to easily navigate through your course. Each component from the course is covered in a separate chapter that makes clear what you are learning and how this will contribute to your assessment. There are opportunities for you to test your understanding of key areas, as well as activities that will challenge and extend your knowledge and skills. You will get the most from this book if you use each feature as part of your study. The different features will also help you develop the skills that will be important in completing your assignments as well as preparing you for your external assessment.

Features of the book

This book is designed in spreads, which means that each pair of facing pages represents a topic of learning. Each spread is about one hour of lesson time. Your teacher may ask you to work through a spread during a lesson or in your own time. Each spread contains a number of features that will help you to check what you are learning and offer opportunities to practise new skills.

Getting started A short activity or discussion that will introduce you to what you will be covering in the lesson.

Activity These will help you learn about the topic. You may be asked to work in pairs, groups or on your own.

Link it up This indicates where what you're learning about is covered in another part of the course.

Key terms Important words or terms are defined.

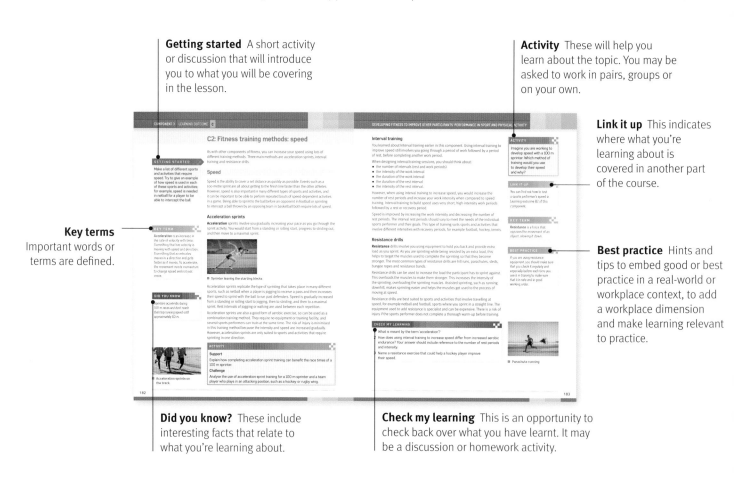

Best practice Hints and tips to embed good or best practice in a real-world or workplace context, to add a workplace dimension and make learning relevant to practice.

Did you know? These include interesting facts that relate to what you're learning about.

Check my learning This is an opportunity to check back over what you have learnt. It may be a discussion or homework activity.

At the end of each learning aim there is a section that outlines how you will be assessed and provides opportunities for you to build skills for assessment.

Checkpoint This feature is designed to allow you to assess your learning. The 'strengthen' question helps you to check your knowledge and understanding of what you have been studying, while the 'challenge' questions are an opportunity to extend your learning.

Assessment Activity This is a practice assessment that reflects the style and approach of an assignment brief. In Component 2, tasks in the assessment activity features will be similar to those you should expect in your external assessment.

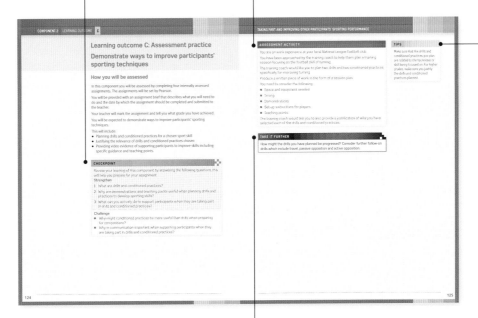

Tip A hint or tip that will help you with your assessment.

Take it further This provides suggestions for what you can do to further the work you've done in the practice assessment.

01 Preparing participants to take part in sport and physical activity

Introduction

Participating in sport and physical activity is a key ingredient in physical and mental well-being. In 2021, it was reported that 28 million adults, and 3.2 million children and young people, met the expected weekly participation levels. The use of technology continues to attract people to participate in sport and physical activity. Watching their role models enhance their performance also helps.

In Component 1, you will initially focus on the types of sports available for everyone to participate in and enjoy. While learning about the types of sports and physical activities available, you will explore the benefits of participation for various target groups. Although the number of children and young people taking part in sport is 3.2 million, this is only 44.6 per cent of the cohort. Component 1 investigates the barriers to participation and ways to address these for each target group.

You will investigate the clothing and equipment needed for participation, as well as technology available to support and enhance performance. Individuals can be motivated by technology, but you will also explore the limitations of technology and the impact on performance.

Concluding the component, you will appreciate the components of a warm-up before delivering a warm-up session to your group.

LEARNING OUTCOMES

In this component you will:

A	explore types and provision of sport and physical activity for different types of participant
B	examine equipment and technology required for participants to use when taking part in sport and physical activity
C	be able to prepare participants to take part in sport and physical activity.

A1: Types and providers of sport and physical activities 1: types of sports and NGBs

KEY TERMS

Team sports are sports which can only be played as a team, they cannot be played individually. An example of a team sport is football.

Individual sports are sports that a participant can play on their own against an opponent. An example of an individual sport is tennis.

Sport can be defined as a group or individual activity which involves physical exertion, while having a competitive edge with rules and regulations to guide the performance. In this section, you will discover examples of team and individual sports as well as the role the National Governing Bodies (NGBs) play in governing a sport on a national level.

ACTIVITY

Challenge

Discuss the difference between a team sport and an individual sport:
- Is it only the number of people playing?
- Do team and individual sports both have rules and regulations?
- Do team and individual sports both have competitions?
- Do team and individual sports both involve physical exertion?
- Do team and individual sports both have an NGB?

◨ A wide variety of team sports and individual sports are available

Team and individual sports

There are many examples of **team sports**, such as football, rugby, netball and hockey, which you may have played at school. Other examples include basketball, volleyball, cricket and rounders. All these team sports need rules, regulations, competition and an NGB. These help individuals work together to achieve goals in their performance and outcome.

In **individual sports**, a person is solely responsible for their own actions. Like team sports, individual sports also need rules, regulations, competition and an NGB to achieve goals in their performance and outcome. Individual sports include athletics, squash, badminton, snooker and boxing.

National governing bodies

NGBs play a key role in supporting each sport to grow on a national level. The focus of the NGB is to control and regulate the sport while developing the sport, promoting participation and developing coaching knowledge and delivery.

One example of an NGB is the RFL, Rugby Football League. The RFL's strategy is 'Committed to developing and growing rugby league at all levels'. The RFL is paramount in signposting the laws of the game and securing discipline within the game as well as supporting players and coaches from grass roots to the professional level. The RFL educates players and coaches on anti-doping, promoting websites to enhance the understanding of drugs and rugby league. It offers medical advice, in particular on concussion injuries. One key area of focus for the RFL is safeguarding all players, coaches, officials and spectators. Another is enhancing knowledge and understanding through education programmes. Rugby league prides itself as an inclusive sport and, through the values of the RFL, is committed to increasing initiatives to include all members of the community in the game.

ACTIVITY

Support

1 Select an NGB, such as England Netball or the Football Association. Create a wall display to highlight the aim of the NGB. Make sure you include information such as:
   - the year NGB was founded
   - current campaigns the NGB is delivering
   - how important the campaigns are to increase participation in the sport.

Challenge

2 How does the NGB support players, coaches, officials and spectators?

3 How does the NGB educate about safeguarding?

BEST PRACTICE

All sports should belong to an NGB. Their importance goes beyond rules and regulations, by monitoring player participation from grass roots to international level.

CHECK MY LEARNING

1 Select one team sport and one individual sport. List five rules from each sport.

2 Why are NGBs important?

3 Select an NBG of your choice. Describe their role when governing the sport.

KEY TERM

National governing bodies (NGBs) are organisations that govern and regulate sports.

DID YOU KNOW?

Sport England reported that, between May 2020 and May 2021, walking was the most participated in physical activity in the UK. About 3.4 million participants recorded two sessions per week within a 28-day period. Cycling also increased in participation levels from 6.3 million participants in 2019–2020 to 7.5 million participants between May 2020 and May 2021.

DID YOU KNOW?

British Cycling, the NGB for cycling and mountain biking, offers valuable advice on the type of bike to use for the terrain you intend to ride. The NGB also educates participants on the different mountain terrains such as downhill, four cross and cross country; providing knowledge and understanding to support new and experienced participants. All outdoor and adventurous activities have an NGB.

A1: Types and providers of sport and physical activities 2: benefits of taking part

☐ Taking part in sport and physical activity has extensive physical benefits

Participating in sport and physical activity has numerous benefits. As stated by Sport England, 'sport does not only have an economic value but a social value including physical and mental health, well-being, individual and community development'. In this section, you will discover the benefits of taking part in sport as well as learning more about outdoor and adventure activities.

The benefits of participating in physical activity

What do we mean when we say that sport participation provides a physical benefit? The NHS offers information on the physical benefits of sport. Research has shown that, by participating in sport and physical activity, a person can reduce their risk of coronary heart disease, a stroke, type 2 diabetes as well as some cancers. Scientists state that participation can lower the rate of an early death by 30 per cent.

Knowing the benefits of sport and physical activity is key in increasing participation. The main benefits include:

- Improved fitness levels: sport and physical activity will improve each element of fitness; your heart will be improved by aerobic activities making blood pump more effectively around the body. The muscles will be stronger but also bones will strengthen, resulting in improved bone density. Flexibility will be improved, reducing the risk of musculoskeletal impacts.
- Development of leadership skills: the leader's role is to unite a team to accomplish a set target. Communication, decision-making and supporting others to overcome adversity are key skills in leading a team and this can be transferred to their life outside of sport.
- Development of teamwork skills: encouraging a positive attitude to the set target, working together to make the target a success while gaining respect can be the recipe for a successful team.
- Building resilience and self-confidence from competition: resilience is the ability to recover quickly from difficulties. Participation in sport and physical activity can often be challenging with decision-making the key to overcoming the challenge. Building resilience, which will develop an individual's confidence, can result in improved performance individually and as a team.
- The chance to meet new people: Age UK reported that 1.4 million older people feel lonely in the UK, with the **ONS** discussing a new survey which suggested that one in 20 people aged over 16 years feel lonely. The figures suggest that meeting new people can have an impact on many individuals, and sport and physical activity are a route to new friendships and an improved social life.

Outdoor activities

Outdoor activities are a key ingredient in the variety of sports offered in the UK that enable everyone to find a sport or physical activity they are interested in. Traditional sports introduced in schools do not attract everyone to participate on a regular basis. By introducing different experiences, all individuals can find a sport or physical activity that motivates them to join. Cycling is currently the most participated in outdoor activity in Great Britain.

Outdoor activities are a selection of recreational activities which take place in an outdoor setting. Most people who regularly participate in an outdoor activity do so for the enjoyment they feel when engaged in the activity. Some individuals also appreciate the challenge, and health and fitness benefits. There are many outdoor activities. The first step is to find the one which would interest you. Would it be: hiking, canoeing, caving, kayaking, rock climbing, sailing or scuba diving?

The benefits of taking part in outdoor activities

Research has concluded that those participating in outdoor and adventure activities benefit from them. The benefits can include (Figure 1.1):

Offers an opportunity to learn new skills which can boost confidence and happiness whilst preventing boredom.

Offers an opportunity to experience a positive risk-taking activity whilst having time away from normal life and more importantly electronic devices.

Benefits of outdoor activities

Finding an environment where new friends who like the same activity can meet. The participant can feel positive about meeting another person who shares their interest and can bond over the experience.

Outdoor activities can improve a person's self-esteem and increase their confidence. A sense of achievment can boost the mental health of the participant.

◘ Figure 1.1: Benefits of outdoor activities

ACTIVITY

Support

Choose a new outdoor and adventure activity. Watch video clips or take part in the activity yourself. Now answer the following questions.

1 Which outdoor and adventure activity did you take part in or watch?
2 Which new skills did you learn, or would you have learned if taking part?
3 Did you or would you have the opportunity to meet new people?

Challenge

4 Would the activity allow you to relax and forget life stresses? Why is this important?

DID YOU KNOW?

The NHS have reported that one in four adults, and one in 10 children, experience a mental health condition at some point in their lifetime. As a result, those directly involved with young people and adults are being encouraged to attend a 'mental health first aid' course.

DID YOU KNOW?

Research suggests that reducing screen time allows a person to spend more time with friends and family, connecting through experiences. As a result, a person can reduce the symptoms of stress, depression and anxiety.

CHECK MY LEARNING

1 State four benefits of participating in sport.
2 Highlight three benefits of participating in an outdoor activity.
3 How can physical health benefit from participating in sport and physical activity?

A1: Types and providers of sport and physical activities 3: physical fitness activities

The World Health Organization (WHO) defines physical activity as 'any bodily movement produced by the skeletal muscles that requires energy expenditure'. WHO states that moderate and vigorous physical activity improves physical and mental health for everyone.

Taking part in sport and physical activity sessions is exciting as well as rewarding. The benefits of sport and physical activity sessions include (Figure 1.2):

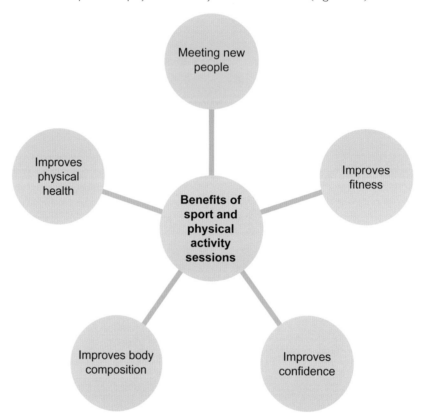

◘ Figure 1.2: Benefits of sport and physical activity sessions

The following case studies show how each of the benefits of taking part in sport and physical activity is met:

1 Deeks is a young adult who has been introduced to mountain biking, he is keen to participate regularly as he appreciates that the benefit of taking part in the activity will allow him to **meet new people**. As a young adult who works full time and has lost touch with his school friends, he feels it is important to participate in an activity which offers an opportunity to meet people who like the same outdoor activity as him while offering the opportunity to meet socially and build friendships.

2 Jessica is an older adult who has been diagnosed with **hypertension**, she is keen to listen to the advice from the NHS and **improve her physical health.** The advice is to participate in regular exercise to lower her blood pressure and Jessica is keen to join a rambling group who also socialise, so that she can make new friends to support her with hypertension.

3 Hetty is a five-year-old with a hearing impairment who has recently started school and is being encouraged by her mum and dad to join the multi sports group which is offered by the local sports development team at her school. Hetty is a shy little girl, and her mum and teachers believe participating in the group will **boost her confidence** to join in and enjoy an unfamiliar activity. Her parents and teachers hope to see Hetty feel more confident around school and with her work as a result.

4 Pedro is 18 years old and has recently had a prosthetic leg fitted. He is feeling very confident and has **set a fitness goal** to motivate him to use the new limb while appreciating how he can adapt activities to be able to participate in sport and physical activity with his friends. Pedro hopes that, by improving the strength in his body, he will make full use of his prosthetic limb and experience outdoor activities for the first time. The fitness goal he has set will hopefully keep him on track, make the activities more effective to enable progress and give him a sense of achievement when targets are met.

5 TJ is 50 years old and is worried about type 2 diabetes after hearing reports in the news and on social media. TJ would like to **improve his body composition** so that he can improve his health and mental well-being to improve how he looks and feels.

ACTIVITY

Support

1 Create a podcast or audio recording. Introduce a case study that includes the benefits of participating in sport and physical activity.

Challenge

2 Interview a member of staff or parent on their opinion of the benefits of participating in sport and physical activity.

3 Share the podcast with the group so that you can listen to each other's. You could use the school's platform to share your podcast.

CHECK MY LEARNING

1 Define the term 'physical activity'.

2 State three benefits of participating in sport and physical activity.

3 Create a case study using a member of your family. Summarise how they would benefit from participating in sport and physical activity. Share the case study with your family member and teacher.

DID YOU KNOW?

Loneliness affects 40 per cent of young people as well as two million aged over 75. The Marmalade Trust, the UK's leading charity supporting loneliness, conducted a study in 2022 concluding that 500,000 older people go at least five or six days a week without seeing or speaking to anyone. A worrying statistic, as loneliness has been linked to a number of health conditions including increased cardiovascular disease, increased hypertension and an increased risk of dementia. One way of tackling loneliness is, where possible, to take part in sport and physical activity, which gives the opportunity to meet people and develop friendships.

A1: Types and providers of sport and physical activities 4: providing activities

With over 60 million people in the UK all being encouraged to play sport, it is essential that facilities and resources are available in each community. The provision of sport is often the key ingredient in encouraging individuals to participate on a regular basis. Sport England helps people and communities across the country to build a 'sporting habit for life' while protecting playing fields from development so that more sports can be in the heart of each community.

The provision for sport and physical activity can be categorised into three areas: public sector provision, private sector provision and voluntary sector provision.

Public sector provision

Public sector provision provides 'sport for all' in local facilities such as leisure centres and schools. The provision is provided by government and local authorities using money from taxes to meet the aim of 'sport for all'. In your community, public sector sport provision could be the local swimming pool, skate park, sports fields within a park or local school or village hall used for martial arts, aerobic sessions or dancing.

Private sector provision

Private sector provision provides sport through individuals or companies who invest their own money to offer a business considering the demands of communities while making a profit. In your community, you may have the opportunity to become a member of a private gym (such as a hotel-run gym or a David Lloyd gym), which offers indoor sports and indoor and outdoor swimming pools. You may be able to go to a privately run climbing wall that uses part of its profits to reinvest in creating more challenging climbs and bouldering walls.

Voluntary sector provision

Whereas the voluntary sector relies on local volunteers to offer sport and physical activities, the facilities are often hired from local authorities. These facilities are usually provided by the public sector. In your community, there may be football teams run by volunteers, for various age groups using pitches within a park owned by the local council (public sector), or church halls offering dance classes for all age groups as well as Scout and Guide groups that offer outdoor activities as part of their provision. Most clubs, like hockey and athletic clubs that people join to enable them to participate in competitive sport, are in the voluntary sector.

◻ A public outdoor swimming pool

◻ A private swimming pool

Characteristics of the public, private and voluntary sectors

What are the characteristics of each sector?

	Aims	Funding source	Quality of the provision	Accessibility
Public	To provide provision in local communities with a low cost to encourage participation	Taxes National Lottery	Purposeful and safe Maintained by a local authority budget	Available in most communities Low cost
Private	To make a profit while meeting the demands of current trends in sport participation	Investors	High-quality changing rooms Enhanced sports hall surface Regularly painted	Only available in areas where there is enough demand Higher cost
Voluntary	To empower local people to come together, be more active	Fund raising Sponsorship Members' subs	Purposeful and safe as facilities are often hired from public sector Maintained by a local authority budget	Available in most communities Low cost, but relies on fundraising and sponsorship

Advantages and disadvantages of public, private and voluntary sector provision

- Cost of participation will vary for each sector.
- Subsidised cost for public sector provision, expensive memberships for private sector provision and a small fee for voluntary sector provision.
- Access to different types of sport and physical activities.
- Public and voluntary sector will offer sport which meets the needs of the community.
- Private sector provision will offer high-standard facilities with sports which are trendy at the moment.
- Additional services such as a crèche or sports therapist.
- Public sector provision will offer a crèche for a short period of time within the day, whereas private sector provision will offer a crèche for longer periods of time, beauty and injury therapists as well as a shop with quality sports clothing and equipment.
- The voluntary sector would not offer additional services due to funding.

ACTIVITY

Support

Select a public, private and voluntary sport sector provider from your local area.

1 Compare the price differences for the same sport or physical activity.

2 How much is a private membership in the facility in your local area? Is the cost a barrier to some local individuals?

Challenge

3 A family would like to go swimming every weekend and send their children to swimming lessons. Calculate the difference in price between a public organisation and a private organisation within your local area.

ACTIVITY

Support

1 Revisit the list you made in 'Getting Started'. Split your list of local sporting facilities into public sector provision, private sector provision and voluntary sector provision. Present your list as a table to share with the group.

Challenge

2 Discuss the differences in the cost of activities, the different types of activities in the list and different facilities available when using public, private and voluntary sports provision.

3 Consider the reason why each facility is public, private or voluntary.

CHECK MY LEARNING

1 State two examples of a public, private and voluntary sport facility.

2 Describe the difference in characteristics of each sector.

3 State one advantage and disadvantage of each sector.

A2: Types and needs of participants

The sports and physical activities that we like or show an interest in can be linked to a person's age and abilities. The government has also released guidance on the recommendations of participation in sport and physical activity to keep us physically and mentally healthy. In this section, you will learn about the types of participants before examining the needs of each group in relation to introducing sport and physical activity into their daily routine.

How often should you take part in physical activity?

The government recommends how much sport or physical activity individuals from different target groups should participate in each week to maintain physical health and well-being.

Government recommendation for sport and physical activity participation:
- Children (5–11 years) and adolescents (12–17 years): 60 minutes of moderate or vigorous activity per day
- Children and young people with a disability: 120–180 minutes per week moderate to vigorous intensity
- Adults (18–49 years): 150 minutes of moderate or 75 minutes of vigorous activity per week
- Older adults (50+ years): 150 minutes of moderate or 75 minutes of vigorous activity or a combination of both per week
- Adults with a disability: 150 minutes of moderate to vigorous exercise per week with no less than 10 minutes for each session.

It is important to use the recommended government guidelines when considering the participation rates of all individuals within a local community. To appreciate the guidelines further, offer Saif advice about how much time he should spend each week participating in sport and physical activity.

Case study: Saif

Saif is eight years old and uses a wheelchair. How much sport and physical activity should he participate in each week?

The government recommends that people with long-term health conditions, such as asthma, type 2 diabetes, hypertension and CHD (coronary heart disease), participate in sport and physical activity. The guidance is to seek medical advice first then build up from 10 minutes per day.

Published in October 2021, Sport England released information from the 'Active Sport' survey conducted in 2020–2021. The report concluded that 60.9 per cent of adults and 44.9 per cent of children and young people met the recommended government target of participating in sport and physical activity. While 44.9 per cent of adults with a disability and 43.1 per cent of adults with long-term health conditions also met the recommended target.

To enable the numbers to increase further, the needs of participants must be considered when planning for enhanced sport and physical activity provision. Review the case studies:

Greg is 55 years old and his physical health needs are:
- To improve his fitness
- To improve his body composition
- To have a better night's sleep
- Build an immunity to prevent illness
- To reduce the symptoms of his long-term health condition.

Orla is 40 years old and has social needs which are:
- Would like to meet new people
- Make new friends
- Have fun while developing leadership and teamwork skills
- Decreasing her loneliness.

Kian is 16 years old and has mental health needs, he would like to:
- Decrease his stress levels
- Improve his work/life balance, he is struggling with exams, his part-time job, family and friends' time
- Decrease his risk of depression
- Improve his mood
- Increase his levels of self-confidence and self-esteem.

ACTIVITY

1 What are Greg's recommended levels of participation?
2 Which sport or physical activity might you suggest for him?
3 What are Orla's recommended levels of participation?
4 Which sport or physical activity might you suggest for her?

ACTIVITY

Support
1 What are Kian's recommended levels of participation?
2 Which sport or physical activity might you suggest for him?

Challenge
3 Create further case studies for participants with other needs. Consider their physical, social and mental health needs.

CHECK MY LEARNING

State the government guidelines for the following target groups:
- Primary school children aged 5–11 years
- Adolescents aged 12–17 years
- Adults aged 18–49 years
- Older adults aged 50+.

A3: Barriers to participation in sport and physical activity

GETTING STARTED

In small groups, produce a collage. Present barriers there may be for participating in sport or physical activity in the UK.

Think about the barriers faced by:
- children
- adolescents
- adults
- older adults
- those with a disability
- those with long-term health conditions.

ACTIVITY

The English Federation of Disability Sport conducted a survey in 2021 on the barriers to participation. A visually impaired adolescent shared that 'More and more we are finding that health and safety is thrown up as a reason to exclude us'.

Should health and safety be a barrier? How could facilities and activities be adapted to support those who are visually impaired?

Share your thoughts with your teacher.

DID YOU KNOW?

In the UK more than half of girls aged 12–16 years do not play sport (BBC). The barriers they reported were that they did not feel good enough or that no one encouraged them to play.

Sport England's 'Inactive People' study concluded that one in four people participate in sport and physical activity less than 30 minutes each week, with data suggesting that one in six deaths are caused by inactivity. Appreciating the barriers is an essential step in increasing the numbers participating, so that the benefits can be experienced by more of the UK population.

Barriers to participation

Initially, when individuals are asked why they do not participate in sport and physical activity, the barriers are often cost, access and time.

Cost

When selecting a sport or physical activity, it is important to consider the clothing and equipment needed. The cost of the required clothing and equipment could be a reason why individuals cannot participate in their chosen sport. A pair of trainers needed for most sports and physical activities can cost between £20 for a child's size to £35 for an adult's size and more expensive if high-end brands are your choice. Equipment could also be a barrier as ropes for climbing can cost from £50, paddleboards for water activities £300, and dinghies for sailing from £500.

The cost of transport must also be considered. Can you afford the petrol for training and competition journeys? How do you transport the dinghy for sailing trips? Is public transport affordable? These are all questions an individual must consider when selecting the sport or physical activity they would like to participate in.

Access

It is important to consider the location of the activity. The location may determine whether you can attend. How far is the activity from your home? Can you travel to away fixtures or competitions? If there is limited availability to accessible transport, how would this impact your participation in the sport or physical activity?

A participant would also have to consider the types of sports and physical activities available in their local area. What is on offer? Are they able to access the resources needed to participate? Lack of availability in the local area may be a barrier to participation.

Time

Everyone has time commitments, whether they work long hours, have school or college and a part-time job or family that requires care and attention. The impact on time can be enormous. The question that many people ask is, 'when do I have time to exercise?'

LINK IT UP

In A1, the benefits of exercise for each type of participant were investigated. What advice would you share with Siena and Usman?

ACTIVITY

Support

1 Select a sport of your choice. Create a PowerPoint presentation on the barriers regarding cost, accessibility and time. Present your findings to your peers.

Challenge

2 Explain the impact of cost, accessibility and time on an individual's ability to meet the government's recommendation for participating in sport or physical activity.

ACTIVITY

Support

1 Research the types of clothing appropriate for individuals from a diverse range of cultural backgrounds Which sports are they for? How much do they cost? Are the clothes easily accessible?

Challenge

2 Research role models from different cultural backgrounds. Which sport or physical activity do they represent? Offer an example of a sport or physical activity that lacks a role model.

Personal barriers to participation in sport and physical activity

There are many examples why each type of participant has a barrier to their motivation to participate in sport and physical activity. Read the examples below to appreciate the barriers people may face:

Case study: Siena

Siena does not participate in sport or physical activity as she worries about her body image. She has lost her self-confidence and her parents/guardians do not encourage her to play.

Case study: Usman

Usman would like to participate in sport and physical activity after being diagnosed with type 2 diabetes but is concerned that his fitness levels are low. He has limited previous experience and believes participating may make his condition worse.

Cultural barriers

Cultural barriers are experienced by those who have specific social practices, beliefs and traditions which impact their ability to participate in sport and physical activity.

Cultural barriers associated with sport are:

* Limited access to single-sex sessions for sport or physical activity. Private, public and voluntary sectors often hold mixed sessions to increase participation. Single-sex sessions may also be a concern to some participants due to safety of arriving and reaching home after the session.
* Limited access to appropriate sports clothing. Availability in local shops and online stores as well as affordability. The social norms of participating while wearing clothing that may be viewed as unconventional by some people, such as a burka, may be a barrier due to participants hearing comments about their clothing.
* Limited role models from a diverse range of cultural backgrounds.
* Limited access to male-dominated sports for women from a diverse range of cultural backgrounds (e.g. football or cricket).

CHECK MY LEARNING

1 State a reason why cost may be a barrier to participation in sport or physical activity.

2 State two reasons why accessibility may be a barrier to participation in sport or physical activity.

3 State a reason why time may be a barrier to participation in sport or physical activity.

4 Describe how personal barriers affect participation in sport or physical activity.

5 State a reason why culture may be a barrier to participation in sport or physical activity.

A4: Methods to address barriers to participation

Sport and physical activity should be available to all individuals in all communities. Sport England and government ministers have secured a strategy to move sport and physical activities forward in each community. The focus of the strategy is to use sport and physical activity to enable individuals to connect with their health and well-being while connecting to their community with positive experiences for children and young people. The aim of ensuring 'active environments' in all communities will reduce the existing barriers to participation and offer more opportunities to participate in sport and physical activity.

Reducing the barriers to participation

Access

The location and transport considerations when selecting a sport or physical activity can influence your decision about whether to participate. Removing or reducing the barrier will enable individuals to access more choices and hopefully find an interest.

By addressing the barriers, sport and physical activity can become more accessible. Increasing the range of provision in all communities, as well as enabling individuals with a disability to access the provision, will allow each target group to meet the government's recommendation of participation levels in sport and physical activity.

Cost and time

How can sport and physical activity facilities address the barrier of cost and time for local people? Let's think how the barriers of cost and time can be reduced (Figure 1.3):

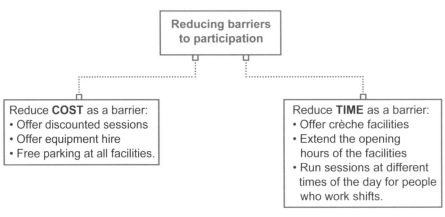

Figure 1.3: Reducing barriers to participation

National governing bodies

The Lawn Tennis Association (LTA) has started a campaign to work with local authorities to secure tennis courts within local communities. The LTA hopes to reduce the barriers of time, access, cost, and personal and cultural barriers through the partnership.

Personal and cultural barriers

Personal and cultural barriers must also be addressed to raise participation levels. A number of ideas to reduce the barriers are:

Reduce the barrier	
Personal barriers	Cultural barriers
Offer private changing rooms in all facilities	Introduce women-only sessions staffed by female staff
Allow participants to wear clothing they feel most comfortable in	Ask employers to reflect on the diversity of their staff
Create profiles of people with different body shapes and share their journey in sport with others	All employers should offer staff training in cultural awareness
Offer parent and child sessions to create a familial culture of sport	Create podcasts from role models from different cultural backgrounds

■ Children's tennis class

LINK IT UP

In A1, you learned about the role of NGBs and the important role they play in supporting participation in sport and physical activity.

ACTIVITY

Support

1   Interview a family member and discuss the barriers they face when participating in sport and physical activity. Do they meet the government's recommended time for participation in sport or physical activity? To end the interview, offer them ideas on reducing the barriers.

Challenge

2   Research a professional athlete and their journey through sport and physical activity. Create a podcast about their journey, showing the barriers they faced and how they addressed the barriers.

CHECK MY LEARNING

1   State three initiatives that could be used to reduce the cost of participating in sport.

2   State three personal barriers an individual could face when wanting to participate in sport and physical activity.

3   Which facilities in your area offer women-only sessions?

Learning outcome A: Assessment practice Explore types and provision of sport and physical activity for different types of participant

How you will be assessed

In this component you will be assessed by completing one internally assessed assignment. The assignment will be set by Pearson. This assignment will be one of three tasks for Component 1 and it will take one hour to complete.

You will be provided with an assignment brief that describes what you need to do and the date by which you must submit the completed work to the teacher.

Your teacher will mark the assignment and tell you what grade you have achieved.

You will be expected to show that you understand the different types of physical activities and providers, the needs of participants, barriers to participation and ways to overcome these barriers.

This will include:
- explaining the type of sport and physical activity appropriate for a selected participant
- explaining the benefits of participating in sport and physical activity for a selected participant.

CHECKPOINT

Review your learning of this component by answering the following questions, this will help you prepare for the assignment.

Strengthen
- Highlight four team and four individual sports and physical activities (including outdoor activities).
- From your examples, what is the provision for the sport and physical activity? Public, private and voluntary opportunities to participate?
- State the benefits of participating in sport and physical activity.

Challenge
- Name the physical, social and mental needs of an adolescent.
- Describe the barriers faced by an adolescent.
- How could an adolescent overcome the barriers?

ASSESSMENT PRACTICE

A primary-school-aged child with asthma has been encouraged by the asthma nurse to take part in sport and physical activity. Produce an information booklet giving the child advice on participating in sport and physical activity. The information booklet should be two A4 pages in length.

To create the information booklet, you must complete the following tasks:

1 Describe the government recommendations for a primary-aged child taking part in sport and physical activity.

2 Highlight four examples of team sports and physical activities that the child could join.

3 Highlight four examples of individual sports or physical activities the child could join.

4 For each of the sport and physical activity examples, discuss the provision, would the child participate in a public, private or voluntary facility?

5 Describe the characteristics and the advantages and disadvantages of each provision.

6 Describe the benefits of taking part in sport and physical activity.

7 Discuss the physical, social and mental needs of the child.

8 Describe the barriers the child may face when participating in sport and physical activity.

9 End the information leaflet by describing ways to address the barriers.

TIPS

- Interview a primary school child and ask about their favourite sports and physical activities. Offer suggestions during the interview to encourage the response. This will help you appreciate which sports and physical activities you could select for the child in the task.

- Or watch a video on the type of activities primary school children enjoy participating in. You can use the suggestions in the task.

- In your assessment, make sure you justify why you have selected the sport or physical activity for the child.

TAKE IT FURTHER

At a primary school the teacher offers a group of parents information on sport and physical activity. The teacher suggests that to make sport and physical activity available to the parents and guardians, the school will hold a sports fair where local provision will offer taster sessions on their activities. Most of the parents are 35 years old and above and work full or part time.

1. State the government recommendations for the parents.

2. What team and individual sports could be held at the school?

3. Would the activities at the school be public, private or voluntary?

4. What barriers would the parents face?

5. What solutions would you suggest for the barriers?

B1: Different types of sports clothing and equipment required for participation 1: clothing and footwear

GETTING STARTED

In small groups choose a sport and research how footwear has developed over time in your selected sport.

◘ Waterproof clothing is important for all-weather activities like hiking

Sports clothing and footwear has seen technology used to improve products for athletes to not only wear comfortably but to enhance performance. The leading sports brands in manufacturing sportswear invest in the latest technology to offer performers the most up-to-date clothing and footwear available.

The different types of sports clothing

The kinds of sports kits available have grown in choice, colour and material to enable a performer to meet the requirements of their chosen activity. Playing a team sport where everyone wears the same clothing to work out in, or wearing the latest fashion in the gym, is critical for some to enjoy their experience. The clothing selected is important.

Waterproof clothing has been designed to reduce the barrier of weather preventing individuals participating in outdoor activities as well as to keep training in outdoor sports. The use of GORE-TEX enabled participants to purchase clothing that is waterproof and breathable, as the microporous properties repel water from the outside, while letting it breathe on the inside to avoid condensation. Likewise, football shorts that are lightweight and temperature sensitive, and gym leggings that are stretchy and enable movement, make sure participants are more comfortable and therefore motivated to participate in an outdoor sport or activity.

Different types of footwear

1914

◘ **The technology used in studded boots has developed greatly since they were first used**

The use of studded boots to allow a player to grip the playing surface more effectively was introduced in 1886. Technology has helped develop the design of the studded boot. Today, metal or plastic moulded studs are used to enable a player to grip the surface and perform their skills to the highest level.

Trainers are a popular shoe for those participating in sport, with Statista reporting that in 2020, 7.65 million trainers with the Adidas logo were sold in Great Britain. Trainers offer comfort, grip, increased friction and style to the outfit worn by participants.

ACTIVITY

Create a storyboard or podcast describing the clothing and footwear needed for different outdoor and adventure activities.

For example:

Sailing: goggles, gloves, wetsuit, water shoes, sailing hat, sailing jacket (inshore, coastal and offshore all have different linings)

Mountain climbing: climbing shoes, warm clothing, gloves, helmet, headlamp

Share the storyboard or podcast with your peers and teacher.

Clothing needed for specific sports

Different sports require different specific clothing and footwear. Look at the three case studies below to discover the requirements of clothing and footwear for gymnastics, cricket and tennis.

Case study: Claude

Claude would like to participate in gymnastics. The clothing and footwear he would need are a leotard (with male participants preferring to use the term 'competition vest'), stirrup pants and co-ordinating socks so that the outfit has a layered look. Claude may also choose to wear gymnastic shoes, which are tight slippers made from leather with some traction on the bottom to reduce the risk of slipping.

Case study: Lucas

Lucas would like to participate in cricket. The clothing and footwear he would need are 'whites' consisting of trousers, a shirt, a tank top for keeping warm while fielding or waiting to bat and 'spikes' (a type of trainer with spikes for reducing the risk of slipping).

Case study: Serafina

Serafina would like to participate in tennis. The clothing and footwear she would need is a tennis one-piece suit and a pair of trainers suitable for the surface (e.g. grass, clay or AstroTurf). The term 'tennis whites' may be used to discuss tennis clothing: this was once a symbol of class as keeping white clothing clean was expensive.

CHECK MY LEARNING

1 State the different types of clothing and footwear needed for rugby, badminton and hiking.

2 State the importance of waterproof clothing.

3 State the importance of studded boots.

B1: Different types of sports clothing and equipment required for participation 2: sport-specific equipment and protection

In small groups or as an individual, research sport-specific equipment for:

One team sport

One individual sport

One outdoor and adventure activity.

Think about:
- Participation equipment
- Travel-related equipment
- Scoring equipment.

Share the research with your peers and teacher.

Sport and physical activity require certain pieces of equipment to be able to participate. For example, netball participants need a ball, goal posts, appropriate flooring marked out and a scoring table.

Safety is also a huge aspect of sport. Many NGBs recommend protective equipment to reduce the risk of injury. This also enhances the enjoyment and participation in sport and physical activity.

Equipment needed for specific sports

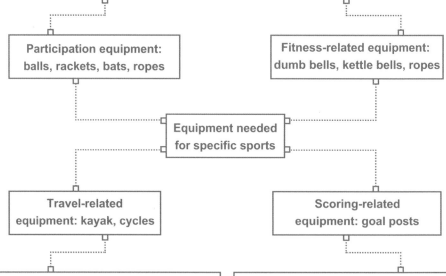

It is important that the appropriate equipment is available for the sport or physical activity. E.g.:
Tennis requires a racket and ball
Baseball requires a bat and a ball
Netball requires a net and a ball
Climbing requires a harness, ropes and carabiners.

It is reported that over 10 million people in the UK go to the gym on a regular basis.
Therefore, it is essential that the gym equipment offered meets the requirement to train each element of fitness.

Participation equipment: balls, rackets, bats, ropes

Fitness-related equipment: dumb bells, kettle bells, ropes

Equipment needed for specific sports

Travel-related equipment: kayak, cycles

Scoring-related equipment: goal posts

When a sport or physical activity requires the performer to travel, it is vital that the appropriate equipment is available.
When sailing, a dinghy or yacht is required, when travelling down a river, a canoe or kayak is needed.
Cycling is the most popular activity in the UK, therefore different-sized cycles are needed.

Scoring equipment is needed to enable players to register the competitive element of the sport.
Football and rugby require goal posts.
Rounders requires four posts.
Basketball has a scoreboard to notify the players, coaches and spectators of the score.

◻ Figure 1.4: Equipment needed for specific sports

In A1, you explored the role of an NGB, in Learning outcome B you will discover the importance of the NGB.

◻ Eye protection is important for a number of activities

Protection and safety equipment

Protective equipment in sport is designed to protect against impact, which is critical for the safety of the players. Mouth guards are used in several sports including rugby, American football and hockey to reduce the risk of injury to a player's teeth and biting into the lip or internal cheek. Head guards are encouraged in rugby, cricket, American football and ice hockey to reduce the risk of concussion when participating in these sports. Many sports have introduced eye protection, including safety glasses in squash and cycling, to reduce the risk of impact on the eye. Water sports require the use of safety equipment, such as flotation devices in sailing and life jackets.

ACTIVITY

Support

1 Find out the history of the mouth guard. Create a leaflet encouraging sports performers to purchase a mouth guard from a dentist. Highlight the benefits of having the mouth guard made to match your mouth and teeth.

Challenge

2 Research the investigation by the sport of rugby into the lasting consequences of concussion on players. A mouth guard is being trialled which can measure the impact of concussion. Saracens Rugby Football Club are trialling a chip behind a player's ear to gather data for analysis.

  Share the findings with your peers and teacher.

First aid equipment

Coaches and first aiders must be present at training and competitive games. It is vital they have a first aid kit to support any injured players. Below are some examples.

Ice packs are normally available in the first aid box which can be used on participants who have a swelling due to an injury. The ice pack will reduce the swelling until further medical treatment is made available.

Bandages should also be in the first aid kit, offering protection should a participant have an injury that is bleeding. The bandage will stop the bleeding as well as reduce the risk of infection until further treatment can be made available. It will also provide support for an injury such as a sprained ankle or wrist.

A defibrillator should be used if a performer is in cardiac arrest as it gives a high-energy shock to the heart to increase the chance of recovery. The device sends an electrical shock or pulse to the heart to restore a normal heartbeat.

CHECK MY LEARNING

1 State the type of equipment needed to attend a spinning class and an aqua aerobics class.

2 State the equipment needed to play hockey and racketball.

3 If an individual wanted to play ice hockey, state the protective equipment they would need.

4 Describe the importance of ice packs and bandages when a player is injured.

▣ A defibrillator should be used if a performer is in cardiac arrest

B1: Different types of sports clothing and equipment required for participation 3: people with disabilities and assistive technology

DID YOU KNOW?

Sport England explored disabled sport concluding that, in the UK, one in five people have a long-standing limiting disability or illness with 70 per cent of disabled people aged over 50. There are also slightly more females with disabilities than males and 75 per cent of people with disabilities having more than one impairment.

Active Nation 'Disability Sport' states, 'Disability sport is extraordinary: tearing up clichés and breaking down barriers for people with intellectual disabilities. Disability is about much more than physical and mental difference. It's about the limits everyday life imposes. It's about what people think disabled people can do. And these can change.' The development of equipment or assistive technology for people with a disability supports the future of disabled athletes, enabling barriers to be addressed as well as participation rates to increase.

There is a range of assistive technology available for athletes, from clothing to mechanical serving equipment. The technology helps to support all athletes to participate in sport. The wheelchairs in tennis are specially designed to allow increased speed of movement and agility across the field, court or pitch.

Case study: Sophia

Sophia can play tennis using an adapted wheelchair for wheelchair tennis. Adapted wheelchairs have 4–5 wheels: 2 large wheels at the back, 2 small wheels at the front and usually an anti-roll fifth wheel at the back.

◻ Sophia playing wheelchair tennis

Boccia is a sport played by individuals, pairs or teams of three. Boccia is suitable for participants who use a wheelchair, as it is played while sitting down. Boccia expects each player/team to have six balls and with a throwing action release each ball to reach the 'jack'. The individual or team closest to the 'jack' wins.

LINK IT UP

In A3, you investigated the barriers to sport with cost of equipment being discussed. How much does an adapted wheelchair cost?

Case study: Ahmed

Ahmed is playing Boccia. In Boccia you can use serving ramps which allow athletes with limited mobility to compete.

Visual and hearing impairments

Sports participants with a hearing impairment may have access to assistive listening devices (ALDs), which amplify sound and are especially useful when there is background noise. AAC devices (augmentative and alternative communication) include picture boards and computer programs to support communication. Alerting devices can be used to support the participant with safety, such as alarms with flashing lights.

For those with visual impairments, smart watches or GPS with voice assistance can help guide participants, along with equipment that includes sound devices such as balls with bells inside that the participant can follow.

ACTIVITY

Support

1 Define the term 'assistive technologies'.
2 Discuss the assistive technologies that can support athletes who have:
   • A hearing impairment
   • A visual impairment.
   Summarise your findings to your peers and teacher.

Challenge

3 A child with a hearing impairment would like to join the school football team. Create a poster, using appropriate pictures, to highlight the clothing, footwear and equipment needed to play the sport.

CHECK MY LEARNING

1 Name the sports which are accessible for participants who use a wheelchair.
2 State two examples of assistive technology for participants with a visual or hearing impairment.
3 Describe the impact of prosthetics on sport and physical activity.

B1: Different types of sports clothing and equipment required for participation 4: facilities, officiating equipment and performance analysis

GETTING STARTED

In small groups, research the national sports facilities in the UK. Discover the role the facility plays in developing athletes as well as the additional support and guidance offered at the centre for each participant.

Think:

Bisham Abbey

Lilleshall

Plas Y Brenin

Centres of Excellence for Sport.

How do the centres encourage participation?

Share your findings with your peers and teacher.

In the UK, in 2013, there were 151,000 indoor sports facilities, with many outdoor facilities as well as national parks where outdoor and adventure activities can take place. In 2021, the government announced that £100 million was allocated to local authorities to support the recovery of public-owned leisure centres with grass roots and the physical activity sector benefitting from £270 million from Sport England. The government also allocated an additional £25 million to grow grass roots football, allowing 700 new pitches to be built. Also important is training officials for each sport to enable the competitive element to be governed in line with the NGB rules, and performance analysis, which is key for motivating individuals to offer greater performance.

☐ **Table 1.1: Types of indoor and outdoor facilities**

Indoor facilities	Outdoor facilities
Sports halls	Pitches
Gyms	Climbing walls
Squash courts	Mountain bike trails
Swimming pools	Lakes
Gymnastic pits	Rivers
Snow domes	

What equipment does an official need?

Officials need a surprising amount of equipment in a game and the higher the level of competition, the greater the amount of equipment required. Consider a netball umpire, a cricket umpire and a rugby referee and what equipment they need.

☐ Equipment needed to be an effective official: whistle, earpiece, microphone, disciplinary cards, flags

Performance analysis

GPS, heart rate monitors and apps form an enhanced edge to sport and physical activity performance. The technology provides valid, reliable and detailed information on an individual's performance, enabling adaptations to training as well as motivation for personal goals. The technology offers the performer information on metres per second, overall metres, intensity worked and heart rate as well as information about performance under fatigue, all vital elements in an individual's drive to improve their performance.

Sports clubs use the GPS data to assess the in-game and post-game performance of a player. The sport science team and data analysts can highlight to the coaching team if a player is at increased risk of injury and whether their distance-covered running statistics are lower than normal.

Garmin sales have increased from revenue of 3 billion US dollars in 2016 to 5 billion US dollars in 2021, a significant increase in sales as more participants appreciate the information covered by using the technology.

Types of performance analysis technology

Types of technology enabling performance analysis include:

- **Smartwatches**
- Heart rate monitors
- **GPS** systems
- Smartphone fitness apps.

KEY TERMS

Indoor sport facilities are buildings available to play indoor sports.

National parks are outdoor facilities offering outdoor and adventure activities.

Smartwatch features technology to monitor heart rate and other vital signs.

GPS tracks a player's health and fitness as well as distance covered and position during the game.

DID YOU KNOW?

Due to ever-growing revenues in sport from broadcasting deals and a global audience, a player's performance has never been so critical in attracting major investment in a specific sport.

ACTIVITY

Using one of the four types of performance technology listed, participate in a warm-up and sports session.

Once the session has been completed, write down the information the technology has provided on your performance.

Discuss with your peers what you have discovered.

Set yourself a target for a future sport and activity session from the information you have gained from the performance technology.

CHECK MY LEARNING

1 Name three indoor and three outdoor facilities used to play sport or take part in physical activities.
2 State the equipment needed to officiate a netball game.
3 Describe the importance of performance analysis.

B2: Different types of technology and their benefits for participation and performance 1: clothing and footwear

Thermoregulation is defined as the maintenance of a stable core body temperature. It is vital that participants prevent **hyperthermia** or **hypothermia**. The type of clothing worn by a participant affects how well air can circulate over their skin as well as allowing heat and moisture to evaporate.

As a group, discuss the benefits of clothing that can regulate body temperature. What impact might it have for the sports and physical activity participant?

KEY TERMS

Hyperthermia is a result of overexertion in hot temperatures, when the body absorbs or generates more heat than it releases.

Hypothermia is a drop in body temperature below 35°C.

Sport clothing has developed considerably over the years. If you compare the clothing worn by Edmund Hillary in 1953 to scale Everest to the clothing worn today by climbers, there are significant differences in terms of lightweight, additional warmth and waterproofing. Footwear has also seen dramatic developments in the design and materials used, with improved grip and rebound, all allowing an enhanced performance for each participant. Footwear is also important to reduce the risk of injury in a participant (e.g. reduce slipping through increased grip), which is critical to allow an individual to stay active.

Aerodynamic clothing

Aerodynamic clothing means it reduces the forces of air moving past it. When a person or object moves through the air, drag forces are created which act as to resist the movement. The faster a person or object travels, the greater the drag forces are that act upon them.

▫ Pierre must wear tight clothing as a cyclist. As he will travel very fast, loose clothing can create extra drag force from air resistance

Compression clothing

Compression clothing is worn so that it fits tightly around the skin. The benefits are that it helps to increase blood flow to the area covered by this clothing, and this helps to improve performance and recovery time. This is because blood brings oxygen and nutrients to working muscles and removes waste products. Therefore, having more blood flow to the area is going to help to increase the delivery of oxygen and nutrients for the muscles to use when exercising. More blood flow also increases the removal of the waste products, such as carbon dioxide and lactic acid, which are produced by the working muscles.

Many people who take part in non-competitive sports and activities, such as fun runners, wear compression clothing as they believe it helps to improve their running performance and recovery.

Footwear

Footwear has also developed since players wore thick leather boots which doubled in weight when wet, whereas today players wear a combination of synthetic and leather boots.

ACTIVITY

Support

1 Complete the table below to illustrate the types of footwear used in sport. Share the table with your teacher.

Sport	Material used in footwear	Has the grip helped performance?	Does the footwear have rebound?
Netball			
Ice hockey			
Basketball			
Mountain biking			
Wind surfing			

Challenge

2 Create a similar table for clothing using the same sports.

DID YOU KNOW?

Rebound shoes absorb up to 80 per cent of the shock when jumping in exercises like aerobics. These shoes can mean that the user is able to burn up to 20 per cent more calories and reduces the risk of injury.

CHECK MY LEARNING

1 Define the term thermoregulation.
2 Define the terms hypothermia and hyperthermia.
3 State the purpose of aerodynamic clothing.
4 Describe the benefits of compression clothing.

B2: Different types of technology and their benefits for participation and performance 2: sport-specific equipment

The equipment used to take part in sport and physical activity has advanced over the years. Instead of wooden tennis rackets, players use rackets made from graphite, javelins are now designed using carbon fibre rather than wood or metal, and the creation of resistance bands from latex has allowed performers to enhance their flexibility while contributing to their recovery from injury.

Tennis, badminton and squash: how the equipment has changed

Tennis, badminton and squash have changed over the years with advances in science and technology. Players are hitting the ball harder and faster to overcome their opponent. Therefore, the design of the racket is paramount for the participant as they want to serve the ball as fast as possible before reacting to the return shot with accuracy and force.

◻ A squash racket

Squash rackets are made from graphite and titanium for a light racket that is easy to swing while being good for vibration absorption. The grip is made from artificial fibres, which increases the grip on the racket, securing improved performance.

ACTIVITY

Support

1 Select a sport or physical activity: how has the equipment used in the sport or physical activity changed over the years?
    • Is the equipment lighter?
    • Is the equipment stronger?

Challenge

2 How has this changed or enhanced performance?

3 Which materials have the manufactures started to use? What did they use before?

New designs to improve performance

Golf drivers have been modernised in recent years with significant impact on the game. Modern drivers now offer a larger face, which in turn enables a golfer to increase the speed and distance of the ball on off-centre strikes. As the head and shaft are lighter, the golfer finds it easier to generate more swing to enable greater impact on the ball. Designers now design the head of the driver with aerodynamics in mind, allowing a golfer to hit the ball longer and straighter. As a result, performance has improved, and more participants join the sport.

Some facts about golf drivers:
- New drivers come with a titanium club face
- The club face is either inserted or welded to the club frame
- Drivers come in varying thicknesses to increase the springiness
- Drivers come with internal support behind the face to increase strength
- The crown (top section of the driver) is made from titanium or carbon, making it the lightest section of the club.

🔲 Golf drivers are very carefully constructed to perform optimally

LINK IT UP

In A1, you examined the provision of sport. Are golf courses offered by public, private or voluntary organisations?

In A3, you investigated the barriers to sport. How much does a golf driver cost? Does the cost impact on accessibility to the sport?

In A3, you investigated the access to sport. Do all communities have access to a golf course?

BEST PRACTICE

Professional golfers now have all of their clubs and assistive technology specially designed for their own performance with longer grips. Despite this, the golfer's caddie provides invaluable performance support.

ACTIVITY

Support

1 Can you add more points to the golf driver list above? Create a display in the classroom using all the points from the group.

Challenge

2 Research another sport-specific piece of equipment that has had a design improvement.

   What has been the impact?

CHECK MY LEARNING

1 Describe the benefit of squash rackets being made from graphite and titanium.
2 How has a golf driver developed over the years?
3 Discuss the impact on performance due to the changes to a golf driver.

B2: Different types of technology and their benefits for participation and performance 3: protection and safety equipment

Identify what protective equipment the ice hockey goalkeeper is wearing. Which areas of the body is it protecting?

Discuss in small groups why the protective equipment is needed by an ice hockey player.

Ask your teacher to play a clip from a game of ice hockey to enhance your understanding.

Taking part in sport and physical activity, as we know, can occasionally result in participants getting injured. Taking part in certain sports and physical activities has a greater risk of injury for a participant due to the nature of the game. As a result, scientists and manufacturers continually seek to improve protective equipment for the safety of all participants.

In 2021, *Rugby World* magazine included a report entitled 'New Rugby Concussion Reports calls for Action on Brain Trauma'. The report highlighted the urgent need for research and investigation into brain trauma from the game of rugby. The Drake Foundation has invested over £2.2 million since 2014 into research examing the effects of head injuries in football and rugby. Recent reports suggest that 23 per cent of elite rugby players have brain structure abnormalities due to brain impacts. This has prompted the Department for Digital, Culture, Media & Sport (DCMS) to call for a government investigation into the issue.

ACTIVITY

Support

1   Produce a poster on the protective equipment available for rugby players to wear.
    Think: helmet and mouth guard.

Challenge

2   On the poster, include a section about the chip to be included in some mouth guards to measure impact from the game.

Mouth guards

One example of protective equipment for sports such as rugby and hockey is the mouth guard. The British Dental Association supports the use of mouth guards to help absorb shock and prevent some sports-related concussions.

Lighter weight so more comfortable to wear → **Improved protection design** → Individually measured for personal use, for example mouth guards produced from mouldings of an individual's teeth and gums

■ Figure 1.5: Protective and safety equipment: development of the mouth guard

Cycling safety and protection

◨ Full face helmet for mountain biking ◨ Aerodynamic helmet for road cycling

Protective and safety equipment has not only been designed to reduce the risk of injury for cyclists but to also improve performance. The key function of a helmet is to absorb impact and stay on your head if a collision occurs. As stated by Dr John Black, an emergency doctor, 'If someone's unprotected head strikes a solid surface, such as the roadside or the pavement, even if it's a ground-level fall, patients can sustain devastating head and brain injuries.' ... 'We know that the wearing of cycling helmets can reduce the risk of that by up to two-thirds.'

His comments have been supported by Rune Elvik, a Norwegian academic and road safety expert, who reviewed a study from 2001 which concluded that helmets reduce the risk of a head injury by 60 per cent. While most riders have opted for a cycle helmet with aerodynamic design paired with small vents up-front for breathability to enhance performance, safety is also a key factor in their decision when selecting a helmet.

Athletics and martial arts

Athletes can purchase and choose to wear the protective equipment available for their safety, but the sport can choose to reduce the risk of injury too. Gymnastics, trampolining and martial arts all use landing mats which are designed to cushion the impact of landing from a fall, move or throw. The technology of the foam inside the mat has improved over the years so that it can absorb the landing shock to a higher degree. As a result, the risk of injury has been reduced and participants have gained confidence in improving their performance in the knowledge that the safety equipment is sufficient to meet their needs and reduce injury.

BEST PRACTICE

PPE is essential for participants in many sports. For example, an under 18-year-old cricketer must wear a helmet when batting. This reduces the risk of injury and head trauma. The coach has a duty of care to ensure PPE constraints are followed.

CHECK MY LEARNING

1 Describe the importance of a personally fitted mouth guard.
2 State the purpose of protective equipment.
3 Suggest the protective equipment needed for a field sport in athletics and weight training in a gym.

LINK IT UP

In B1 you explore the use of protective equipment for participation in sport and physical activity.

B2: Different types of technology and their benefits for participation and performance 4: equipment for people with disabilities or assistive technology

GETTING STARTED

Research three different sports that can be adapted so that anyone can participate in them with the addition of assistive equipment or technology.

Produce a podcast of your findings to share with your peers.

'Activity Alliance', the national charity and leading voice for disabled people in sport and physical activity, states that the UK has 12.2 million people with disabilities accounting for more than one in five of the total population. The prevalence of disability rises with age, with nine per cent of children being disabled, 21 per cent of working-age adults and 42 per cent of the older adults, all leading to a focus on providing appropriate equipment to enable 'sport for all' to be a national endeavour.

According to the Activity Alliance, two-thirds (67 per cent) of people with disabilities are motivated to be active to improve or maintain their physical health. Specialist equipment and assistive technology can help disabled people participate in sport.

The impact of adaptations for wheelchair participants

Case study:

Martin is a wheelchair user and would like to join his local gym. During his induction, he asks the instructor to demonstrate the equipment he can use and how it can be adapted to meet his needs.

The instructor explains that the gym has been working with the IFI (Inclusive Fitness Initiative) and provides equipment that is inclusive to enable both disabled and non-disabled participants to access a full body, cardiovascular and resistance workout during their gym session.

◻ Wheelchair-bound athletes are able to use this machine as the seat has been removed. An able-bodied athlete can then reinstate the seat. In this way, the equipment is accessible for all users.

Sport wheelchairs can enable an individual to perform to the standard they expect of themselves. Sport wheelchairs are usually non-folding to increase the solidity with a pronounced angle for the wheels that provide stability for turning and are lightweight to aid reaction to the play.

◻ Sport wheelchairs are designed for stability when turning

Prosthetics

In sport and physical activity, specific prosthetics, such as the Eagle for golf and blades for runners, can be used to support the participants' ability to play and enhance their performance.

Technology to support visual and hearing impairment

Radio aids can be very helpful to those with a hearing impairment. A radio aid helps to reduce the impact of background noise. It is made up of a transmitter and receiver. The instructor or coach wears the transmitter, which sends sounds wirelessly to the receiver worn by the participant. A hearing loop is a sound system in a space such as a sports hall that works in a similar way, by providing a wireless signal that is picked up by hearing aids.

Standard hearing aids can't be fully submersed in water, but some cochlear implants can be used with waterproof accessories for swimming. For example, a waterproof swimming cap to protect the implant, a silicone sleeve to contain the sound processor or a microphone that an instructor can wear and stream directly to the implant.

Equipment has also been developed to enable those with visual impairments to take part in sports, such as balls with sound devices inside, so that participants can follow the location of the ball in short tennis, football or goalball. In goalball, the object of the game is to roll a basketball sized ball with bells inside over the opponent's goal line. Your opponents listen for the oncoming ball and attempt to block it with their bodies.

Smart watches with voice assistance and GPS systems with audio could also be used to guide visually impaired users, alongside equipment such as a long cane.

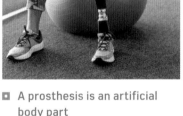

◻ A prosthesis is an artificial body part

CHECK MY LEARNING

1   Define the term 'prosthetics'.

2   Give examples of prosthetics for sport.

3   How can equipment be adapted to support disabled and non-disabled participants?

4   How do sport wheelchairs differ to everyday wheelchairs?

B2: Different types of technology and their benefits for participation and performance 5: facilities and officiating

The British weather can be wet, cold and windy with little sunshine and humidity at certain times of the year. How do sports performers prepare for events where the weather is extremely cold (ski resorts), or hot and humid like the Qatar Football World Cup where in the summer the region has temperatures of 35°C? The answer is often to train in areas where the temperature will be similar, but cost, accessibility and commitments are often a barrier. This is why the UK has created facilities which simulate environments to replicate the areas where the sport or physical activity is being offered.

The aim of the snow dome is to offer an environment which is consistent with the environments in ski resorts, enabling a participant to maintain and develop their skill level, while offering race training and competitions to simulate the events available to the performers.

ACTIVITY

If possible, arrange a visit to a snow dome or watch a promotional video to investigate whether the snow dome meets the aim of enabling participants to take part in their chosen discipline in an environment which simulates competition and events in authentic ski resorts.

Share your opinion with your peers and teacher. Remember to give reasons for your thoughts.

ACTIVITY

Support

1 The football World Cup is usually held in July. However, the 2022 football World Cup hosted in in Qatar played in November and December. Discuss in small groups the reason for the change.

Challenge

2 Discuss the clothing that the players should wear to play in high temperatures.

Facilities

Sports surfaces have developed over the years with sprung and rubber floors being added to inside venues and 3G pitches being built for outside participation.

Sprung floors have been developed to help absorb some of the impact experienced by high impact sports and physical activities. Rubber flooring is used in weight rooms within a gym to absorb the shock from the weights being placed back on the floor. The rubber floor also has anti-slip properties, which lowers the risk of injury and is water resistant to cope with spilt drinks and sweat.

3G pitches supplemented the availability of pitches when the weather made playing conditions unacceptable or unsafe. The development of 3G pitches enabled a hard-wearing, durable and resilient facility to be available, therefore increasing the playing opportunities for sports that required a pitch.

Officials and technology

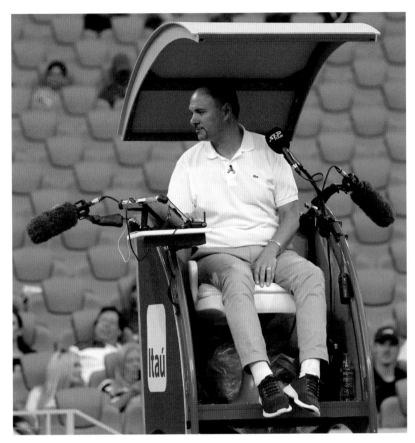

◻ A tennis official is supported by line technology to reduce errors in their decisions. The score, game, set and match are also displayed for umpire, player and spectator enhancement of the game

Officials use a range of equipment that means participation increases in sport. For example, in long jump, laser technology is used to track jumps. In swimming, timing pads are used to clock times and microphones are used in rugby to hear the match officials. All of these technologies increase accessibility, help sport be fair and remove barriers for participants.

ACTIVITY

Support

The use of VAR (Video Assistant Referee) in football started in the 2017–18 season in Italy and Germany, with Spain, France and England accepting the new technology in the 2018–19 season. This came after the technology was tested in the Dutch season 2012–13.

1 Research VAR.
- What is it?
- Why was it developed?

Challenge

2 In your opinion, does it help or hinder the role of the official?

Share your thoughts and opinions with your peers and teacher.

DID YOU KNOW?

In the 2019–20 Premier League season VAR checked 2400 incidents with 109 decisions overturned by VAR.

BEST PRACTICE

In football, VAR reviews are conducted by a team of qualified officials at Stockley Park. These officials receive technical support to add in lines to offside decisions and review incidents from different angles.

CHECK MY LEARNING

1 Describe the benefits of a sprung floor.

2 Describe the benefits of a 3G pitch.

3 Explain how VAR is used in football.

B2: Different types of technology and their benefits for participation and performance 6: performance analysis

How did I play? How did I perform? What was my time? All these questions are asked by sport and physical activity participants. Coaches, officials and parents used to be able to give their opinion but now technology can offer an analysis of a participant's performance to enable goals to be set for future participation. Being able to monitor and receive feedback on your performance is key to improving as well as motivating an individual to push their performance to the next level. Identifying strengths and weaknesses as well as comparisons with others has enabled individuals to set targets and secure goals while accepting their performance.

Action camera

An action camera is a digital camera that can be worn by participants when they are taking part in sport or physical activity. They are usually waterproof and can withstand some impact, while being attached to the performer's clothing, chest harness, cycling handlebars or helmet. The action camera provides footage of what the person sees when they are taking part in sport or physical activity. It can also be used by a coach to record an individual so that their performance can be analysed, enabling skills and techniques to be reflected upon.

Global positioning system (GPS)

This uses satellites to track the location of a person or object and is often incorporated into devices such as an Apple Watch or Garmin. GPS availability to athletes has enhanced the information available about their performance. GPS can detect fatigue during a game or performance, which could indicate an injury, while information is also available on appropriate intensity during the expected performance, which is vital in changing training routines to enhance success in the sport or physical activity.

◘ A skier wearing an action camera on their helmet to film their decent

Sensors

Performance analysis equipment to improve performance includes:

1 Sensors on clothing: Smart clothing can monitor heart activity as well as temperature during the performance.

2 Sensors on equipment: gathering information on grip, stroke and impact which allows a participant to reflect on their performance.

Sensors are used in footballs, located under the ball's laces, which capture information on velocity, acceleration and distance. This delivers vital information that the coaches and players can use to adapt training and skill development drills.

GPS data can produce a heat map for a player. This shows the coach and the player their basic positioning and the areas of the pitch they explored the most. This can be used to change tactics and change players in game position to make them more effective.

ACTIVITY

Support

1 Research clothing and equipment that have integrated sensors.

2 Produce a leaflet on your findings, offer your leaflet to your peers and ask for feedback.

Challenge

3 Within the leaflet, discuss the impact of integrated sensors on a participant's clothing and equipment.

Gait analysis

Some sport shoemakers offer a gait analysis on footwear. Gait analysis offers the participant information on their running style but more importantly on the degree of pronation (the way your foot rolls when you walk, the roll acting as a natural shock absorber). This is key information when selecting the footwear to support a participants' performance.

Pronation affects how much the foot rolls outwards or inwards while walking or running. Footwear can be used to correct this (e.g. supportive insoles or overpronators). This will help participants to run or walk efficiently and prevent common injuries to the foot, such as plantar fasciitis.

CHECK MY LEARNING

1 Describe the purpose of an action camera.

2 How would using an action camera impact a participant's performance in sport or physical activity?

3 Describe the role of GPS in sport or physical activity.

B3: The limitations of using technology in sport and physical activity

While technology has provided huge advances in sports performance, it can also have its limitations and a negative effect on the performance and playing opportunities of some participants. An initial concern is the cost of the new and advancing technology. Are all participants able to afford the information to develop their performance? While the mental health impact of technology is widely discussed, the impact on participants may be that emotional well-being is not as well-considered due to the information given on the actual performer by the technology. For instance, using GPS tracking means tracking a participant's movements or whereabouts constantly.

A GPS vest: an example

Cost

A GPS vest uses Smart technology to measure data such as distance covered, top speed, sprint distance or total number of sprints. With a starting cost of £160, the GPS vest has its limitations, illustrating that access to technology can be a major factor in an athlete's participation. This may feel to an athlete that cannot afford a vest that their opposition or teammates have an unfair advantage, which raises the question of equality in sport.

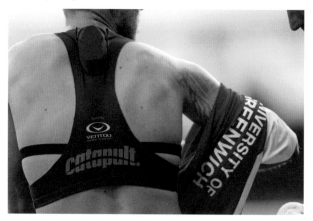

◻ A sportsperson wearing a GPS vest

Accuracy of data

Another concern would be the accuracy of the data, as all technology can have issues. What impact would this have on participants and coaches requiring the information? The impact could be: has the device captured all the data, has the data recorded or printed off appropriately? This could impact others as the information may not paint a clear picture of the participant's performance, making the feedback inaccurate, causing frustration.

Time

Alongside the GPS vest, the player could have video analysis set up during the training session or game, which is time-consuming as well as needing an individual to monitor the equipment and then time would be needed for feedback to enable the information to benefit the participant and coaching plans.

Usability

Finally, the use of technology requires those using it to understand the instructions for use and the maintenance required to receive the intended information.

ACTIVITY

During a practical sports performance, use a GPS vest or watch that monitors and records fitness.

Once completed, make a list of the potential limitations of the technology you have used.

Think about the limitations of:
- Time
- Access to the technology
- Accuracy of the data
- Usability of the technology.

Advantages and disadvantages of GPS vests

- Advantages: record performance data, you can share your data, compare against other players, can be worn in all conditions.
- Disadvantages: high costs, lots of maintenance, staff member needs to monitor data, not as accessible unless professional.

BEST PRACTICE

GPS vests can be complex to use and require the assistance of a sport scientist or analyst to set up, maintain and record the equipment.

CHECK MY LEARNING

1 Why is time a limitation?
2 Do all sports have access to technology? Research some examples.
3 What is the impact of inaccurate data from the technology?
4 Why is usability of technology an issue?

Learning outcome B: Assessment practice
Examine equipment and technology required for participants to use when taking part in sport and physical activity

How you will be assessed

In this component you will be assessed by completing one internally assessed assignment. The assignment will be set by Pearson. This assignment will be one of three tasks for Component 1 and it will take one hour to complete.

You will be provided with an assignment brief that describes what you need to do and the date by which you must submit the completed work to the teacher.

Your teacher will mark the assignment and tell you what grade you have achieved.

You will be expected to show that you understand how technology would be selected to affect the provision of sport and physical activity participants.

This will include:
- Different types of sports clothing and equipment
- Different types of technology and their benefits in improving sport and physical activity performance and participation
- The limitations of using technology for sport and physical activity.

CHECKPOINT

Review your learning of this component by answering the following questions, this will help you prepare for the assignment.

Strengthen
- State three type of sports clothing and footwear. Which sports would the items be appropriate for?
- State examples of protective and safety equipment.
- Discuss the types of equipment available for individuals with a disability.
- Discuss aerodynamic clothing and equipment.
- State three limitations of technology for sport and physical activity.

Challenge
- Discuss materials used for sports equipment and how this has impacted on the sport or physical activity.
- How do prosthetics help an athlete with a disability to participate in sport and physical activity?

ASSESSMENT PRACTICE

Assessment practice text

A group of adolescents are taking part in a sailing session. Produce a booklet or PowerPoint presentation which offers information on clothing, equipment and technology needed to participate in the session.

Remember to include:

1 Appropriate clothing and footwear

2 Sport-specific equipment

3 Protective and safety items

4 Technology that could enhance the experience

5 The benefits and limitations the group may experience with use of the technology in the clothing, footwear and equipment

6 A justification for the choices of clothing, equipment and technology suggested.

TIPS

- Watch a video clip on a sailing session to develop your knowledge and understanding of the sport.
- In your assessment, consider the use of technology, such as the use of an action camera. What benefits would the camera provide? What are the limitations, frustrations and consequences of the technology?
- Offer costing and availability information in the booklet to provide further guidance for the adolescents.
- When offering a justification, make sure you discuss the impact of the clothing, equipment and technology on the experience.

TAKE IT FURTHER

Consider why it is is important for a sailor to be aerodynamic when sailing and suggest what types of equipment, clothing and technology could help both the sailor and the boat be aerodynamic in a race.

C1: Planning a warm-up 1: pulse raiser activities

Performing a warm-up is beneficial to the sport or physical activity an individual is about to take part in. The NHS advise that a warm-up should be no less than six minutes and include three stages: a pulse raiser, a mobiliser and preparation stretches. It is important to warm up to lower the risk of injury while preparing the mind for the movement ahead.

ACTIVITY

Find your pulse on your wrist or your neck.

Use a stopwatch to time 60 seconds, or six seconds and then times by 10 (number of beats × 10). As you watch the time, count the number of beats you feel, your pulse rate.

Make a note of the number.

Now take part in a five-minute speed walk or jog, starting at walking pace then speeding up.

As soon as you stop, find your pulse and take your pulse for 60 seconds, or six seconds and then times by 10 (number of beats × 10).

Create a table to record your results.

Compare your results with the rest of the class to find the average resting heart rate and pulse rates after exercise.

The warm-up

A warm-up is designed to increase blood flow to deliver oxygen to the exercising muscle groups, while increasing the body temperature to reduce the risk of injury to the muscles and tendons.

As the muscles contract, they generate heat, increasing the temperature of the blood surrounding the working muscles. As your muscles become warmer, they become more pliable, which reduces the risk of injury. This means they are less likely to tear when they are stretched during the sport or physical activity, reducing the risk of injury.

Pulse raisers

The pulse raiser section of a warm-up should be designed to gradually increase the heart rate and body temperature ready for exercise. The pulse raiser should be age and sport specific to ready both the body and mind for exercise.

Pulse raiser ideas for different sports

An older adult attending a walking rugby session: walking relay race with rugby equipment.

A participant attending wheelchair basketball: create treasure island by placing 'treasure' at one end of the court and a hoop at the other and they must transport their 'treasure'.

An adolescent attending a kayak session: once in the kayaks, place an enlarged ball in the water and ask group to use their kayak to push the ball back into an area.

A child aged 5–11 years attending gymnastics: design hoops on the floor that the participants can jump into. One participant is a shark and must catch each person as they run and jump between the hoops.

An adult attending a spinning session: time trial on the bike.

◻ Figure 1.6: Pulse raiser ideas

◻ Table 1.2: Some pulse raiser ideas

Sport/physical activity	Type of participant	Pulse raiser idea
Football	A group of six-year-old children	Play shark-infested waters – participants run around a marked area, two sharks pass the ball between each other to be able to tag another participant. The one tagged replaces the shark who caught them
Gym	16-year-old adolescent	Five-minute row on a rowing machine
Swimming	35-year-old adult	Swim six lengths of the pool
Tennis	Group of 50-year-old adults with type 2 diabetes	Serve ball and run around to the other side of the net and return Whole group returns ball before running to other side of the net
Wheelchair basketball	A group of young adults with a disability	Chest passes in groups, throw the pass and follow the ball and re-join the opposite line

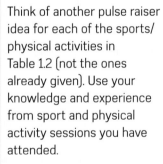

ACTIVITY

Think of another pulse raiser idea for each of the sports/physical activities in Table 1.2 (not the ones already given). Use your knowledge and experience from sport and physical activity sessions you have attended.

Ask your group for advice if unsure or need an idea.

CHECK MY LEARNING

1 Why is a warm-up important when participating in sport or physical activity?

2 Define the term 'pulse raiser'.

3 Suggest a pulse raiser for a climbing activity, a game of table tennis and a swimming session.

C1: Planning a warm-up 2: pulse raiser response of the cardiorespiratory and musculoskeletal systems

Performing a pulse raiser as part of the warm-up will have a response from the cardiorespiratory and musculoskeletal systems. The cardiorespiratory system is responsible for getting oxygen to the working muscles and removing carbon dioxide.

The cardiorespiratory system

The cardiorespiratory system consists of the heart and blood vessels working with the lungs and airways to carry oxygen and remove waste. The musculoskeletal system enables the body to move and offers protection while generating heat and enabling blood circulation. To enable blood flow to be increased, the pulse raiser has an effect on the cardiorespiratory system.

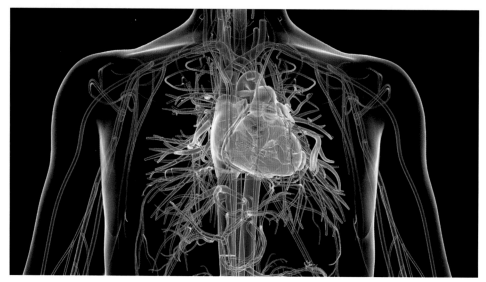

☐ **The cardiorespiratory system**

The pulse raiser will initiate a response from the cardiorespiratory system:
* Heart rate will increase as the body moves faster from rest, so when performing a pulse raiser, the participant will begin to run, which will increase their heart rate.
* Breathing rate and depth of breathing will increase as we take in more air as when the pulse raiser is performed, the body asks for more air so the rate you breathe increases.
* The working muscles will have an increase to the supply of oxygen they receive as the heart is pumping blood around the body faster, getting to the muscles and increasing their supply of oxygen.
* As a result, an increase in the removal of carbon dioxide will occur as we breathe out faster.

The benefit is that the working muscles will be warmer so will react and contract ready for exercise.

The musculoskeletal system

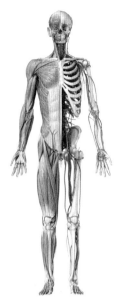

☐ The musculoskeletal system

☐ Muscles increasing in temperature

☐ Pliable muscles

The musculoskeletal system consists of the skeletal system and the muscular system. To complement the response of the cardiorespiratory system, the musculoskeletal system will respond by:

- increasing the temperature of the muscles, which allows the muscle to increase its elasticity
- increasing the pliability of the muscles, allowing muscles to move to make the movements for the sport or physical activity
- reducing the risk of muscle strain due to increased blood flow and lessening the risk of injury.

DID YOU KNOW?

The term 'pliability' means that the muscle can stretch and bend without breaking. Pliable muscles have high elasticity.

ACTIVITY

Support

1 Your teacher informs the class that the next sport session will be short tennis. Before the session starts, use the wipe board in the sports hall to offer an idea on an appropriate warm-up.

Challenge

2 When offering your idea, write one response of the cardiorespiratory system and one response of the musculoskeletal system.

CHECK MY LEARNING

1 State four responses of the cardiorespiratory system after a pulse raiser has been performed.

2 State three responses of the musculoskeletal system after a pulse raiser has been performed.

C1: Planning a warm-up 3: mobiliser activities

Mobiliser activities are exercises which take the joint through their range of movement, starting with small movements before making the movements bigger as you progress through the warm-up. The movement should be performed slowly to encourage focus and correct performance. The mobiliser section of the warm-up features exercises to improve the range of motion of joints and muscles.

Mobiliser activities could include stretching, jogging, and repetition of skills required in your sport. The increase in mobility helps participants reduce and prevent the risk of injury.

Mobiliser activities should be planned to suit a participant's individual needs. Look at the case study below and the suggestions for mobiliser activities that accompany the case study.

Case study: Rose

Rose is 65 years old and enjoys the chair aerobics offered by the day care centre she attends. To start the session, the instructor asks Rose to warm up her wrists, elbows and shoulders using mobiliser exercises.

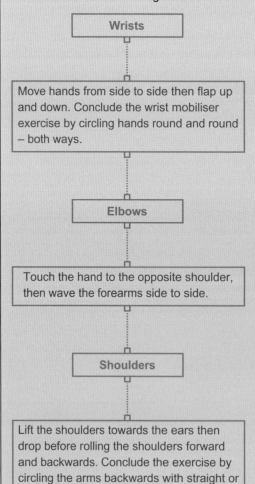

Wrists

Move hands from side to side then flap up and down. Conclude the wrist mobiliser exercise by circling hands round and round – both ways.

Elbows

Touch the hand to the opposite shoulder, then wave the forearms side to side.

Shoulders

Lift the shoulders towards the ears then drop before rolling the shoulders forward and backwards. Conclude the exercise by circling the arms backwards with straight or bent arms.

■ Figure 1.7: Mobiliser flow chart

ACTIVITY

Support

1 Complete the table offering Rose mobiliser exercises for the following areas:

Area	Suggested mobiliser exercise
Spine	
Hips	
Knees	
Ankles	

Challenge

2 You have suggested mobiliser activities for an older adult. Complete the activity again suggesting ideas for an adolescent or adult.

☐ A mobiliser activity for the shoulders

Response of the body systems to mobiliser activities

In the pulse raiser section, you examined the response of the cardiorespiratory and musculoskeletal systems. The cardiorespiratory and musculoskeletal systems will also have a response after an individual has completed mobiliser exercises as part of the warm-up routine.

Response of the cardiorespiratory system to mobiliser exercises:
- Slight drop in heart rate as intensity of exercise lowers as the tissues demand less oxygen to complete the exercises.
- Slight drop in breathing rate as intensity of exercise lowers. When we exercise, the body demands more oxygen and therefore instead of breathing 15 times per minute we breath 40–60 times per minute. When completing a mobiliser, the breathing rate lowers as the demand for oxygen lowers as the body asks for less oxygen.

Response of the musculoskeletal system during the completion of mobiliser exercises:
- Increased production of synovial fluid in the joints to increase lubrication of the joint and increases range of movement at the joint. When the body performs exercises, the soft tissue surrounding the joint called the synovial membrane produces more fluid to allow the bones to move more smoothly.

Examples of mobiliser activities

High kicks, lunges, squats, and shoulder rotations are basic examples of mobiliser activities for many sports. In specific sports such as gymnastics, participants even need to mobilise their wrists, fingers and arms to prepare them for the nature of their high-impact sport.

CHECK MY LEARNING

1 During a practical session, demonstrate a mobiliser activity.
2 While performing the activity, inform the group of a response of the cardiorespiratory and musculoskeletal system.

BEST PRACTICE

Football follows a specific set of warm-up and mobilisation exercises for young athletes. The FIFA 11+ warm-up builds strength and conditions the body for football. Planning these activities is usually the role of a strength and conditioning coach or a sport scientist.

C1: Planning a warm-up 4: preparation stretches

Preparation stretches are completed as part of a warm-up to stretch the main muscles that will be used in the sport or physical activity the individual is going to perform. The preparation stretches should always be performed after the warm-up activities but before the main session as the muscles must be warm to enable a participant to perform the stretches correctly.

Preparatory stretches are a type of stretching that take place before the training session or match takes place. The aim is to complete stretches on all the muscles required in your sport. Each stretch should be held for 10-15 seconds at a time and are sometimes repeated in multiple sets.

The muscular system

The following diagram shows you the muscular system and the major muscles in the human body:

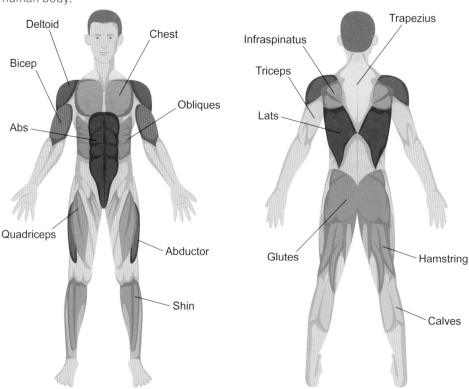

◻ Figure 1.8: The muscular system: major muscles in the human body

Static and dynamic stretches

An example of **static stretching** is bending over and touching your toes and holding the position.

An example of **dynamic stretching** is bending over and touching your toes but then bending and straightening the knee during the stretch. More examples are given in Table 1.3.

◘ Table 1.3: Some examples of static and dynamic stretches

Muscle	Example of a static stretch	Example of a dynamic stretch
Deltoids	Bring a straight arm across your chest, use the other arm to hook the straight arm above the elbow. Push straight arm towards the chest	Hold arms straight to the side of the body, in the shape of a cross. Swing arms to hug the body, swing back to starting position
Biceps & Triceps	Sit on the floor, knees bent, hands placed on the floor behind the body fingers pointing down the body, lift hips, hold	Feet shoulder-width apart, arms straight at shoulder height, thumbs up and rotate, starting slowly, pointing thumbs backwards
Erector Spinae	Kneel down, lie forward keeping the knees bent, stretch arms, hold and breathe	Curl body forward and perform rotational movements
Abdominals	Chair stretch: sit down, lean your back against the back of the chair. Lift each leg in turn	Chair stretch: legs together, lift legs, arms behind the head twist towards the legs
Obliques	Feet shoulder-width apart, twist torso and hold	Lie down face upwards. Lift knees to right angle, arms extended to the side at shoulder level. Twist knees to right and left side
Hip flexors	Lie on your back, legs straight, bend left leg towards the body, arms holding below the knee and hold. Repeat with the right leg	Perform a lunge position. One arm above your head, the other across the abdominals. Twist to each side
Gluteus maximus	Lie on your back, knees bent, left ankle over right knee. Pull right knee towards the body and hold. Repeat with right ankle over left knee	Hold the back of a chair, stand with feet shoulder-width apart, swing right leg in front of the left leg, leading with the inside of the foot. Repeat with the left leg.
Quadriceps	Hold a chair or wall. Feet together. Bend the right leg, hold foot and pull towards the gluteus maximus. Push foot into the hand. Repeat using the left leg	Perform jump squats
Hamstrings	Sit on the floor, legs straight. Reach arms forward to touch the toes	Standing shoulder-width apart, swing left leg upwards (straight), touch toes with stretched right arm. Repeat using right leg
Gastrocnemius	Hands placed on a wall, feet shoulder-width apart, step back with left leg, heel on the floor and hold. Repeat with right leg	Seated stretch. Perform calf raises

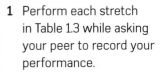

ACTIVITY

Support

1 Create a table like Table 1.3. Include another example of a stretch for each muscle group.

Challenge

2 Produce an instructor guide for each stretch in Table 1.3. How would a participant perform the stretch?

ACTIVITY

1 Perform each stretch in Table 1.3 while asking your peer to record your performance.

2 Reflect on the strengths and weaknesses of your performance. Did you perform the stretch correctly? Are there any improvements to the movement you need to complete?

3 Make notes of teaching points to offer others when performing the stretch.

BEST PRACTICE

Warming up muscles isn't as simple as just conducting a pulse raiser and a few stretches. The body needs to be conditioned from a period of training. To maximise the benefits of a pre-game warm-up, it should be repeated before training sessions as well.

CHECK MY LEARNING

1 Define the term 'preparation stretch'.
2 Describe a static stretch.
3 Describe a dynamic stretch.

C1: Planning a warm-up 5: preparation stretch response of the cardiorespiratory and musculoskeletal systems

Static and dynamic stretching enable a participant to focus on muscles which will be used in the performance they are undertaking. Static stretching is important as it allows a participant flexibility and range of motion in the joint, resulting in improved performance of their activity. Dynamic stretching also benefits the participant as it increases joint and muscle mobility, which can reduce the risk of injury.

Response of the cardiorespiratory system

The cardiorespiratory system responds to the preparatory stretching by elevating your heart rate to pump more oxygenated blood around the body to your working muscles. The increased blood flow delivers more nutrients to the muscles, tendons and ligaments, helping them to become more supple.

Case study: Edward

Edward's cardiorespiratory system has had a response to the static and dynamic stretches:

Slight drop in heart rate

Slight drop in breathing rate

Maintained elevated heart and breathing rate for dynamic stretches.

Response of the musculoskeletal system

The musculoskeletal system responds to preparatory stretching by increasing the range of motion at joints to help your body withstand the rigour and stress of exercise. The tendons and ligaments at the joints become pliable and reduce the risk of you getting injured. In addition, your muscles increase in temperature, preparing you for the game or training session.

Case study: Helena

Helena's musculoskeletal system has had a response to the static and dynamic stretching she has participated in. She has extended muscles so that they are fully stretched so less likely to tear during sport or physical activity.

ACTIVITY

Support

1 Create a booklet with diagrams and pointers on performing static and dynamic stretches.

Challenge

2 Produce a booklet on different stretches including the coaching points for participation in the stretch.

A coach or instructor would share coaching points with participants to reduce the risk of injury.

For example, when touching their toes:

- Stand with feet hip-width apart
- Move hips slightly backwards
- Slide arms down their thighs and shins towards the feet
- Keep back straight
- Continue until point of mild discomfort
- Hold the position for 10–15 seconds.

By offering coaching points the participant can appreciate how to perform the stretch correctly, reducing the risk of injury while achieving the aim of a static stretch.

CHECK MY LEARNING

1 State the response of the cardiorespiratory system when performing the preparation stretches.

2 State the response of the musculoskeletal system when performing the preparation phase.

BEST PRACTICE

The coach or the instructor should ensure participants are fully warmed up before starting the exercise. Failure to warm up sufficiently leads to muscle tears, sprains and strains that prevent participants from exercising.

C2: Adapting warm-ups for different types of participants and activities 1: specific to the participants

Adapting the warm-up for different participants allows the session to be accessible for all. Engaging activities which motivate a participant to join in while working to appreciate the benefits of sport and physical activity are crucial in preparing an athlete for the movements expected by the activities they want to participate in.

Adapting warm-ups for different participants

Warm-ups can be adapted for different participants and different physical activities in various ways. For participants you can vary:
- the intenstity of the activity (**moderate intensity** or **vigorous intensity**)
- the impact (high or low)
- the timing
- the type of stretch.

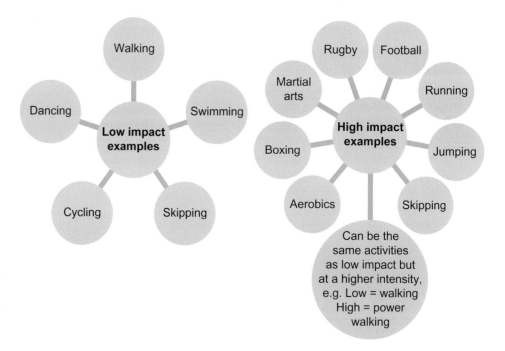

◻ Figure 1.9: Low- and high-impact options

1 During a practical session, take part in a variety of low-impact and high-impact activities.
- Discuss with your peers the differences.
- Ask a peer to record you participating in a low- or high-impact activity.
- Use the recording to highlight coaching points for each activity.

2 Ask an individual or small group to take part in your low- or high-impact activity. Initially observe the activity. Next, practise instructing using the coaching points:
- What difference did it make to the activity once you added coaching points? How did the participants feel?
- Record their comments and reflect on the points given.
- Share the points with your teacher. Ask for feedback.

ACTIVITY

Support

1 Research the time a primary-aged child with a disability should warm up before taking part in their chosen activity.

Challenge

2 Prepare a podcast which informs the listener on the expected duration of a warm up for each type of participant.

Adapting the timing

The duration and intensity of the warm-up differs from person to person. The warm-up should match the individual needs of the participants, being sport-specific and including the participant's own injury prevention exercises. For example, a netballer who has just come back from a hamstring strain will need to spend longer warming up their hamstrings to help reduce the risk of further injury.

The length of time needed to warm up is different depending on the participant:
- Primary age = 6 minutes
- Adolescent = 6 minutes
- Adult = 6 minutes
- Older adult = 10–15 minutes
- Individuals with long-term health conditions = 10–15 minutes.

Adapting the stretches

Participants new to sport and physical activities or trying a new activity will be unsure of the types and techniques of different warm-up stretches. Be sure to use simple stretches for beginners. By developing a participant's technique in simple stretches, you will build their confidence to attempt complex stretches. For example, a static hamstring stretch, where participants stand upright and gently bend one knee as if they are going into a sitting position. Using demonstrations and discussing technique will support the participant to develop their ability in completing simple stretches. Once the participant is confident and able to perform the stretches correctly, you can include additional stretches in their routine. Once a beginner gains experience in the sport or physical activity, you can introduce compound stretches. As an advanced participant the compound exercises which work multiple muscle groups at the same time can be introduced to the participant. For example, a squat that works the quadriceps, glutes and calves can be developed into a stretch with a roundhouse kick, engaging the participant to stretch further but also limit the boredom of completing the required stretches.

DID YOU KNOW?

A participant may ask you how they know if they are working at **moderate intensity**. The easiest answer is that they can still talk but cannot sing.
A participant may ask you how they know if they are working at **vigorous intensity**. The easiest answer is that they will not be able to say more than a few words without pausing for breath.

LINK IT UP

In A2, you explored the different types of participants and government recommendations for sport and physical activity.

CHECK MY LEARNING

1 Define moderate intensity levels.
2 Define vigorous intensity levels.
3 State four low-impact and four high-impact activities.
4 Describe how you would adapt the low- and high-impact activities for participants with a disability.

C2: Adapting warm-ups for different types of participants and activities: specific to the physical activity

In C1, you investigated the importance of a warm-up. There is also a benefit of offering participants a warm-up specific to the sport or physical activity they are going to participate in, which will engage the correct muscles as well as their mental approach to the activities about to be performed.

Make the warm-up sport specific

It is important to design the warm-up for the requirements of the sport or physical activity as well as the needs of the participants. By performing a warm-up appropriate for the sport, you will focus the body by stretching the correct muscles as well as the mind by mentally preparing the participant on the performance they are going to take part in.

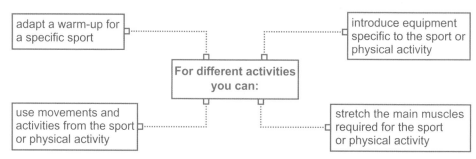

▣ Figure 1.10: Adapting a warm-up for different physical activities

▣ Table 1.4: Examples of warm-ups adapted to different physical activities

Sport or physical activity	Pulse raiser suggestion – sport specific
Volleyball	Place hoops on either side of the volleyball court. Participants to use the service line to serve, aiming for the colour hoop that the instructor shouts for that round. Once the participants have served, they must run to the other side of the court and repeat
Boxing	Ghost boxing, front, side and upper cuts combined with squats and roundhouse kicks – leader to shout out number of reps
Gymnastics	Bands and hoops to be placed on the matted area, leaps and turns to be completed to music
Boccia	Leader to set up a number of goal areas, participant to be offered different-sized balls to roll into the goal areas
Surfing	Participants start by laying on their board, jump to surf position on the board then run to the shoreline, lay down and jump to surf position in the sand, return to the board. Repeat

Case study: Cooper

Cooper enjoys the surfing sessions he attends during the school holidays. He asks if he can help warm up the young children to gain experience in leading a group. What activities would you suggest he offers as a sport-specific pulse raiser?

ACTIVITY

Choose three of the sports or physical activities in the table and identify at least one other specific warm-up example appropriate to each activity.

Show your teacher.

ACTIVITY

Support

1 Plan a sport-specific warm-up for an adult playing badminton.

Show your teacher the plan and ask for feedback.

Challenge

2 Plan a sport specific warm-up for an adult participating in an outdoor activity such as white-water rafting or abseiling.

BEST PRACTICE

Warm-ups don't just prepare you for the physical aspects of sport, they prepare you mentally for the demands of the training session or game ahead. The warm-up for a coach or sport scientist is known as the performance-enhancing process.

CHECK MY LEARNING

1 Define the term 'sport-specific warm-up'.

2 Describe a pulse raiser for a hockey participant.

3 Describe a mobiliser for a group going trampolining.

4 Describe a preparation stretch for a climber.

C3: Delivering a warm-up to prepare participants for physical activity 1

In this component you are going to deliver a warm-up to your peers and hopefully to an unfamiliar group. Your focus is to feel confident with good communication skills alongside appropriately planned activities. Initially you will practise delivering and supporting a pulse raiser before demonstrating mobiliser stretches and preparation exercises.

Organising the warm-up

Warm-ups should be methodically planned and set up ready for the participants to start as soon as they arrive at the session. This saves time and allows for a smooth and purposeful session to take place.

When organising a warm-up, you need to think about the organisation. For example:

- Space – which area are you going to use? Will you use the whole sports hall or field area, or will you create a space using cones or lines on the floor?
- Indoor or outdoor space – what facilities are available to you, would you be able to change if the weather was too hot, too cold or raining?
- What equipment do you need? Think about the focus of the session – which resources do you need?
- How will you organise the participants? Once you have created the activities in your plan, think about how you will arrange the participants: as individuals, a whole group or smaller groups?
- How much time for pulse raiser, mobiliser and preparation stretch phase? In a six- or 10-minute warm-up, how much time would you give to each section of the warm-up? Practise timing your activities.

Steps to a purposeful warm-up

1 Gradual pulse raiser

2 Group stretching

3 Individual injury prevention work/stretching

4 Skill-based practice

5 Mental preparation

6 Consider if you're ready.

ACTIVITY

Support

1 In pairs, plan the organisation of a pulse raiser, use an activity you are familiar with.

Show the plan to your teacher and ask for feedback.

Challenge

2 In pairs, plan the organisation of a pulse raiser, use an activity you are unfamiliar with.

Show the plan to your teacher and ask for feedback.

Demonstrating and positioning

You will need to demonstrate the warm-up to your participant/s:

- Demonstrate movements in the pulse raiser
- Demonstrate movements in the mobiliser
- Demonstrate stretches in the preparation phase.

It is also important to consider your positioning. For example, where should you stand when delivering and demonstrating to the participants so that they can carry out the warm-up safely and effectively?

BEST PRACTICE

When conducting a warm-up session, you would need to consider how the session could be adapted to best suit the needs of the participant. For example, for an older person the session could be a chair warm-up. You could also ask the person how they are feeling after each activity, and whether the exercise is too easy or too hard.

ACTIVITY

Support

1 Plan to deliver the pulse raiser element.
- For the activity, stand in different areas of the space you have created when instructing and demonstrating.
- Which position offered the most effective delivery of the pulse raiser element?
- Ask for feedback from the participants.
- Discuss the outcome with your teacher.

Challenge

2 Plan to deliver a mobiliser element – select two or three activities.
- For each activity, stand in a different place when instructing and demonstrating.
- Which position offered the most effective delivery of the mobiliser element?
- Ask for feedback from the participants.
- Discuss the outcome with your teacher.

CHECK MY LEARNING

1 How should the warm-up session be organised?
2 What is the importance of positioning when delivering the warm-up?

C3: Delivering a warm-up to prepare participants for physical activity 2

GETTING STARTED

Watch a video clip of a warm-up session. You could search for 'warm-up' and look at NGB websites.

What did you observe from the participants?

What feedback would you have given to each participant on their performance during the warm-up?

Discuss your thoughts with your peers.

The motivation to take part in sport and physical activity is driven by learning a new skill, improving fitness levels and being part of a team. Helping an individual realise the goal they've set while achieving the benefits is often the role of the coach or instructor. Offering feedback and motivational comments can encourage an individual to meet government expectations of participation in sport and physical activity while experiencing the benefits of taking part in sport.

Supporting the participants during the warm-up

Coaches or instructors can support participants by:

1   Observing their performance – introduce the exercise, then stand back and observe the participants.

2   Providing instructions on movements performed – offer a demonstration to confirm technique of the activity/exercise.

3   Offering teaching points to each individual – once you have observed the participants, if you notice incorrect technique go and offer guidance to change their position in the activity/exercise.

4   Providing feedback to each participant – offer individual or group feedback on their performance during the warm-up, be a critical friend while offering praise.

ACTIVITY

Consider the coaching points you might give for a badminton pulse raiser.

List the points you may observe and the feedback you could give to the participant.

◘ A warm-up session is a good time to demonstrate technique

Participants should receive immediate feedback during the warm-up to ensure it remains effective. Regular praise sandwiched between constructive feedback helps motivate and develop the participants during the session. You can also increase participant motivation by adding a competitive element to the warm-up such as linking an activity to the skill-based elements of the warm-up. For example, the first team to complete 20 chest passes in the basketball warm-up.

By observing participants, you can offer praise as well as strengths and areas for improvement in their performance. This will allow the participant to set goals for future performance, which is a benefit of taking part in sport and physical activity.

ACTIVITY

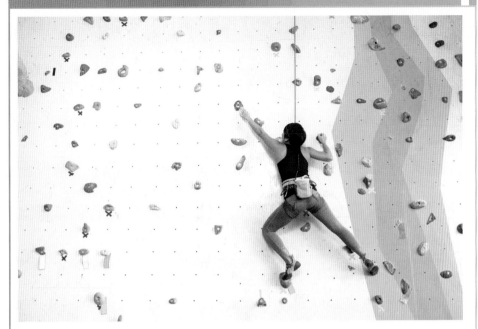

Harriet is participating in a climbing wall activity.

In pairs, discuss the teaching points of climbing.

Agree on what feedback you would you give to this participant.

DID YOU KNOW?

When planning a warm-up session, practise the pulse raiser, mobiliser and preparation activities first, this will help you understand the teaching points.

ACTIVITY

Support

1 Design a pulse raiser activity and describe how you would support the participants during the activity.

Challenge

2 In pairs, design a pulse raiser activity. Label the pair A and B.

   A should deliver the activity while B observes.

   Discuss the observations.

   Did person A support the participants effectively?

CHECK MY LEARNING

1 State four ways that the instructor could support participants taking part in a warm-up.

2 Describe the benefits of observing participants during the warm-up.

Learning outcome C: Assessment practice
Be able to prepare participants to take part in physical activity

How you will be assessed

In this component you will be assessed by completing one internally assessed assignment. The assignment will be set by Pearson. This assignment will be one of three tasks for Component 1 and it will take one hour to complete.

You will be provided with an assignment brief that describes what you need to do and the date by which you must submit the completed work to the teacher.

Your teacher will mark the assignment and tell you what grade you have achieved.

You will be expected to show that you understand how to prepare participants to take part in physical activity.

This will include:

- Being able to prepare participants to take part in sport and physical activity
- Planning a warm-up
- Adapting a warm-up for different categories of participants and different types of physical activity
- Delivering a warm-up to prepare participants for physical activity.

CHECKPOINT

Review your learning of this component by answering the following questions, this will help you prepare for the assignment.

Strengthen

- State the response of the cardiorespiratory and musculoskeletal systems to a pulse raiser.
- State the response of the cardiorespiratory and musculoskeletal systems to a mobiliser.
- State the response of the cardiorespiratory and musculoskeletal systems to a preparation stretch.

Challenge

- Select a pulse raiser for a sport-specific warm-up.
- Select a mobiliser for a sport-specific warm-up.
- Select a preparation stretch for a sport-specific warm-up.

ASSESSMENT PRACTICE

An older adult would like to participate in walking football.

1 Describe a suitable pulse raiser for this activity, including the coaching points.

2 Describe a suitable set of mobiliser activities for the older adult for taking part in this activity.

3 Describe a suitable set of preparation stretches suitable for this activity.

4 Justify the choice of activities in the warm-up, how do the activities meet the needs of the participant?

5 Discuss the responses of the cardiorespiratory and musculoskeletal system for each element of the warm-up.

Another older adult asks to join the group, the individual has asthma.

How would you adapt the activities to meet the needs of this participant?

How would you organise the warm-up?

How would you support the participants?

Design a feedback form you could offer the participants for additional feedback.

TIPS

- Interview older adults about the choices they could make when selecting a sport or physical activity to participate in.
- Produce a video or audio recording to show how you would deliver your planned warm-up.
- In your assessment, make sure you justify why you have selected the sport or physical activity.

TAKE IT FURTHER

Consider why a participant may need to complete their own individual stretches and justify how and when you would incorporate this into a group warm-up activity. Then discuss how you could motivate a participant to warm up who dislikes completing the warm-up.

COMPONENT

02

Taking part and improving other participants' sporting performance

Introduction

Participation in sport continues to grow, as we become more aware of the benefits of taking part in regular physical activity.

Component 2 will focus on learning about sport from the perspectives of both a participating player and a coach learning about ways to improve participants' sporting skills and performance.

You will investigate the different components of physical fitness as well as the skill-related components of fitness, examine how they apply to different sports and explore their potential impact on sporting performance.

You will develop your own sporting skills by researching, practising and demonstrating the skills required to be able to participate effectively in different sports. This will include examining the roles and responsibilities of officials and researching the rules and regulations of different sports and how these are applied in different situations.

Lastly, this component will help you to explore ways to improve other participants' performance. This will be achieved through learning drills and practices to develop specific sports skills, practising setting up drills and supporting participants, and using demonstrations and teaching points to develop and improve performance.

LEARNING OUTCOMES

In this component you will:

A	understand how different components of fitness are used in different physical activities
B	be able to participate in sport and understand the roles and responsibilities of officials
C	demonstrate ways to improve participants' sporting techniques.

A1: Components of physical fitness 1: aerobic endurance and muscular endurance

GETTING STARTED

What do we mean by physical fitness? Is fitness measurable and if so how do we assess it? Discuss fitness with classmates in a small group. Write a paragraph explaining what fitness means to you.

Hold your hands out in front of you and keep your head up and back straight. Bend your legs until your knees reach 90 degrees. Stand up again. Repeat this process as many times as you can in two minutes. Compare your results with your classmates. What is it that allows some people to perform more repetitions than others?

■ A person can have high levels of fitness in some areas, such as flexibility, but less in others

KEY TERM

Aerobic endurance is your ability to exercise at moderate intensity for extended periods of time. Exercise intensity is a measure of how hard a physical activity feels while you're doing it.

LINK IT UP

In Component 1 C1 you looked at the response of the cardiorespiratory system to the different phases of a warm-up.

There are different definitions of fitness, and it can mean different things depending on what is important to you and the sport(s) you play. In broad terms, it means the condition of being physically healthy because of exercise.

Physical fitness is a complicated subject. Many people consider it to be simply how far we can run, swim, cycle or row. However, the distance a person can complete is only a part of the overall elements that make someone fit. Someone can have high levels of physical fitness in one area and low levels in another area.

Physical fitness can be broken down into six different components, as shown in Figure 2.1.

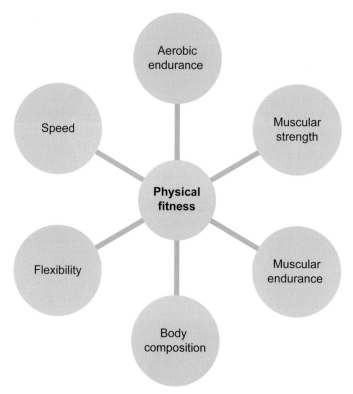

■ Figure 2.1: Physical fitness is made up of six components

Aerobic endurance

Aerobic endurance is your ability to keep performing an activity, such as running, cycling or swimming, without becoming fatigued. This relies on having a high level of cardiovascular fitness.

The cardiovascular system is made up of the circulatory system and the respiratory system. The circulatory system comprises the heart, blood and blood vessels, and the respiratory system is made up of the lungs and airways – see Figure 2.2. These two systems work together to take oxygen from the air we breathe, carry oxygen and nutrients to the muscles and organs of the body, and remove waste products, such as carbon dioxide.

Support

Identify which of the following sports require high levels of aerobic endurance:

- archery
- hockey
- netball
- swimming 1600 metres
- 100-metre sprint
- football
- high jump
- basketball
- ironman triathlon.

Challenge

Explain which sport you think requires the highest levels of aerobic endurance, giving reasons for your choice.

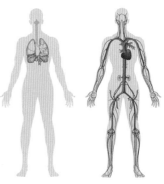

Respiratory system   Circulatory system

■ Figure 2.2: Aerobic endurance relies on the circulatory and respiratory systems working efficiently together

Muscular endurance

Our muscular system is complex: it is made up of a large number of muscles. **Muscular endurance** is related to how efficiently your muscular system works. The greater a person's muscular endurance, the increased ability they have to perform an exercise that involves repetitive contractions of a muscle over an extended period of time. Because there are many muscles in our body, it is possible to have good muscular endurance over one movement but poor over another. Movements could include squatting, performing a pull-up, doing a press-up or doing sit-ups.

KEY TERM

Muscular endurance is where a muscle can continue contracting over a period of time against a light to moderate fixed resistance or load.

■ Table 2.1: Examples of sports that require good levels of muscular endurance

Individual sport	Team sport
Rock climbing to hold on to the rock face	Rugby to be able to keep pushing in a ruck or scrum
Hurdles to maintain the ability to jump	Hockey to ensure that participants can keep moving at speed
Swimming to keep up speed	Rowing to keep stroke rate high
Sailing to allow the person to lean out and keep the boat flat	Netball to allow athletes to keep jumping to catch the ball
Cycling to keep pushing the pedals and keep the bike moving	Football to allow competitors to keep kicking the ball hard

Muscular endurance is needed in everyday life. For example, when climbing a flight of stairs your leg muscles are repeatedly contracting to take you all the way to the top. Can you give any other examples of when muscular endurance might be needed in everyday life?

DID YOU KNOW?

There are over 650 muscles found within the human body, but this figure can be higher, depending on what we count as being a muscle. The range in number is largely down to the difficulty in separating muscles that are grouped together and those that are distinct individual muscles.

CHECK MY LEARNING

1 List the six components of physical fitness.

2 Explain why aerobic endurance is needed for any sports that have sustained physical activity.

3 For two sports of your choice, describe why specific areas of your body require high levels of muscular endurance.

A1: Components of physical fitness 2: muscular strength and speed

GETTING STARTED

■ Elite 100-metre sprinters

Examine the photo of 100-metre women sprinters and identify key features of the sprinters' physiques. Explain how these features help them to run at high speed over a short distance.

KEY TERMS

Muscular strength is the maximum force (in kg or N) that can be generated by a muscle or muscle group.

Speed is when a person travels very fast over a short distance, calculated as distance covered divided by the time taken to cover the distance.

BEST PRACTICE

To protect your bones and prevent injuries from falls, all people should take part in resistance training to maintain their muscle mass.

Depending on the sport you play, it can be important to train your muscles to have a high level of strength or to be able to move quickly.

Muscular strength

Muscular strength is related to how much muscle mass a person has – the larger the muscle mass, the more strength the person has. This is because muscle tissue produces force. The more muscle tissues that a person has, the more force their muscles can produce.

ACTIVITY

Support

Identify two individual sports and two team sports that require high levels of strength.

Challenge

For each sport, describe why a person playing that sport needs high levels of strength to perform well in their sport.

While it is not necessary to have high levels of strength for health reasons, a certain level of strength is required in order to support daily activities. Strong postural muscles are required to keep an upright stance and prevent back pain; strong leg muscles are required to allow us to hold our body weight and move around. Muscle tissue has a higher metabolic rate compared to other body tissues so it helps to 'burn calories' to prevent a person from becoming overweight.

It is important to note that as a person gets older, from about the age of 30, their muscle mass naturally starts to reduce unless the person takes part in resistance training to try to maintain or increase their muscle mass. Strength training can help protect your bones and prevent fractures from falls, as it helps to maintain balance and coordination, which is crucial in preventing falls.

Speed

Speed is where a person travels very fast over a short distance. Speed is worked out by measuring distance covered divided by the time taken to cover the distance. Travelling at high speed can take place in various forms such as cycling, swimming, rowing or running over a short distance. Speed is also required in a range of team and individual sports and activities, such as having to sprint to get to the ball in football or to intercept a pass in netball.

◘ Athletes who require a wheelchair can take part in wheelchair racing, which competes over short distances and requires high levels of speed

Speed training puts your muscles through a greater range of motion. This helps build strength, increase mobility and increase the number of muscle fibers in the body. This can make your body more balanced and increase the quality of your daily life and not just your performance in sport.

ACTIVITY

Support

There are many sports that benefit from an athlete having speed. In a small group, create a list of sports that require high levels of speed, from both team and individual sports and activities.

Challenge

Next to each of the sports identified above, explain why high levels of speed are required.

CHECK MY LEARNING

1 For two sports of your choice, describe why specific areas of your body require high levels of muscular strength.
2 Identify three individual sports and three team sports that require speed.

LINK IT UP

In Component 1 you studied how to prepare participants for sport. Preparing for speed training needs a unique warm-up.

BEST PRACTICE

In some sports, timing gates are used to monitor the speed of an athlete in training. In addition, GPS can be used to track player speeds during competitions.

A1: Components of physical fitness 3: flexibility and body composition

The body is amazing, and can be trained in different ways to change and improve. Keeping the body supple and having an optimum fat ratio is important to everyday life as well as to sport.

Flexibility

Flexibility is an area of fitness that is sometimes overlooked in favour of increasing other components of physical fitness. However, being flexible is directly linked to success in almost every sport.

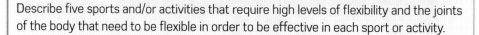

ACTIVITY

Describe five sports and/or activities that require high levels of flexibility and the joints of the body that need to be flexible in order to be effective in each sport or activity.

We have a greater range of motion available in some joints, such as the shoulder compared to the elbow. You can move your whole arm in a circular motion because of the type of joint at the shoulder, whereas it is only possible to bend and straighten the elbow joint. Muscle and ligaments surround a joint and will affect how much movement a person can produce at a joint. The less flexible a person is, the less movement they have at various joints in their body because their muscle tissues and ligaments are stiffer and shorter compared to a more flexible person.

Flexibility, like many other components of fitness, can be good across one area of a person's body but weak in another. Ensuring adequate flexibility is an important part of injury prevention. Forcing muscles to make movements that they are unused to can lead to damage and injury. Conditioning muscles with flexibility training can protect the body from injuries through overextension. During a warm-up, gently stretching muscles to prepare them for exercise should be an integral element.

Body composition

Body composition is what your body is made of. The main components of your body include bone, muscle and fat.

ACTIVITY

Mark Cavendish (Tour de France cyclist), Dina Asher-Smith (track and field athlete) and Owen Farrell (rugby player) are very clearly different athletes. What is it about their body compositions that make them effective at their chosen sports?

To a certain extent we are born with a body type and this will define our capabilities, strengths and weaknesses as an athlete. When you measure body composition, the main area that is considered is the amount of body fat a person has. You need to have some body fat to be healthy; however, too much body fat can result in health problems. An excess of body fat also increases our body's weight, which in turn means that we have to carry more load. This extra load can make some sports, physical activities or daily tasks more difficult to complete.

Body composition can have a significant effect on a sportsperson's performance and varies depending on the sport, with different sports having an 'optimum' body composition for performance, as shown in Table 2.2.

◻ **Table 2.2: Examples of sports that favour different body compositions**

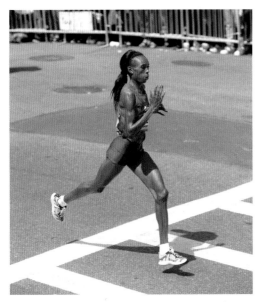

Rita Jeptoo of Kenya runs the Boston marathon

Long-distance runners tend to have slight frames with lean muscles and carry very little body fat. This means that their legs need to work less hard to carry their frames than if they had muscular bodies or excess body fat

Sanne Wevers during Balance Beam in Doha, Qatar

Gymnasts have powerful frames with a lot of muscle tissue and very little body fat. By having low levels of body fat, gymnasts remain as light as possible but still have the muscle strength to jump high enough and with sufficient power to perform somersaults in the air

Konrad Bukowiecki competing in the shot put in the 2022 World Indoor Championships

An athlete that throws the shot put needs high levels of muscle tissue to throw the shot with force so it will travel a long distance. As they do not have to move their body any significant distance, excess body fat does not reduce the shot putter's performance

LINK IT UP

In Component 1 A1 you studied types of sports available to everyone. This provides you with a good list of sporting examples.

CHECK MY LEARNING

1 Thinking about your own body, which areas are the most flexible and which areas are the least flexible? Explain why you think this is.

2 Explain how body composition affects performance in different sports and activities.

A1: Components of physical fitness 4: types of activity and impact on performance

The six components of physical fitness and five elements of skill-related fitness contribute to a person's overall fitness and will have a direct impact on their performance in a particular sport or activity.

Benefits of fitness

There are many benefits of having a good level of physical **fitness**. In everyday life this includes being able to climb steps or stairs, walking or cycling to school or the workplace, or carrying out regular tasks such as shopping and cleaning. For athletes, having a good level of fitness means that they will be able to participate in their sport effectively and to a high level. The relationship between physical fitness, exercise and health is shown in Figure 2.3.

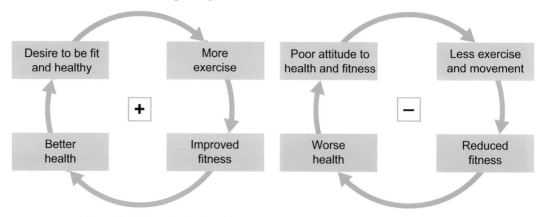

◻ Figure 2.3: The relationship between physical fitness, exercise and health can be positive or negative

Impact of fitness on performance

Increased physical fitness leads to better athletic performance, as a physically fit athlete is likely to perform better in their sport. Athletes who have good physical fitness can not only have improved performance, but can also reduce the incidence of injuries and accidents caused by the movement performed in their sport, as their body will be in the optimum physical condition needed to play the sport.

◻ Table 2.3: Examples of how the components of fitness are used in different sports and activities and how they impact performance

Sport/activity	Most important components of physical and skill-related fitness	Impact on performance
Individual sport: golf	Flexibility	Flexibility ensures the athlete has the mobility in the shoulder joint required to swing the club. Limited flexibility will hamper the ability to swing

	Power	Power is needed to swing the club to propel the ball through the air towards the target. Insufficient power will result in the ball not travelling far enough
	Coordination	Coordination is needed to connect the club to the ball. If the athlete does not have good hand-eye coordination, then they will likely not be able to strike the ball
Team sport: curling	Muscular strength	Muscular strength is important to ensure correct technique and delivery. Shoulder and upper body strength are vital for sweeping the stone and lower body strength is vital for a good delivery technique
	Aerobic endurance	In a game, players can sweep up to 80 stones. Good aerobic endurance is needed for the repeated bouts of hard exercise followed by active rest
	Balance	Athletes need to perform the stone delivery and sweeping actions on slippery ice. Good balance and stability are needed so they can perform these actions without falling
Outdoor activity: parkour	Aerobic endurance	Parkour requires constant running, moving and jumping. To meet the demands of the activity a high level of cardiovascular fitness is needed to supply the body with the oxygen and nutrients needed to keep going
	Power	With all the jumping, leaping and running, power is necessary to produce the explosive movements needed to travel between obstacles
	Coordination	Parkour is about efficient movement through the environment, using jumps, swings and vaults. Coordination is needed to make sure that take-offs and landings are well-timed and successful
Physical fitness activity: Zumba	Aerobic endurance	Aerobic endurance is needed to keep dancing and moving for prolonged periods of time
	Muscular endurance	Muscular endurance is needed to keep moving the body in repeated motions throughout the length of the session
	Balance	Balance is needed so that the person will stay on their feet whilst changing movements and steps, often at speed

Assessing fitness

Having low levels of the components of fitness can have a negative impact on sport or activity performance. It may well mean that other people taking part in that sport or activity will perform better because they have higher levels of fitness in specific components. It is therefore important to carry out fitness testing in order to identify which components of fitness need to be improved.

Fitness testing is essential to fitness training as it identifies areas of weakness, which can then be focused on. Training programmes can also be designed to work on these areas. Fitness tests are used before training begins to assess the level of a component, during the training programme to assess progress, and again at the end of the training programme to measure improvement.

ACTIVITY

The components of physical fitness are used in team sports, individual sports, outdoor activities and physical fitness activities.

Support

For each of the following sports and activities, identify the components of fitness that are most important:

1 Volleyball

2 Tennis

3 Rock climbing

4 Crossfit.

Challenge

For each of the four sports and activities listed above, explain how performance is impacted by the components of fitness that you have identified as most important.

LINK IT UP

In Component 2 you have looked at some of the benefits of participating in sport, and in Component 3 you will explore how to assess the components of fitness and different training methods for improving the physical components of fitness.

CHECK MY LEARNING

1 Outline what it means to be physically fit.

2 For a sport or an activity of your choice, describe how the component of physical and skill-related fitness impacts performance.

A2: Components of skill-related fitness 1: introduction and power

Fitness can be broken down into different components. We have already looked at the components of physical fitness. Now we will look at the components of skill-related fitness.

Skill-related fitness refers to additional aspects of fitness beyond the six components of physical fitness. These skills are important to be able to perform successfully the more technical aspects of many sports and activities.

Skill-related fitness can be broken down into five different components:

🔲 Figure 2.4: The five components of skill-related fitness

Power

Power is a combination of strength and speed. In sport and activity terms, power is the ability to apply the maximum force possible in as fast a time as possible, to use strength at speed. The force produced can be applied into our own body, into someone else or into an object.

🔲 Table 2.4: Examples of individual sports that require high levels of power

Golf needs power when a competitor has to hit the ball a long distance	Shot put requires power to throw the shot	Tennis requires power when hitting the ball, especially in the serve
Sprinting involves high levels of power to accelerate from the blocks	Powerlifting is the ability to lift a weight quickly from the floor, often to above the head	High jump needs power to push off the floor to generate height to get over the bar

◘ Table 2.5: Examples of team sports that require high levels of power

Football players need power to kick the ball hard	When rugby players are in the scrum and pushing against the other team they need power	When playing netball, players need to have power to jump high enough to catch a pass
Basketball requires lots of power to jump to the height of the basket and score	Rowing requires power to accelerate up to speed and keep the boat moving quickly	Hockey involves lots of changes of direction. After every extreme change, a player needs power to accelerate again

There are multiple benefits to having power, especially for athletes in sports. You can run faster, swing the bat harder, jump higher and lift more weight. Powerful athletes are often the most sought-after athletes for teams as they are often very dynamic and exciting for crowds to watch. For example, the boxer Deontay Wilder is well followed due to his powerful and explosive punching.

◘ Petra Kvitová uses power to hit a backhand shot

BEST PRACTICE

People often get confused between strength and power. In sport, they work closely to ensure athletes are able to create the best performance that they can. In weightlifting strength and power is essential. Tom Stoltman is currently the World's Strongest Man.

ACTIVITY

Support

For three selected sports or activities that require a high level of power, describe how power is used in that sport.

◘ Power is used in basketball to jump up to shoot

CHECK MY LEARNING

1 Outline what skill-related fitness is.

2 Explain how power is different from muscular strength.

A2: Components of skill-related fitness 2: agility and reaction time

GETTING STARTED

In small groups, discuss and make a list of sports that require a high level of agility and quick reaction times.

KEY TERMS

Agility is the ability to rapidly change body direction, accelerate, or decelerate.

Reaction time describes how fast an athlete is able to respond to an external signal or stimulus.

◻ Slalom skiers require agility to respond to obstacles

LINK IT UP

In Component 2 C2 you learn how to incorporate these skills into isolated, competitive and conditioned practices to help build your athlete's performances.

Agility and reaction time are two components of skill-related fitness that are fundamental to many sports and activities; these skills both involve being able to move the body.

Agility

Agility is all about being able to change the direction and the speed at which you are travelling, with speed and accuracy. Most sports require a degree of agility; for example, in football and rugby where the player with the ball dodges a defender, or in badminton or tennis, moving around the court quickly to reach the shuttlecock/ball in time. In contrast, static sports, such as Boccia and curling, do not require agility, other skills are more important in these sports.

Training to improve agility commonly involves exercises that develop faster foot speed and direction change. For example, an agility ladder is used to practise quick and accurate foot placement.

ACTIVITY

Support

Describe how athletes use agility in each of the following sports:
- Basketball
- Skiing
- Table tennis
- Ice hockey.

Challenge

Explain why agility also relies on cognitive functions such as interpreting visual information, timing and using the senses to anticipate what is about to happen.

Reaction time

Reaction time is the time taken between a stimulus and the start of a response. This is important in a great many sports; for example, it is useful for fast-paced sports and quick decision-making, such as sprinters responding to the gun at the start of a race, a goalkeeper saving a penalty, or a badminton player reacting to a smash shot.

How quickly your brain can respond to a stimulus and initiate a response is a complex process:

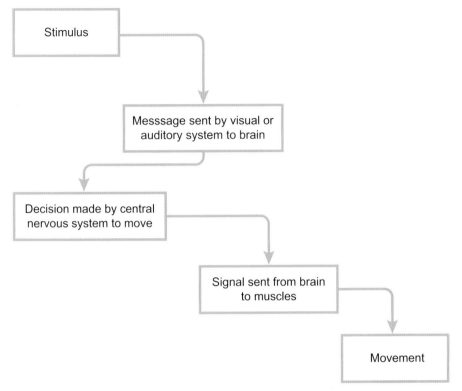

■ Figure 2.5: Reaction time involves processing information and initiating action as quickly as possible

All of this happens almost instantly. By training and improving the speed at which their brain processes the stimulus and initiates a response, athletes can gain vital extra time. Reaction-time training tends to be sport specific and often comes down to gaining experience in the sport to develop knowledge in order to interpret and predict movements and therefore be able to react more quickly and accurately.

ACTIVITY

Support

Describe two sports that require quick reaction times.

Challenge

Explain how gaining experience in sport and developing a deeper understanding of the sport can improve reaction times.

CHECK MY LEARNING

1 Describe why agility is required in judo and football.
2 Explain why reaction time is important to performance, giving a sporting example.

DID YOU KNOW?

Any condition or disorder that is characterised by perception, information processing or motor problems will affect reaction time. For example, a visual or hearing impairment will impact being able to see or hear a stimulus to have good reaction time; dementia will impact at the processing stage; and ADHD or Parkinson's disease can cause problems at the reaction stage. Other general factors that can lower and weaken reaction time include tiredness, low mood, anxiety or lack of concentration.

A2: Components of skill-related fitness 3: balance and coordination

The final components of skill-related fitness are balance and coordination. These components are fundamental to being able to move the body with accuracy and precision.

Balance

Balance is the ability to maintain your centre of mass over a base of support. In other words, it is the ability to be able to control your body's position. Balance is important in everyday life, not just in sport. Without good balance you would not be able to walk, stand up from a chair or bend over.

There are two types of balance, static and dynamic (Figure. 2.6).

Static balance: a yoga pose

Dynamic balance: lateral weight shift

◻ Figure 2.6: Types of balance

Static balance refers to the ability to maintain a position. **Dynamic balance** refers to the ability to remain upright when moving. Balance is closely linked to agility, as to be able to change direction quickly and accurately relies on you maintaining your balance.

◻ Practising yoga can improve balance

Athletes can benefit from balance training to improve movement and technique, to prevent injury and enhance performance. Balance training exercises can include standing on one foot, yoga poses, tai chi or Bosu ball exercises. By performing strength training movements on an unstable surface, or on one leg, you can train your strength and balance simultaneously. For example, a goblet squat on a Bosu ball, or a one-leg dumbbell deadlift.

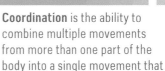

ACTIVITY

Support

In small groups, make a list of different sports and activities that involve static and dynamic balance.

Challenge

Choose one sport or activity from each category and describe why balance is fundamental to performing it successfully.

Coordination

Coordination is the ability to move two or more body parts at the same time smoothly and efficiently. It involves being able to use the body parts and senses together to perform techniques effectively. A high level of coordination is vital in sport, the terms hand-eye coordination or hand-foot coordination are commonly used.

ACTIVITY

Support

Test your own hand-eye coordination by carrying out the tennis ball test.

Method:

1   Make a mark on a wall with some tape.

2   Stand two metres away from the wall.

3   Throw the ball from an underarm position against the wall, aiming for the marker, and catch it in the opposite hand.

4   Alternate between the hands, always aiming for the mark.

Test yourself for 30 seconds, recording the number of successful catches.

Results:

>35 Excellent

30–35 Above average

25–29 Average

20–24 Below Average

<20 Poor.

Challenge

Explain what training you could undertake to improve your hand-eye coordination.

The impact of coordination is that the more coordinated a person, the more efficient their movements are, which will result in better performance, as the coordinated athlete can move more precisely and save energy with their movements.

Often, the way to improve coordination is sport specific and involves repeatedly practising a particular movement. For example, hitting a golf ball, dribbling a ball, or hitting/throwing a ball at a target.

KEY TERM

Coordination is the ability to combine multiple movements from more than one part of the body into a single movement that is smooth and efficient.

BEST PRACTICE

When working with children, you should encourage the development of balance and coordination. These are two of the most important gross motor skills in a child's physical development because they allow children to participate in sports and physical activities with a degree of success. This reduces their risk of injury and improves their ability to perform everyday tasks.

CHECK MY LEARNING

1   Make two lists of sports:
   a. sports that require hand to eye coordination
   b. sports that require hand to foot coordination.

2   Explain the differences between balance and coordination.

Learning outcome A: Assessment practice
Understand how different components
of fitness are used in different physical
activities

How you will be assessed

In this component you will be assessed by a completing one internally assessed assignment. The assignment will be set by Pearson.

You will be provided with an assignment brief that describes what you will need to do and the date by which the assignment should be completed and submitted to the teacher.

Your teacher will mark the assignment and tell you what grade you have achieved.

You will be expected to show that you understand how different components of fitness are used in different physical activities.

This will include:
- explaining how different components of physical fitness and skill-related fitness are used in a physical activity
- explaining how different components of physical fitness and skill-related fitness impact on performance in a specific physical activity.

CHECKPOINT

Review your learning of this component by answering the following questions. This will help you to prepare for your assignment.

Strengthen
- Outline the six different components of physical fitness.
- Describe the five different components of skill-related fitness.
- Describe how the components of physical and skill-related fitness are related to sports performance.

Challenge
- Explain how the components of physical and skill-related fitness impact performance in one individual sport and one team sport.
- Explain how the components of skill-related fitness are related to the technical aspects of sport, using a sporting example to illustrate your answer.

ASSESSMENT ACTIVITY

You are an amateur swimmer who wants to start assisting the club with coaching the development squad, which is made up of younger members. The club coach has asked you to help the young people understand the different components of fitness they require for participation in swimming at a more competitive level.

Produce a written response that includes the following:

- Describe the six components of physical fitness, highlighting the ones that are most relevant to swimming.
- Describe the five components of skill-related fitness, highlighting the ones that are most relevant to swimming.
- Explain the impact these components of fitness have on swimming performance.

TIPS

In your answers, make sure you include all six components of physical fitness, and all five components of skill-related fitness. You can include images to help support your responses.

TAKE IT FURTHER

To expand your answers, include examples of other sports or activities. For example, if muscular endurance is not relevant to your chosen sport, give an example of a sport it is important to and describe why. Also try to use examples from a range of individual and team sports.

B1: Techniques, strategies and fitness required for different sports 1: skills

In order to be able to play sports or perform activities successfully, there are a number of skills that are needed. Learning, practising and mastering the basic skills of a sport are a fundamental element of sports performance.

Skills

Skills are the expertise or talent that are needed to perform a sport. Each sport and physical activity requires a different set of skills to be able to participate, although there may be similarities. Skills have many characteristics that will change depending on the complexity, environment and pace at which the skill is being carried out.

Basic and complex skills

Basic, or simple skills, are often generic to many sports and only have a small number of parts. Athletes need to master basic skills before they attempt more complex skills, as basic skills form the foundation of complex skills. Examples of basic skills are catching, sprinting, jumping or throwing.

Complex skills are more difficult. They are complicated movements made up of many parts or several basic skills. Complex skills are normally more sport specific. Examples of complex skills are a tennis serve, kicking a conversion in rugby or a lay-up shot in basketball.

Mental skills, such as decision-making, judgment and interpretation, are also needed in sport. The more mental skills needed to carry out a movement, the more complex the skill becomes. For example, when returning a shot in tennis the athlete must judge the best shot based on the speed and position of the ball and also where their opponent is.

Open and closed skills

The environment in which a skill is performed determines whether a skill is open or closed.

- A closed skill is a skill which is not affected by the environment and occurs in a familiar and stable environment.
- An open skill is a skill which is highly influenced by the environment. They occur when performers have to adapt their skills to a changing or unpredictable environment.

For example, performing ball dribbling drills during football practice would be classified as a closed skill because it is being performed in a stable and predictable environment. However, when this same skill is performed during a competitive match, the skill becomes open as the addition of opponents makes the environment unpredictable and unstable.

Self-paced and externally paced skills

Pacing refers to the participant's control over the timing of performing the skill.

- Self-paced skills are where the athlete determines the time and pace of executing the skill.
- Externally paced skills are where factors external to the athlete determine the timing of execution of the skill.

◻ Diving is a self-paced skill as the athlete determines the timing of performing the skill

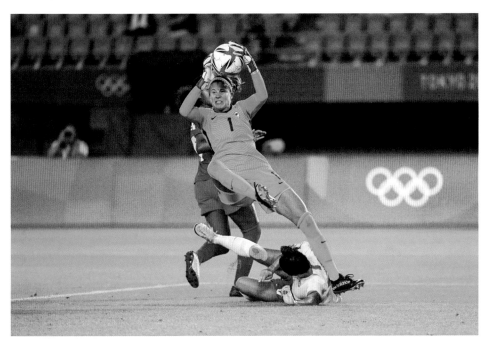

◻ Goalkeeping is externally paced as the reaction and decision-making of the athlete is determined by the actions of the opponent when taking a shot

Selecting skills

In sports, it is essential for athletes to select the best skills for the activity or task they must complete. Picking the right skill will lead to skilled performance. This needs to be effective, efficient and responsive to ensure the athlete has an advantage over their competitors.

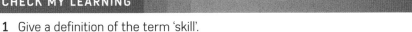

ACTIVITY

Support

Working in small groups, make a list of the skills needed in diving, rugby and golf.

Challenge

Identify whether these skills are basic or complex, open or closed and self-paced or externally paced.

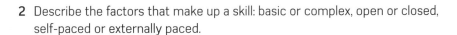

CHECK MY LEARNING

1 Give a definition of the term 'skill'.
2 Describe the factors that make up a skill: basic or complex, open or closed, self-paced or externally paced.

B1: Techniques, strategies and fitness required for different sports 2: strategies

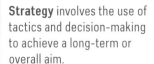
A strategy is a plan of action designed to achieve a long-term or overall aim. In sport, this may be winning a match or tournament. Tactics are the smaller short-term specific actions that are undertaken to accomplish the strategy.

Strategy

You may put in place a **strategy** for how to use **tactics** and decision-making to achieve a long-term or overall aim like winning a tournament. You may then select and perform appropriate strategies during competitive situations, helping you to accomplish the overarching aims.

Why are strategies useful?

Strategies and tactics help coaches and athletes to maximise their chances of success, which in sport means winning. They can include aspects such as the way to play, where they should be at a particular time and what to do. For example, a football coach will need to consider which set play to use at a corner during a football match.

The purpose of strategies and tactics is to assess and apply different ways to gain an advantage over an opponent.

Pre-planning

Strategies and tactics may be employed during competitive situations, or they may be pre-planned. Developing strategies involves assessing a number of aspects. These can include the strengths and weaknesses of the opponent, the strengths and weaknesses of the team or player, the importance of the match, and even the weather. The technical and tactical skills that are going to be needed can then be identified and plans can be made to ensure the athlete or team is well prepared.

◘ Jockeys will assess the other riders and horses, as well as the weather and conditions, before deciding on the best tactics for the race

In Premier League football, many clubs now use match analysis tools to help teams plan their tactics against an opposition. These analysis software tools convert data from a match into graphics and statistics so that tactics can be agreed. Teams can then practise set moves and improve their knowledge of the opponent to assist their decision-making within the game.

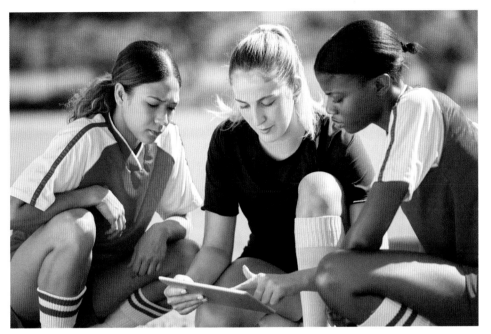

◨ Tactics may need to change during a game to maximise the chance of winning

Adapting strategies

Although strategies and tactics may be pre-planned or rehearsed, athletes also need to be able to adapt or change them during a performance, depending on how the play is going. This requires good interpretation, problem-solving and decision-making skills; for example, a distance runner may change their normal tactic of leading the race from the front to sitting behind another runner in order to pace themselves and leave enough energy to sprint finish.

ACTIVITY

Support

In pairs, choose a sport and pick a real-life team/player. Research what their current overall aim is (strategy). You could either research a famous team, like a professional football team, or interview a coach or athlete you know locally.

Challenge

Explain what strategy and tactics are and how they are used.

CHECK MY LEARNING

1 Define the terms 'strategy' and 'tactics'.
2 Explain the factors a tennis player may assess before a tournament final to maximise their chance of winning.

B1: Techniques, strategies and fitness required for different sports 3: isolated practice

Sports people will need to develop a number of skills to be able to play well. For instance, a basketball player will need to be able to run while bouncing the ball, throw and catch accurately, and jump high to score. To get better, they will need to practise these skills to improve their ability.

Isolated practice

The type of practice chosen has a major influence on the development of sport skills. The traditional approach to teaching or breaking down a sport is to perform practices or drills that focus on one skill at a time. This is called **isolated practice**.

This type of practice is ideal for skills that are always performed in the same way, as it allows for the technique and motor sequence to be perfected.

◘ An example of an isolated practice would be a footballer practising dribbling the ball around cones

Advantages and disadvantages

The use of **isolated practices** can be beneficial, but they are not perfect. The table below sets out some of the advantages and disadvantages.

◘ Table 2.6: Advantages and disadvantages of isolated practices

Advantages	Disadvantages
• Players do not have to worry about an opponent • Can focus on the skill and practice • Removes the complexity of a game situation • Easy way to introduce a sport • Good when space is restricted • Some skills can be practised individually so do not need lots of players	• Not realistic • Does not practise the skills needed in a game such as judgment, interpretation and decision-making • Isolated practices can become boring for players

Isolated practices are a traditional approach to skill development. Despite their lack of match realism, they are still a useful tool for coaches and athletes to use. They help players to develop a high level of technique. They can also be useful to show players different possible moves that they wouldn't think of by themselves.

 Tennis players can use isolated practices to improve the accuracy and placement of their serves

BEST PRACTICE

Coaches use a combination of isolated, conditioned, and competitive practice to prepare athletes for sports performance. For example, a cricket player may practise the straight drive against a feeder, or bowling machine, in the nets with a bowler and in a semi-competitive format with fielders as part of their training.

ACTIVITY

Support

Give an example of an isolated practice for the following sports:
- Swimming
- Badminton
- Netball
- American football.

Challenge

Imagine you are a hurdler preparing for a competition. Explain when it is most useful to use isolated practices.

LINK IT UP

Designing and setting up isolated practice drills will be explored further in Component 2 C2.

In the Assessment practice for Learning outcome B, you will have the chance to plan an isolated practice drill for a sport or physical activity of your choice.

CHECK MY LEARNING

1 Describe the term 'isolated practice' and give an example from an individual and team sport.
2 Explain the advantages and disadvantages of isolated practices.

B1: Techniques, strategies and fitness required for different sports 4: competitive situations

GETTING STARTED

Working in pairs, choose a sport and list as many differences as you can between a practice session and a competitive match. Discuss the effect these different factors could have on an athlete.

Competitions are very different from practice; the pressure, the audience and the opponent are just a few factors that differ. Competitive situation practices seek to replicate matchday conditions for athletes to prepare fully.

Competitive situations

Learning a sports skill is the first step in the process of being able to participate in a sport. If the main strategy is to win, then it will not be enough for the athlete to just be technically excellent. They need to be able to apply and perform these skills in competition conditions.

When you think about a competition, such as a 90-minute football match, athletes will need to be able to perform skills at speed, while facing opponents, when they feel fatigued and are under pressure to perform in front of an audience.

A good example of this is USA Olympic gymnast Simone Biles, who withdrew from five of her six finals at the Tokyo Olympics in July 2021. She stated that she felt immense pressure and anxiety and was not able to perform to her best and so chose to withdraw in order to focus on her mental health and not injure herself physically when competing not at her peak.

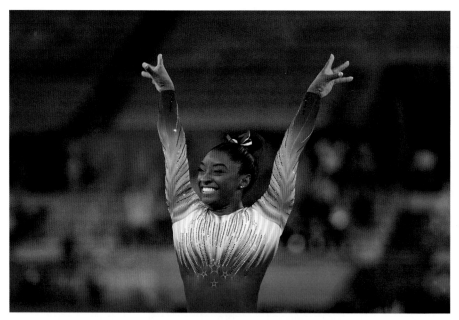

◻ Although technically excellent, Simone Biles was not able to perform at the 2021 Tokyo Olympics due to the pressure and anxiety she felt

Implementing a competition situation

Competition situation practices seek to replicate conditions of real matches, such as the number of players, introducing opponents, using the full area of play and having the presence of an official.

Sports psychology aims to help athletes to learn how to perform as well in a competition as they do in practice. There are several factors that can affect competition performance, such as motivation, anxiety, stress and concentration. However, one relatively simple strategy to overcome these is to make competitions and practices more similar to each other.

Ways to make practices more like a competition can include:

- Increasing the stakes – this involves increasing the level of pressure. This can be done by creating matchday scenarios in your head or imagining yourself performing at a competition.
- Invite an audience – you can increase the pressure felt at a practice by asking people to watch. This could be friends, family, teammates or coaches.
- Asking for analysis of performance and feedback – asking for a critique of performance will increase pressure and anxiety as the athlete knows they are being watched and judged.
- Participate in mock or friendly competitions – by practising performing in competitions, athletes will be able to practise managing anxiety.

Ways to make a competition more like practice can include:

- Familiarisation – it is fairly obvious to state that we feel more comfortable in familiar surroundings. To make match grounds more familiar, athletes could train at the ground, or if this isn't possible, visit it to become familiar with the set-up and surroundings.
- Keep behaviour consistent – some athletes swear by a pre-match routine, a set of actions they take before playing. If this is something that makes athletes feel more relaxed and comfortable then they should establish their routine during practice and make sure is it continued into competition.
- Consistent self-talk – we all say things to ourselves to keep us motivated or focused. During practice, athletes could establish words or phrases that work to enhance performance, and use the same self-talk during competitions.
- Optimum energy levels – some athletes need to keep calm before a competition whereas others need to hype themselves up. Work out when you perform best and incorporate actions to achieve this state before a competition.

ACTIVITY

Support

Working in small groups, design a competition situation practice or drill for the following sports:

- Hockey
- Football
- Rowing.

Challenge

Choose one of these sports and explain the ways that a practice could be made more like a competition.

BEST PRACTICE

Coaches generally agree that the most effective training makes use of a range of isolated practices to teach and develop skills, and then competitive situations so that these skills can be improved upon in realistic conditions, where other skills such as judgment and decision-making will also be needed.

CHECK MY LEARNING

1 Define what a competition situation practice is.

2 Explain why competition situation practices are a good training tool.

Learning outcome B1: Assessment practice

Techniques, strategies and fitness required for different sports

How you will be assessed

In this component you will be assessed by a completing four internally assessed assignments. The assignments will be set by Pearson.

You will be provided with an assignment brief that describes what you will need to do and the date by which the assignment should be completed and submitted to the teacher.

Your teacher will mark the assignment and tell you what grade you have achieved.

You will be expected to show that you understand how different techniques and strategies help athletes to perform well.

This will include:

- Demonstrating the skills needed to participate in a selected sport.
- Demonstrating strategies used in a selected sport.
- Participating effectively in isolated practices and competitive situation practices used in a selected sport.

CHECKPOINT

Review your learning of this component by answering the following questions. This will help you prepare for your assignment.

Strengthen

- What are the different ways that skills can be described?
- How are strategies broken down?
- What is the difference between isolated practice and competition situation practice?

Challenge

- What is the difference between strategy and tactics?
- Why is competition situation practice beneficial?

ASSESSMENT ACTIVITY

You are gaining coaching and work experience by volunteering with a local sports team. You have been asked by the lead coach to demonstrate some of what you have learned by planning a practice session for the group.

For a sport of your choice, carry out the following tasks.

1 Plan an isolated practice for three skills required for your selected sport.

2 Give your plan to a partner, demonstrate the isolated practices to them and ask them to mark your ability out of 5, where 1 = poor and 5 = excellent.

3 Devise a strategy and tactics for a competitive situation friendly match.

4 Gather a group of players together and brief them on the tactics for the match. Once they have been briefed, the match should be played to practise putting the strategy into action.

TIPS

Choose a sport that you are knowledgeable about and confident in demonstrating your practical ability. This will also make it easier for you to plan drills, strategy and tactics, and justify your choices.

TAKE IT FURTHER

Provide an explanation on video or a written explanation justifying why you have chosen the tactics and decision-making you have chosen for your competitive situation practice. Discuss your decisions with a group and ask for critical feedback.

B2: Key officials and roles 1: referee, umpire, assistant referee, line umpire

GETTING STARTED

In pairs, choose a sport and discuss it.

What rules do you know for that sport? And what officials are there to enforce these rules?

KEY TERM

Officials control how a sports match is played and administer the rules.

DID YOU KNOW?

A few sports, such as American football and Canadian football, have both a referee **and** an umpire.

◻ In cricket, umpires show their decisions through arm signals

For sports to be played fairly and safely, there need to be clear rules and officials who ensure these rules are followed. Officials are an essential part of sport.

Officials

In sport, an **official** is someone who manages the play of a competition and ensures the rules and laws of the sport are followed correctly. This is to make sure the sporting fixture is conducted fairly, in accordance with the rules and in a safe environment.

Different sports require different types of official, each with their own roles and responsibilities. The number of officials can vary too, with some sports requiring more officials than there are players, such as tennis.

Referee/umpire

In general, the role of a referee or umpire overlaps. They are both officials who watch a match or game closely to ensure all players follow the rules and regulations and enforce these rules to maintain fair game play. They ensure that all of the rules (or laws) of the game are followed by the participants. This includes making a decision on whether an act is legal or not, according to the sporting rules.

Examples of sports that use a referee are:
- football, rugby, boxing, snooker, basketball, ice hockey, lacrosse and wrestling.

Examples of sports that use an umpire are:
- hockey, tennis, cricket, sailing, badminton, netball, rowing and baseball.

Good referees and umpires are knowledgeable on the rules, confident in their ability and decisive at applying the rules. They must be clear, calm, communicate well and not allow players to question their decisions.

Some sports make use of additional assistant officials, such as assistant referees or line umpires.

Assistant referee

In association football, there are two assistant referees, whose role it is to support the referee with decisions. They assist the referee in controlling the match in accordance with the rules of the game; however, the final decision lies with the referee. Their responsibilities are to indicate when:
- the ball leaves the field of play and which team is entitled to a corner kick, goal kick or throw-in
- a player is in an offside position
- a substitution request has been made and monitor the procedure
- at penalty kicks, if the goalkeeper moves off the goal line before the ball is kicked and if the ball has crossed the line.

Line umpire

Tennis has a number of line umpires who work on court as part of a team. Each line umpire is assigned to one line or a position on court and makes decisions on all shots relating to their assigned line. Line umpires are a mandatory requirement for professional tennis games.

■ Heather Watson at Wimbledon. The line umpire's primary role, as a member of the on-court officiating team, is to assist the chair umpire in determining if a ball falls within or outside of the boundaries of the court

Third/fourth umpire

The third umpire or official is common in sports. In football, there is a fourth official who manages the technical area and displays substitutions. In cricket, the third umpire is off-field and monitors video replays for no balls, dismissals and boundaries. The officials are essential for the smooth running and management of sports.

ACTIVITY

Support

Working in small groups, draw a diagram of a tennis court, and mark where the line umpires should be positioned.

Challenge

Consider what would happen in a football match if there was no referee. Evaluate the advantages and disadvantages of playing a match that has no referee present.

CHECK MY LEARNING

1 Define the term 'sports official'.

2 Describe the role and responsibilities of a referee or umpire.

B2: Key officials and roles 2: scorers, timekeepers, video reviewers

GETTING STARTED

Make two lists of sports:

1 One for sports that are judged by a panel who allocate a score.

2 One for sports that are measured, e.g. distance, goals, speed/time.

So that a sport can run fully and efficiently, a number of key officials are needed to help maintain standards of play. Scorers, judges, timekeepers and video review officials play a key part in this.

Scorers

The score is an essential part of every sports game. The role of the scorer is to keep an accurate record of the points scored in a game and publish/update the posted score. Sports that have an official scorer include basketball, baseball, football, cricket and American football.

Judges

Some sports use judges to officiate. Sports such as track running events and tennis, are clear cut and not subjective. The fastest runner is the fastest, or the player that scores the most points scored is the winner. However, some sports are subjective, such as gymnastics and diving. In these sports, a number of judges will sit on a panel and make decisions together on the score to be awarded. Other sports that have judges include archery, showjumping, boxing, judo, figure skating and fencing.

Starters

In sports such as swimming and athletics, the starter has a pivotal role in the race. The starter informs the participants to get into position, when the race is nearly ready, and when to start. They also monitor false starts and provide sanctions for athletes who false start or break rules. This is to ensure the rules are adhered to by all participants and no one gets an unfair advantage.

DID YOU KNOW?

Different sports call video review different names. These include video assisted referee (VAR), video referee, video umpire, instant replay official, television match official, third umpire or challenge.

Timekeepers

Many sports have a restriction on the amount of time allocated to a match or competitive situation. The timekeeper has the sole responsibility to stop and start the clock. The role of the timekeeper is to measure the duration of the game, the intervals of play, the rest periods, and to start and stop the clock at various stages, ensuring accurate time is kept. Depending on the sport, these stoppages may be for injury, substitutions, when the ball goes out of play or for time outs.

LINK IT UP

In Component 1 B2, you explored the technology used as part of officiating equipment.

Video review officials

Some sports allow referees or other officials to consult video replay footage before making or revising a decision about an unclear or dubious play. The role of the video review official is to watch the video replay and advise the referee or umpire on what occurred. Sports that utilise video review official decision-making include hockey, football, basketball, baseball, tennis and rugby. However, due to the high cost associated with the equipment needed for video review, it is generally only used in top-class, professional, or high-profile international competitions.

 Video technology is routinely used in top-level football to assist with decision-making

ACTIVITY

Support

Working in pairs, choose a sport and research the number and role of the key officials that are used in high-level or professional matches.

Challenge

Explain why sport played at an amateur level does not usually have specific scorers, timekeepers or video reviewers. Detail who takes on these roles in amateur matches.

BEST PRACTICE

In football, all Premier League VAR decisions are referred to Stockley Park. A team of qualified officials and analysts will review the footage and camera angles available to them to support the referee with a decision. This is often used for checking goals, violent tackles, and offside decisions.

CHECK MY LEARNING

1 Describe the role of the timekeeper.
2 Explain the purpose of video review and the benefits this can bring to a game.

B2: Responsibilities of officials 1: appearance, fitness, equipment

Sports officials are integral to playing sport safely and fairly. Good officials are fair-minded, impartial and have a thorough understanding of the sports they officiate.

In order to officiate in sport, a person must have a thorough knowledge of the rules of the sport as well as keeping up to date with any changes. To be an effective and respected official, there are also other responsibilities to fulfil.

Appearance

For the majority of sports, it is a requirement that officials wear a specific uniform. This uniform differentiates them from the athletes and reinforces their importance. The uniform worn by officials must be distinguishable and different from the colours of the sport participants.

The National Governing Body (NGB) for the sport will stipulate what officials must wear. For example, England Boxing states the dress code for a referee is a white button shirt with black bow tie, black trousers (not jeans) and black flat-soled shoes.

◘ Key officials must ensure they wear the correct uniform as specified by the specific sport governing body

Fitness

Some sports require officials to be on the field of play. Obviously, they must therefore have a certain level of fitness to be able to keep up with the play and ensure that they are close at hand to make quick decisions. Some sports are played at a fast pace, so referees must have a high level of fitness. In some sports, officials are not full-time match officials and therefore having the time commitment to building and maintaining fitness can be difficult.

FIFA has two fitness tests for men and women that referees must pass at least once a year. These tests measure their ability to perform repeated sprints over 40 m and their capacity to perform a series of 75 m high-speed runs interspersed with 25 m walking intervals.

Equipment

Officials need specific equipment to carry out their role. It is each official's responsibility to bring the appropriate kit to every competition or game. For example, a netball umpire will need a whistle to stop/start play, a stopwatch to time the game, a coin to decide which team starts first and a pen and scorecard to record the goals scored. A rugby union referee requires a whistle to stop/start play and red and yellow penalty cards to caution or dismiss players.

◨ Officials must be prepared with the correct equipment to enable them to apply and enforce the rules of the game

CHECK MY LEARNING

Describe why appearance, fitness and equipment are key responsibilities of sport officials.

B2: Responsibilities of officials 2: communication, control, health & safety

GETTING STARTED

Discuss in small groups what the consequences would be if sports officials did not communicate clearly, did not control players, and allowed players to question and dispute their decisions.

It is a core responsibility of sports officials to ensure that the game is played fairly, safely and according to the rules. They need to communicate their decision-making clearly and without ambiguity to players and spectators.

Officiating sports can be complex and challenging. It involves strong knowledge of the game, appropriate fitness, good positioning, and accurate perceptual judgment skills to make accurate decisions in the fast and dynamic context of the game. We will now look at some core responsibilities that help with this.

Communication

The best referees and umpires are those who are able to communicate efficiently and effectively with players. Communication is a two-way process that involves sending and receiving information. A key trait that can set exceptional officials apart is their ability to relate to and communicate with players.

Effective communication on the sports field requires confidence. Officials need to demonstrate confidence in their decisions both through what they say and how they say it:

- Language should be clear, accurate and concise.
- Tone of voice should be neutral but firm.
- Hand signals need to be strong and clear.

Confidence can be demonstrated through body language, establishing eye contact and using positive facial expressions. Keeping the head neutral or upright and the posture strong will project confidence.

It can be difficult to make quick accurate decisions during a fast-paced match. Players and spectators may disagree with your decisions. It is when situations are more difficult that skilled communication is most important.

It is also important for officials to communicate clearly with each other, so that the rules and regulations of the game are followed, and the game is played smoothly and fairly. For example, in netball the timekeeper will signal that the period of play has ended at the end of each quarter by signalling with a horn or similar. They will also be watching the umpire throughout the match so that time can be stopped for injury.

BEST PRACTICE

Make sure you are confident and strong in your communications when officiating. A good decision can be communicated badly and create a perception of unfairness, yet a contentious decision that is communicated effectively can be well accepted by players.

Video reviewers also need to maintain a clear method of communication with other officials. In rugby, the television match official can communicate with the referee via an earpiece to pass on information to assist with making accurate decisions, such as foul play or whether a try has been scored or not.

Control

Officials maintain control of sports games by applying regulations correctly. This ensures a safe playing environment is maintained. The key to keeping control is to demonstrate confidence and authority, making good decisions which show a strong knowledge of the laws of the game.

Sometimes, decisions that officials make will be unpopular. Officials need to be decisive and resistant to pressures from other players, and not cave to the pressures of players or the crowd but stand firm behind their decisions. In some sports, if the rules are broken because of serious foul play, the officials have the power to discipline the player(s) involved by sending them off the field of play.

There will be times when the intensity of the game rises and players can start to become frustrated. Recognising this is starting and taking measures to prevent the situation from escalating is crucial to maintaining control.

Health and safety

A major responsibility of officials in sport is to ensure that every event is carried out safely. This is in order to protect players, spectators, coaches and officials.

Prior to games starting, officials must carry out checks on uniform, equipment and facilities. These verify compliance with safety rules and ensure there is no risk of injury to participants and spectators. For example, prior to a netball match starting, checks will be carried out on the condition of the court, that the net is fixed at the correct height, that only a regulation ball is used, that players' fingernails are short and smooth, that long hair is tied back and that no jewellery is being worn.

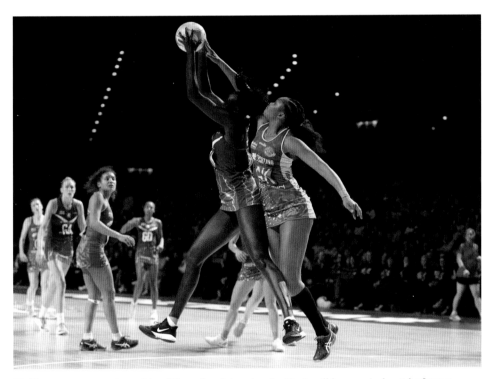

▣ There are a number of health and safety checks that will be carried out before a netball match starts

ACTIVITY

Support

Select a sport that you play or have a keen interest in. Research and describe the health and safety checks that officials carry out before the sport can be played.

Challenge

Explain what the consequences may be for players if health and safety checks were not carried out before a match or game. Give examples.

CHECK MY LEARNING

1 Describe why health and safety checks are needed before a sport is played.

2 Explain how the key responsibilities of communication and control are related.

B3: NGBs, key rules and regulations 1: number of players and length of play

GETTING STARTED

Think of a sport you like to play. Describe the key rules and regulations of that sport.

To be able to play a sport, particularly at a high level, you need to know the key rules and regulations of the sport and understand how they are applied.

National governing bodies (NGBs)

A national governing body (NGB) is an organisation that governs and administers a particular sport on a national basis. Their key responsibilities include overseeing rules, clubs, coaching and competitions, as well as developing participation in the sport. Examples include the Lawn Tennis Association (LTA) and England Athletics (EA).

Number of players

The number of players in a sports team differs according to the specific sport. Table 2.7 details the rules on the number of players in a team for some common sports.

Many sports allow player substitutions. This means replacing one player with another during a match. Substitutions are generally made to replace a player who has become tired or injured, or who is performing poorly, or for tactical reasons. They can be rolling or a set number. Rolling substitutions allow players to enter and leave the game for other players an unlimited number of times during the course of the game, as allowed in ice hockey. In sports that use set substitutions, a fixed number is allowed during a game and only at certain times, such as after an interval or when play has stopped.

■ Table 2.7: Number of players and types of substitutions allowed for different sports

Sport	Number of players (per team)	Type of substitutions
Football	11	Set – 5
Netball	7	Rolling – there is no limit to the number of substitutions a team can make
Hockey	11	Rolling – 5
Cricket	11	Set – one tactical substitute can be named at the toss
Basketball	5	Rolling – there is no limit to the number of substitutions a team can make
Rugby union	15	Set – 8

Sports that can seem similar can have different rules on the number of players. For example, although the rules of beach volleyball are mostly consistent with the indoor version, professional beach volleyball teams consist of only two players, rather than six players, which is the norm for the indoor version. Other sports can have variations on the number of players allowed depending on the format of the game being played; for example, the number of players allowed to participate in lacrosse depends on the variant being played, box, women's, or field.

Length of play

The length of play differs according to the specific sport. Some games, such as hockey and rugby, have a specified amount of playing time and the match finishes when that has ended. Other sports, such as tennis, will be played until a player or team reaches the number of points needed to win.

Most games are divided into a fixed number of periods, such as halves in football or quarters in netball. Other sports are divided into playing periods not based on time but on a specified amount of playing, such as sets in tennis or innings in cricket.

▣ **Table 2.8: Length and structure of play for different sports**

Sport	Length of game	Periods of play	Rest period
Football	90 minutes	2 halves of 45 minutes	15-minute half-time interval
Netball	60 minutes	4 quarters of 15 minutes	4 minutes between the first and second then third and fourth quarters 12-minute half-time interval
Hockey	70 minutes	2 halves of 35 minutes	5-minute half-time interval
Basketball	48 minutes	4 quarters of 12 minutes	15-minute half-time interval
Rugby union	80 minutes	2 halves of 40 minutes	10-minute half-time interval

It is the responsibility of the score keeper and/or timekeeper to keep track of the length of play.

In some sports, extra time is allowed, this is an additional period of play added to a game if the score is tied at the end of normal time. The aim is to bring a game to a decision and avoid declaring the match a draw where the scores are the same. Sports that have rules for extra time include football, rugby and field hockey.

DID YOU KNOW?

The longest tennis match lasted for 11 hours and 5 minutes. It was contested over three days between John Isner and Nicolas Mahut at the 2010 Wimbledon Championships.

ACTIVITY

Support

Working in pairs, make two lists:

1 A list of sports that play a fixed amount of time.
2 A list of sports that are played until a certain number of points mean a player or team has won.

Challenge

Explain why not all sports allow substitutions.

CHECK MY LEARNING

1 Describe the difference between rolling and set substitutions.
2 Explain how the length of play of a sports game is determined by time or score and give examples.

B3: NGBs' key rules and regulations 2: scoring system and playing area

As we know, the rules and regulations for different sports are set by their respective national governing body. This includes detailing how the sport is played and scored as well as the area it should be played on.

Scoring systems

There are many different ways that scoring can be done in sport, it can be quite complex and rarely are two sports the same.

Methods of scoring

The methods of scoring vary across sports. In some games, players need to gain a territorial advantage to target a specific goal, for example the touchdown endzone in American football and the net in netball. In other games, the distance equipment is moved will determine the number of points achieved by the performer, for example how far the ball is hit in cricket and baseball, or how far a discus is thrown in athletics.

Some sports have clear-cut and objective methods of scoring, meaning that it is usually obvious when a point is scored. For instance, a try scored in rugby, a goal scored in hockey or a net scored in basketball.

Other sports are more subjective, and judges assess performance to award points. For example, in gymnastics and figure skating a panel of judges will award a score on the technique and skill level shown in the performance.

In tennis, scoring is done in points, games and sets

Differing awarding of points

Depending on the sport, the score will be determined by the number of points won (volleyball), the number of goals scored (football), the time (running), the distance (javelin) or the accuracy (archery).

Generally in sport, there is only one way to score a point. However, in some sports, a different number of points are awarded depending on how the points were scored. A good example of this is basketball, where there are three ways to score points:

1 Three points are awarded if a shot is successfully scored from outside the three-point line.

2 Two points are awarded if a shot is successfully scored from inside the three-point line.

3 If free shots have been awarded for a foul, then each shot successfully scored will be awarded one point.

How a winner is determined

In most sports, the winner is determined by the team or player who scores the most points. However, a clear exception to this is in golf where the aim is to hit the lowest number of shots in order to win.

What happens in the event of a tie?

A draw or tie occurs in sport when the results of two teams or players are the same or inconclusive. For example, two horses crossing the finish line at the same time or two divers scoring the same points.

What happens in the event of a tie will depend on the sport. Often, if the game is part of a tournament or competition where points are accrued over many games, certain points will be awarded for a win, a draw and a loss (e.g. three for a win, one for a draw and zero for a loss). In other sports, the game does not finish until a winner is evident, so play will resume until a winner is decided, such as in snooker or tennis.

Playing area

One key regulation set out in all sports is the size of the playing area. Specific sport governing bodies set what the dimensions of the playing area must be.

In some sports there are strict dimensions that must be adhered to, in other sports there is a range that a playing area can fit within. In addition to this, some sports specify how big an area around the playing area must be (referred to as the run-off). Finally, the size of the playing area can differ depending on whether games are being played inside or outside, the age group, and at what level (i.e. recreational, club, county and regional, or national and international).

For example, for international football matches the length of the pitch must be between 100 and 110 m and the width 64 and 75 m. Whereas, the basic size of a badminton court of 13.4 × 6.1 m remains consistent across all playing levels.

ACTIVITY

Support
Research the NGB rules on the size of competition area for the following sports:
- Basketball
- Karate
- Squash
- Volleyball
- Beach volleyball
- Rounders.

How does the size of the competition area influence the result of each sport?

Challenge
For two different sports, describe what happens in the event of a tie or draw.

CHECK MY LEARNING

1 Describe the different ways that sports can be scored.
2 Research the different playing areas permitted for a sport of your choice. Explain why it is important to check the size the playing area must be.

B3: NGBs' key rules and regulations 3: equipment and starting play

In order to participate in sport, you should have an awareness of the equipment that is required as well as the key rules on starting and restarting play.

Equipment

Some sports cannot be played without specific **equipment**. When this is the case, there will be NGB rules about what can and cannot be used.

Sizes and weights of playing equipment

Many sports have set rules on equipment that can be used, so that it is standardised across competitions. For example, size 5 netballs are the official size used by players over the age of 10 years in matches, training sessions and for recreational purposes, they are classed as 'full size' netballs. However, children aged under 10 should use a size 4 netball.

Required protective equipment

Sports injuries are very common in both contact sports and non-contact sports, and this risk can be increased when equipment such as balls and sticks are introduced. Due to this, many sports have strict rules on protective equipment that must be worn by players in order to participate. For example, jockeys must wear a helmet and body protector, and boxers must wear abdominal groin protectors (compulsory for males/discretionary for females), gloves and gum shields. It is the responsibility of officials to ensure the correct required protective equipment is worn by players before the game starts.

Optional protective equipment

As well as required protective equipment, some sports also set rules on additional protective equipment that may be worn by payers if they wish. For example, in rugby, players may choose to wear headguards, shoulder pads and mouthguards. It should be noted that mouthguards are mandatory for junior rugby and are strongly recommended for senior rugby.

Starting and restarting play

The rules about starting and restarting play are different for each sport. Table 2.9 details examples from two different sports.

◻ Table 2.9: Comparison of start and restart rules for football and tennis

	Football	Tennis
How the game begins	A kick-off starts the game 1 The ball must be stationary on the centre mark 2 The referee gives a signal that play can commence, normally a whistle blow 3 The ball is in play when it is kicked and clearly moves The team that takes the first kick-off is decided by whoever wins the toss of a coin. They decide either which way they would like to play first or to take the kick-off	Before each match, a coin-toss takes place. The winner of the coin-toss can decide whether to serve first or receive first, or they can decide which side of the court they want to start on The match begins with one player serving
How play is restarted after scoring	After a team scores a goal, the kick-off is taken by their opponents	Service stays with one side for the duration of each four-point game After a point is scored, the right to serve stays with the same player that started the service game, until it is won The right to serve changes each game
Fouls or infringements	Depending on the foul or infringement, play can be restarted by a free kick, penalty kick, throw-in, goal kick, corner kick or a dropped ball	A foul or infringement can result in a second serve from the player who has the service game, or can result in a point for their opponent, in which case play will resume with the serve again until the game is completed
How and when the game ends	When the 90 minutes of playing time plus any stoppage time are up, the match ends	Tennis is played in points: Four points win a game, six games win a set, and two or three sets win a match The game will end when a player has won two sets for women, or three sets for men

KEY TERM

Foul is inappropriate or unfair behaviour by a player, usually due to a violation of the rules of the game.

ACTIVITY

Support

Choose one individual sport **or** one team sport. Research the rules about the equipment that is used and/or worn.

Challenge

Explain why protective equipment may be optional in some sports.

LINK IT UP

In Component 1 Learning outcome B you examined equipment and technology required for participants to use when taking part in sport. In Component 2 you can link this to rules and regulations in sports. For example, in cycling the bike must be within a specific weight range for certain races.

CHECK MY LEARNING

1 Why is there a difference between required and optional protective equipment? Give examples.

2 Choose a sport. Describe how play is started and how it is restarted after scoring and after a foul or infringement.

B3: NGBs' key rules and regulations 4: applying rules and regulations

There are certain actions an official can take if rules are not adhered to. These actions may vary depending on the situation.

Non-adherence to the rules

Rules are needed in order to control events. Sport is competitive and rules are required to encourage fair play and reduce the possibility of injury.

Rule violations, or fouls, are actions or behaviour that is against the accepted rules of the game. This can be accidental, such as a player being pushed out of bounds by an opposing team member, or intentional, such as holding a player back with your arms in netball. **Violations** can be **direct** or **indirect**.

Some rule violations are sport specific, such as hitting the ball twice in tennis and passing the ball forward in rugby.

Other rule violations are more generic and can be seen in many different sports. For example, kicking a ball out of the play area/offside or intentionally harming another player.

The way in which rule violations are dealt with varies across sports, and may include possession being awarded to the opponent, a free kick/pass, being booked or ultimately a player being sent off.

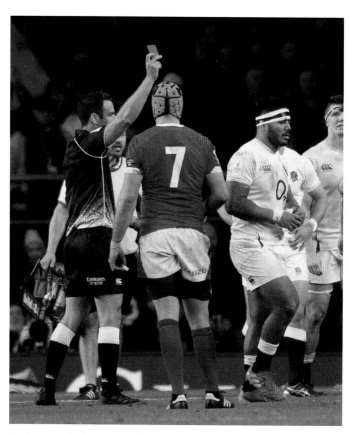

A player being sent off is the ultimate sanction for foul play in many sports. Here England's Manu Tuilagi receives a red card for foul play

Application of rules and regulations by officials

One of the key responsibilities of sports officials is to apply the rules and regulations effectively.

As discussed earlier, good officials are confident and decisive. Officials can make use of a range of techniques to assist their decision-making and communication.

Use of signals

The use of whistles and hand signals allows officials to be clear in their communication. The use of a whistle ensures play stops and they have players' attention. The use of hand signals assists in passing on the message.

Communication of decisions to players and other officials

Umpires will announce rule decisions in the correct sequence. They give concise directions to all players in both teams.

A key role of officials is to use precise and clear terminology to indicate the foul, state the rule infringement, and set the sanction. For example, in football, whistle blow, offside, indirect free kick to other team, or whistle blow, contact, penalty pass in netball.

Use of the whistle, clear voice calls and hand signals means all competitors and spectators receive appropriate and unambiguous enforcement of the regulations being handed out by officials.

Positioning

It is the responsibility of the referee, umpire and other officials to ensure the rules of the game are being followed, and to issue sanctions for violations. To do this effectively, they need to position themselves so that they can clearly see the field of play with no obstructions.

In tennis, the umpire is sat in a raised chair ensuring that they have a good view over the whole court. In football, the referee is not static but continually adjusts their position according to the players and events in the match.

In every sport, the best position for officials is one where they can make the correct decision.

■ Basketball referees use hand signals to indicate certain fouls or violations

LINK IT UP

In Component 1 A3 you considered participation levels in sports and barriers to participation. In Component 2 you are examining rules and regulations. There are some participants who perceive too many rules and regulations as a barrier to sport and they then prefer non-competitive sports.

ACTIVITY

Support

Research the position of the key officials for three different sports.

Challenge

Write a paragraph explaining why this is the best position for the key officials to be in.

CHECK MY LEARNING

1 Describe how rule violations can be dealt with, giving examples from two different sports.

2 Explain how the use of hand signals helps officials to communicate to players.

Learning outcome B2 and B3: Assessment practice

B2: Officials in sport

B3: Rules and regulations in sport

How you will be assessed

In this component you will be assessed by a completing four internally assessed assignments. The assignments will be set by Pearson.

You will be provided with an assignment brief that describes what you will need to do and the date by which the assignment should be completed and submitted to the teacher.

Your teacher will mark the assignment and tell you what grade you have achieved.

You will be expected to participate in sport and show that you understand the roles and responsibilities of officials.

This will include:
- Describing the main officials and the key responsibilities for a selected sport
- Giving an account of the main rules and regulations for a selected sport
- Explaining the actions officials would take to ensure adherence to the rules of the selected sport.

CHECKPOINT

Review your learning of this component by answering the following questions. This will help you prepare for your assignment.

Strengthen

Select a sport of your choice and answer the following questions:

1 What are the key officials in that sport?

2 What are the responsibilities of these officials?

3 What are the key rules that regulate how the sport is played?

Challenge

- What is the role of National Governing Bodies?
- Why do different rule violations have different penalties?

ASSESSMENT ACTIVITY

You are a senior player in your local club with a desire to undertake training to become an official. There are a number of players interested and so, to help them with selection, the club has asked you to give a presentation to demonstrate your knowledge of officiating in sport.

In your presentation you should:

1 Outline the role and responsibilities of two key officials.

2 Describe the five rules you believe are most important in the sport.

3 Give examples of three rule violations and explain the actions the official would take to ensure adherence.

TIPS

Think about when you participate in sport, which rules help the game to be played well and which officials ensure that it is played safely and fairly. In your assessment, make sure you give clear explanations of the officials, rules and rule violations you have chosen.

TAKE IT FURTHER

Examine why clear and strong communication by officials is important when applying the rules and regulations of a sport and for keeping control of the game.

C1: Planning drills and conditioned practices 1: drills for specific techniques

Most athletes want to strive to be the best they can and improve their skills and techniques to enhance their performance. Coaches should plan drills and conditioned practices that help participants develop their sporting skills.

Drills practice

In order to improve performance, athletes need to identify the skills specific to their sport that need improvement. Often, this can be identified by the person themselves, other times it may be highlighted by a coach. By identifying the skills that require work, athletes and coaches can select and plan different **drills** and practices to develop these specific sports skills.

In some sports, one of the most common activities in training programmes is the performance of drills. These activities are designed to train a specific skill or parts of a movement pattern in isolation. For example, the launch of a shot put, the smash shot in badminton or a bounce pass in netball.

Each sport has its own sport-specific skills that are required and will have established drills for developing these skills. The aim of performing drills is that through frequent repetition, the athlete will progress through the stages of skill acquisition towards autonomous skill mastery.

Whole and part drills

Some skills are quite complex to learn. Part practice is when a skill is broken down into smaller parts that are taught and practised separately before bringing the whole skill back together again. Some skills are relatively easy to learn and taught as whole practice, which involves learning the skill as one movement.

- An example of part practice would be a coach breaking down a tennis serve into different components such as grip, stance, toss, backswing, contact and follow-through.
- An example of a whole practice would be practising a dig pass in volleyball.

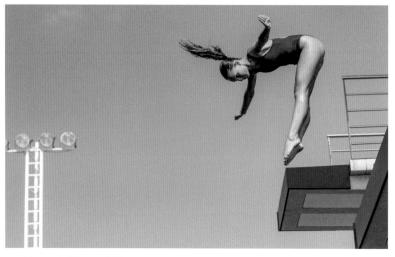

▣ Diving drills would focus on one element of a dive at a time before putting together the complex routine

Progressive drills

When a new sport or skill is being learned, drills should be progressive so that they are broken down into parts and mastered one stage at a time. For example:

- Stage 1 – unopposed stationary drill

At this stage a skill is introduced, and participants are given the chance to practise it in its most simple form, for example when learning to play football, kicking the ball towards a target.

- Stage 2 – drills with the introduction of travel

The same skill is practised whilst on the move, for example travelling with the football towards the target.

- Stage 3 – drills with passive opposition

The addition of a passive opponent forces the player to be more aware of their surroundings, and starts introducing a little pressure. For example, dribbling the football towards a target with another person walking towards them, they will need to go round the opponent and possibly take a feint.

- Stage 4 – drills with active opposition

These drills are designed to add pressure with the presence of an active opponent and force the player to use judgment and practise making a decision. An example would be a 2 v 1 football dribbling drill, where the situation will force the player with the ball to decide whether they should dribble or pass.

BEST PRACTICE

By making drills progressive, and slowly introducing movements and opponents, athletes will be able to learn, practise and eventually master a skill one stage at a time.

ACTIVITY

Support

Describe a whole drill and a part drill that can be used in football.

Challenge

Working in pairs, choose a sport. Design a four-stage drill practice to improve a particular skill or technique in that sport.

CHECK MY LEARNING

1 Describe the purpose of isolated drills.
2 Explain the difference between passive and active opposition.

C1: Planning drills and conditioned practices 2: conditioned games

Coaching is about enabling players to learn and develop their performance. By utilising conditioned practices, players can develop their skills in a more realistic situation.

Conditioned practices

A conditioned practice alters the rules or set up of a game so that a practice can still take place in a game situation but be focused on a particular skill.

An example of a **conditioned practice** in water polo would be to set up a game where players have to make five accurate passes before being allowed to try for goal. The game will be stopped if an inaccurate pass is given, and players given feedback about what caused the game to break down.

Another common technique used for conditioned practices is reducing the number of players in a game, often called small-sided games. They are used to reinforce the transfer of tactical and technical skill practices to game performance. For example, in rugby, by using a smaller number of players or a smaller playing area, players will have more touches of the ball and must think quickly and creatively to get past their opposition.

◻ Conditioned practices give players the opportunity to practise specific skills in more realistic match-like conditions

Outcomes of conditioned games

Conditioned games can be an effective and versatile tool used to motivate players and reinforce learning. Players have the opportunity to practise being more creative in their decision-making and see the effect of those decisions, as it is not a real competition. By providing realistic, match-like scenarios and pressures, players are given decision-making opportunities where they are required to think and react to problems that they will face in real competitions.

Conditioned games have many learning advantages:

- Allows players to practise skills in a game context so they get to see how the skill is dependent on other factors and moments.
- Practise making judgments and decisions. Players can practise solving problems under matchlike conditions.
- Allows learners to recognise the purpose of the skill through its effect on the game.
- Core skills are developed by applying them under realistic conditions.
- Allows players to develop confidence in transferring skills into real game situations.
- Increases motivation. All players want to play more games and perform fewer repetitive drills, conditioned practices encourage greater involvement by more players, meaning there are no queues and less 'waiting around' time.

Disadvantages of conditioned games:

- Players can get demotivated by lots of small games.
- If the games are poorly planned they are ineffective.
- The pitch size must be appropriate to give a fitness benefit.
- The best players may keep the ball too much.
- Poor quality preparation for full-size games if the same stimulus and intensity is not matched.

ACTIVITY

Support

For a sport of your choice, design a conditioned game practice. Specify the skill that will be worked on.

Challenge

Explain how the conditioned game practice will develop the skill.

LINK IT UP

The ways to make practices more like competitions was discussed earlier in Component 2 B1.

CHECK MY LEARNING

1 Describe what a conditioned practice is.
2 Explain three benefits of conditioned practices.

C1: Planning drills and conditioned practices 3: demonstrations

Effective teaching of sports skills involves several steps. The use of an effective demonstration can be key to some players mastering it.

Demonstrating skills

The purpose of a demonstration is to increase the players' understanding of the skill by providing an accurate model from which to learn.

For some athletes, the demonstration step can be the most important part of learning a new sport skill, especially if they have never done anything like it before. These athletes will need a model to replicate. They will need to see what the skill looks like and how it is performed.

Coaches will often demonstrate skills themselves, but they may also use players, sportspersons from outside the team or even videos.

It is recommended that the whole skill is demonstrated initially to provide a visual demonstration of what the skill looks like when performed correctly. It can then be broken down into various skill components, for example breaking down a tennis serve into its various movement components.

An effective skill demonstration requires careful planning by the coach.

◘ **Coaches will use demonstrations to provide a model of how a skill should ideally be performed**

Tips for demonstrations

Some tips to consider to make demonstrations more effective include:
- Prepare ahead.
- Practise the demonstrations beforehand.
- Make sure the correct form is used.
- Demonstrate the skill several times, in full initially and then broken down, ensuring you explain the concept.
- If possible, slow the skill down so athletes can see every movement involved in the performance of the skill.
- Perform the skill at different angles, players need to be able to observe the demonstration from various viewpoints.
- Show both left- and right-handed ways to execute the skill.
- Ensure the demonstrating athlete is positioned so that all participants can see.
- Get the participants involved.
- Encourage responses and questions.
- Repeat if required to encourage participant involvement.

ACTIVITY

Support

Working in a small group, choose a sport that you are all able to play. Individually identify a skill in that sport that you can demonstrate effectively (make sure you all choose different ones). Practise demonstrating the skill to the rest of your group.

Challenge

Review each other's demonstration, highlighting strengths and areas for improvement.

DID YOU KNOW?

You do not have to be an expert in a sport or skill to be able to teach it to others. If you are not able to demonstrate a skill effectively, you can use another athlete who has a high skill level to demonstrate it to others, making sure you point out the relevant parts of the technique.

CHECK MY LEARNING

1 Describe why demonstrations are important.
2 Explain three tips to ensure effective demonstrations.

C1: Planning drills and conditioned practices 4: teaching points

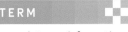
Players each respond differently to instruction and feedback. Some people respond best to demonstration, while others respond best to verbal instructions. Coaches need to make sure that they target the learning styles of all their players.

Teaching points

Although visual demonstrations can be an extremely effective method of teaching, not all athletes will learn best by watching. Demonstrations of skills are only one part in the longer process of teaching and coaching a sport. Much of coaches' communication comes in the form of verbal cues, instructions, and feedback on performance. Understanding how to provide good instructional cues and feedback is key to strong and effective coaching as it increases athlete motivation, dedication and athlete success.

There are many ways to teach a new skill, but it is essential to break it down into the main **teaching points**.

To ensure the information being conveyed is easily understood, coaches should use short sentences and highlight the key points in order of priority.

For example, when coaching a cartwheel, the teaching points might be:
- Lunge forwards
- Put your hands on the ground at 90 degrees
- Kick your feet over your head
- Keep your back straight
- Keep legs straight and point your toes
- Land in lunge facing the opposite direction.

KEY TERM

Teaching points are information about a skill or technique that needs to be conveyed to and understood by the athlete for the skill to be learned and replicated. They are the key aspects that need to be highlighted to ensure the correct and safe way to perform the technique.

◘ Coaches use verbal teaching points, alongside demonstrations, to teach skills

When setting up drills and practices, coaches cannot assume players know why they are being asked to perform a certain drill or conditioned practice. Coaches need to explain how the practice is linked to their ability. The teaching points for drills and practices should be explained and how this links to skill development and the overall performance strategy.

Example teaching points for the bench press might be:

1 Lie back flat on a bench.

2 Grip barbell with hands slightly wider than shoulders.

3 Press feet firmly onto the ground.

4 Engage your core to avoid arching your back.

5 Slowly lift the bar off the rack, lower bar to the chest.

6 Stop when elbows are just below the chest and push the bar up, extending the arms.

7 Perform 9 more repetitions before resting.

BEST PRACTICE

The best coaches use a variety of methods to teach athletes, such as demonstrations and teaching points combined. People learn in different ways and using more than one method ensures everyone is given the opportunity to learn.

ACTIVITY

Support

Choose a drill or conditioned practice for one of these sports:

swimming, squash, volleyball, football.

Write a list of the teaching points for the drill or practice chosen. This should be the instructions the coach would give on how to perform the drill or practice.

Challenge

Describe the importance of being clear and concise with teaching points.

CHECK MY LEARNING

1 Describe why verbal teaching points should be used alongside demonstrations when teaching sport skills, drills and practices.

2 Explain why teaching points should be short and concise.

C2: Organising drills 1: space, equipment, participants

Drills and practices are used to improve participants' sporting techniques. To be effective, it is important to know how to organise and demonstrate them.

Different drills and adapted games can improve sporting techniques and performance. When planning practices, coaches need to identify the skills they will focus on and consider what resources they will need for each drill.

Space

Depending on the drills and practices that are planned, a practice could use all or just part of the full-size playing area. It may be that the full-size playing area is not available, in which case drills and practices need to be planned that can be performed in a reduced area. For example, a half court conditioned game in netball.

Alternatively, the full playing area may be available but there are too many players, in which case drills and practices could be planned where all players are involved but in a smaller area. For example, penalty practice in football.

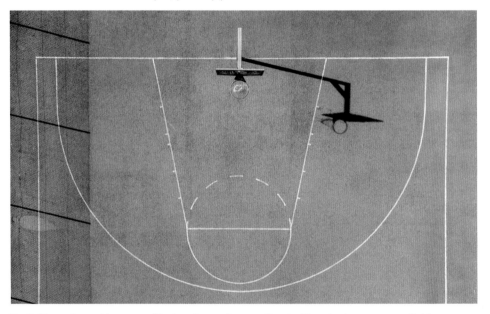

◧ Drills and practices need to be planned according to the playing area available

Equipment

Drills and practices can make use of a range of equipment, if it is available, or equally little equipment if none is available. Coaches must be able to identify what pieces of equipment are needed for each drill, and plan and organise drills and practices to match the resources available.

For example, the T-drill is a basic drill for agility that requires just cones or markers. The cones should be arranged in a T shape, with one at the base, one in the middle of the top line, and one at either end.

To perform the drill:

- Start at the base of the T.
- Sprint forward towards the middle cone.
- Shuffle to the left until you reach the cone on the far left.
- Shuffle to the right, passing the middle cone, until you reach the cone on the far right.
- Shuffle to the left until you reach the middle cone.
- Stay facing forward and shuffle backward until you reach your starting point.
- Repeat the sequence several times, trying to maintain a quick pace and fast feet.

Directional changes should happen quickly, and participants should not stop at any of the cones.

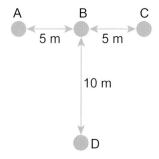

Figure 2.7: Layout of cones for a T-drill

Organisation of participants

Drills and practices can be organised based on the number of players available. Some can be performed individually, for example basketball shooting practice. Another option is working in pairs, for example rugby passing accuracy practice. Finally, players can be organised into small groups to perform a practice, for example, a 2 v 2 football practice in a confined space.

ACTIVITY

Support

Working in pairs, select a sport of your choice. Plan a drill or practice that can be performed in the following conditions:

- Limited space
- Limited equipment
- Limited players.

Challenge

Consider the consequences if a drill or practice is not correctly and effectively planned to the resources available. Give examples.

CHECK MY LEARNING

Describe how space, equipment and participants will affect the drills and practices that a coach plans to develop skills.

C2: Organising drills 2: timing, demonstrations, positioning

Well-organised sports practices are the most effective. Players will be more motivated, more likely to listen and have greater confidence in the coach's ability to improve their performance.

There are additional factors that must be considered when setting up and demonstrating drills and conditioned practices to participants.

Timing

When planning a training session, a coach needs to consider the skills that will be focused on, or which element of technique will be targeted for improvement. A range of drills and practices then need to be planned that meet these aims.

Each coach will develop their own approach to planning a session. In general, most sessions will be based around the following elements:

Sports practices are generally made up of a number of different drills and/or conditioned practices, the timing of these is an important consideration to make sure that players maintain interest and do not become too fatigued in one area. Furthermore, training sessions generally run for a set amount of time, therefore the time each drill and practice will last for needs to be considered so that the session does not overrun.

An example session plan for a football training session focusing on ball manipulation is shown in Figure 2.9.

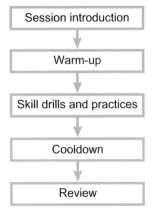

Session introduction

↓

Warm-up

↓

Skill drills and practices

↓

Cooldown

↓

Review

◘ Figure 2.8: Elements of a sports training session

SESSION PLAN			
Session theme: Ball manipulation			
DATE: 06-04	**Group:** under 8's		**Time:** 1 hr
Equipment: balls, bibs, cones, stop-watch, pop-up goals			
Technical skills: running, turning, dribbling		**Psychological skills:** decision making	
Social skills: team work		**Physical skills:** agility, acceleration	

Warm up activity: Dribbling with numbers (10 mins) — 1 ball per player, must run and move with the ball around a small defined area, keeping their head up and avoiding other players. Call out: "1" = change speed, "2" = change direction or "3" = stop.	**Key points:** · Keep head up · Keep ball close to body · Accelerate after turning · Scan the field to see where other players are.
DRILL 1: Ball manipulation (15 mins) — set up cones in a grid pattern. One player with a ball stands in the middle of cone square. Players to practice various ball manipulation techniques. — cone — player with ball	**Key points:** · Speed and control; close control incorporated with speed work on the ball. · Focus on mastering technique
DRILL 2: Canoes (15 mins) — several rivers are set out, players have to 'canoe' through the river and take a shot at goal.	**Key points:** · Travel through the river as fast as possible whilst making sure the ball stays within the boundary.
DRILL 3: 5v5 free game (20 mins) — players play a 5 v 5 free game.	**Key points:** · Practice moving the ball swiftly whilst staying in control.
Adaptations / Progression: · Increase/decrease number of players per side in final free game depending on attendance. · Arlo has just come back to training after a broken arm, he should be encouraged to focus on technique rather than speed.	
Reflections: 1 team member absent, 3 people late — need to work on motivation to attend.	**Improvements:** Add in reward for attending on time e.g. refreshments before we start? Talk to Jo about whether they need a lift here.

◘ Figure 2.9: An example session plan for a football training session

Demonstrations

Demonstrations are used to increase players' understanding of the skill by providing an example of what they are aiming for. Coaches will often demonstrate skills themselves. They may also use other players, sportspersons from outside the team or video recordings.

Positioning

When demonstrating drills or practices, the demonstrating athlete(s) should be positioned so that all participants can see them. The drill or practice should be performed at different angles so that the demonstration can be seen from various viewpoints, and if possible and applicable, both left- and right-handed ways to execute the skill should be demonstrated.

◩ Drills and practices need to be planned and organised well to ensure player motivation and engagement

LINK IT UP

Some key tips to ensure effective demonstrations were discussed earlier in Learning outcome C1 of Component 2.

ACTIVITY

Support

In pairs, plan and set up a drill for a sport of your choice. Deliver this drill to a small group of students from your class. Gather feedback on how the drill was set up and delivered.

Challenge

Plan a progression drill to continue development of the skill practised in the first drill.

CHECK MY LEARNING

Describe why the timing of drills and practices needs to be considered when organising sessions to improve sporting techniques and performance.

C2: Supporting participants during practical drills and conditioned practices

When learning a new skill, or training to improve a skill or technique, sports performers will need support and feedback to allow them to keep making progress.

Supporting participants

The role of a **sports coach** is to help athletes work towards achieving their full potential. They are responsible for training athletes by analysing performances, identifying needs, planning training programmes, instructing in relevant skills and providing encouragement.

Observing participants

By observing players, the performance strengths and weaknesses of athletes and/or teams can be identified and training programmes that will address these can be planned. Observation gives athletes a focus point on where they may need to improve or work harder on. For example, a swimmer may be advised that their tumble turn needs to be refined in order for their time to improve.

Providing instructions

When giving instructions or speaking to players, coaches need to ensure they are in a position where everyone can clearly see them. Clear communication doesn't just rely on words, but also on facial gestures, lip reading and body language.

Instructions need to be clear and concise. Coaches should check that all players have understood, and clarify if necessary. Players should not be singled out when checking, but it is important to ensure that anyone with additional support requirements has heard and understood the instructions.

Providing teaching points

Teaching points are the information about a skill or technique that needs to be understood by an athlete for a drill or conditioned practice to be replicated. They may be given as verbal cues, instructions or feedback on performance.

For example, after setting up a drill, a coach will watch how players are performing it and provide short reminders of the key aspects that need to be focused on, for example when pushing up from a squat, knees pointing over toes, head up, back straight, push through the feet.

Providing feedback to participants

Feedback is an important tool for continuous improvement. It shouldn't be an attack on a player's performance but provide constructive information about the performance of a skill or practice. It is important to discuss what was good and then move on to what could be improved. Feedback should be a motivating tool. For example, you may praise the effort and resilience a player showed in a football match, and then move on to pointing out an area for them to work on, such as increasing their awareness of their teammates' position to be able to pass to them. You would then finish with another positive, such as their strong communication during the match. This is sometimes called a 'praise sandwich'.

Athlete development plan

Development plans and action plans are commonly produced to monitor and improve athletes' performance. These build on the athlete's performance during training sessions by tailoring feedback and producing smarter targets that can help the athlete develop certain skills, aspects of fitness, or performance. Athletes can then focus on specific drills or conditioned practices that will help develop their understanding and performance. This training is often completed after or before usual team training to make the most of the athlete's time.

ACTIVITY

Support

Individually, plan a drill for a sport of your choice, plan out the instructions you need to give and the key teaching points.

Challenge

Pair up with another student to practise delivering the drill. Make sure you give teaching point reminders as they are performing it, and after they have finished, give them some positive feedback and an area to keep working on.

CHECK MY LEARNING

Explain the key role of a coach when supporting sports players to improve their performance.

DID YOU KNOW?

Dr Albert Mehrabian, an American professor, studied the understanding of communications and concluded that how we interpret a message is:

7% from the spoken word

38% from the way that the words are said (for example, tone and volume of voice)

55% body language (for example, facial expression, posture and gestures)

Therefore, 93% of how a message is understood is non-verbal.

BEST PRACTICE

Supporting players to improve their performance involves a number of different abilities: you need to be able to identify strengths and weakness, prepare training programmes, communicate effectively with athletes, give teaching points to develop skills, and evaluate the learning that has taken place. It can be a difficult task.

Learning outcome C: Assessment practice

Demonstrate ways to improve participants' sporting techniques

How you will be assessed

In this component you will be assessed by completing four internally assessed assignments. The assignments will be set by Pearson.

You will be provided with an assignment brief that describes what you will need to do and the date by which the assignment should be completed and submitted to the teacher.

Your teacher will mark the assignment and tell you what grade you have achieved.

You will be expected to demonstrate ways to improve participants' sporting techniques.

This will include:

- Planning drills and conditioned practices for a chosen sport skill
- Justifying the relevance of drills and conditioned practices chosen
- Providing video evidence of supporting participants to improve skills including specific guidance and teaching points.

CHECKPOINT

Review your learning of this component by answering the following questions, this will help you prepare for your assignment.

Strengthen

1 What are drills and conditioned practices?

2 Why are demonstrations and teaching points useful when planning drills and practices to develop sporting skills?

3 What can you actively do to support participants when they are taking part in drills and conditioned practices?

Challenge

- Why might conditioned practices be more useful than drills when preparing for competitions?

- Why is communication important when supporting participants when they are taking part in drills and conditioned practices?

ASSESSMENT ACTIVITY

You are on work experience at your local National League football club.

You have been approached by the training coach to help them plan a training session focusing on the football skill of turning.

The training coach would like you to plan two drills and two conditioned practices specifically for improving turning.

Produce a written piece of work in the form of a session plan.

You need to consider the following:

- Space and equipment needed
- Timing
- Demonstrations
- Set-up instructions for players
- Teaching points.

The training coach would like you to also provide a justification of why you have selected each of the drills and conditioned practices.

TIPS

Make sure that the drills and conditioned practices you plan are related to the technique or skill being focused on. For higher grades, make sure you justify the drills and conditioned practices planned.

TAKE IT FURTHER

How might the drills you have planned be progressed? Consider further follow-on drills which include travel, passive opposition and active opposition.

COMPONENT

03

Developing Fitness to Improve Other Participants' Performance in Sport and Physical Activity

Introduction

Think about people who are the very best in their sport; how important do you think their fitness and training has been for their development? Now think about somebody you think of as being really healthy; what is it about them that makes you think they are healthy? Whether we are looking at elite sport performance or the general health of the population, being fit is an important part of everything we do.

In this component, you will learn about the things that show how fit and healthy we are: the different components of fitness. You will learn about the components of fitness that are important for sports performance and the overall health of the general population, how we can best train and test these different components of fitness, the effects of different fitness training on the body systems and then how you can most effectively prepare programmes to improve fitness and sports performance.

Whether you are interested in moving into coaching, into careers in elite sport, or into careers in personal training, the knowledge, understanding and skills you will gain through this component will help prepare you for the next steps.

LEARNING OUTCOMES

In this component you will:

A	explore the important of fitness for sports performance
B	investigate fitness testing to determine fitness levels
C	investigate different fitness training methods
D	investigate fitness programming to improve fitness and sports performance.

A1: The importance of fitness for successful participation in sport

Whichever sport you play, or you help people to prepare for, understanding the different components of fitness is central to performing at the highest level.

Components of fitness

There are two sets of components for fitness: components of physical fitness and components of skill-related fitness. Different types of sport each require different blends of components of fitness so that you can perform well. Table 3.1 shows the different components of fitness, a description of the types of sport that require those components of fitness and examples of those sports.

◻ **Different sports and positions require different blends of components of fitness**

Types of sport requiring different components of fitness

By breaking fitness down into components it makes it easier to measure a performer's fitness and to identify specific areas where they have strengths and other areas where improvement is needed. A good sportsperson will have high levels of the components of fitness needed for their specific sport or activity.

Physical components of fitness are the basic elements of fitness. Physical components of fitness include aerobic endurance, muscular endurance, muscular strength, speed, flexibility and body composition.

◻ **Table 3.1: Components of physical fitness and the sports they benefit**

Component of fitness	Description of sport	Examples
Aerobic endurance	Events/sports lasting longer than 30 minutes	Marathon running
Muscular endurance	The ability to maintain/repeat a muscular movement; e.g. 12 repetitions with a barbell in the gym	Long-distance cycling
Muscular strength	Activities requiring force	Javelin throwing
Speed	Activities requiring fast movements	100 m sprinting
Flexibility	Activities requiring a wide range of movement around a joint	Gymnastics
Body composition	Each activity requires a different body composition	Low body fat, e.g. gymnastics High muscle mass, e.g. sprinters

Skill-related components of fitness involve movements which allow you to complete an activity or skill. For example, balance is required by a netball player standing on one leg taking a shot at the goal. The skill-related components of fitness include agility, reaction time, balance and coordination.

◻ Table 3.2: Components of skill-related fitness and the sports they benefit

Component of fitness	Description of sport	Examples
Power	Activities requiring explosive movement	Shot put
Agility	Activities requiring quick changes of direction, such as when dodging an opponent or changing direction on a course	Freestyle skiing
Reaction time	Activities where a quick decision or a response to a stimulus is needed	Sprint start
Balance	Activities requiring the control of the distribution of body weight or to remain upright and steady	Skateboarding
Coordination	Activities requiring the movement of two or more body parts and can include the use of sporting equipment	Tennis

ACTIVITY

Tables 3.1 and 3.2 provide some examples of the different sports that require different components of fitness.

Support

Select four different components of fitness. These can be physical or skill-related.

Challenge

Produce additional examples of sports that require your selected components of fitness.

CHECK MY LEARNING

1 Give a definition of the term 'component of fitness'.

2 Describe the difference between physical and skill-related components of fitness.

A2: Fitness training principles

FITT is an acronym for the different principles of training that should be used when designing personal training programmes. FITT stands for Frequency, Intensity, Time and Type.

The basic principles of training

FITT is commonly used to identify the basic principles of training:

- **Frequency** refers to how often the training will take place; for example, the number of training sessions completed over a period of time, usually per week.
- **Intensity** means how hard the sportsperson works during training, which is usually expressed as a percentage of maximum intensity.
- **Time** identifies how long the training will last; for example, how long an individual will train for during each session.
- **Type** shows that the training is relevant to the sportsperson and their chosen sport; for example, the exercise and training method the performer takes part in to improve a specific component of fitness.

The additional principles of training

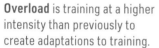

KEY TERMS

Overload is training at a higher intensity than previously to create adaptations to training.

Progressive overload is continuing to increase the intensity of exercise over time to make continued fitness gains.

As well as the FITT principle, there are some additional principles of training that you need to understand to be able to design training programmes effectively.

Progressive overload

So that your body can develop, the training needs to be demanding enough to cause your body to adapt. These adaptations will then help to improve sports performance or overall health and are created by overloading your body. **Overload** means that you must work at a higher intensity than you used to earlier on in your training programme, as your body will have adapted to the training, so doing the same exercise becomes easier. You can overload the body by increasing your intensity of activity, but you should not overload too much if you are a novice trainer, as this may result in injury or a poor technique. When you continue to increase your exercise intensity over a period, this is called **progressive overload**. For instance, a weightlifter will increase the amount of weight they lift on the shoulder press machine during each training session.

Specificity

The principle of specificity means that you should plan your training around the needs of your sport or activity. This means that you should consider factors including: the muscle groups used, the duration of the activity, the movement patterns, and the energy systems used. For example, if you are training for a marathon, you would need to have lots of long-distance running in your training programme. You should also make sure that you set goals that are specific to the activity and components of fitness. The occasional exercise that is not specific to the sport or activity can also be included in a training programme for variation, to prevent tedium and to help develop other components of fitness that are beneficial for general health, injury prevention or all-round sport performance.

Individual differences

Any training programme that you design should be specific to the needs of the individual. Everyone has different ability levels, goals, physical attributes, medical history and training activity preferences; so, you should design training programmes around these individual needs. For example, in netball, a goal shooter and centre have very different roles and require specific training to meet their individual needs.

Adaptation

This is where changes in your body happen in response to training load increase, which enables your body to cope with that increase. For example, a bodybuilder's muscles tear slightly (micro tears) before repairing naturally to make the bodybuilder bigger and stronger to lift the required weights as part of the training programme (hypertrophy). These adaptations allow a participant to improve the component of fitness that is being trained. They occur during recovery periods.

Reversibility

Think about a hockey player who severely sprains their ankle ligaments in their right ankle and has it in a cast for several weeks. When the cast comes off, the injured leg would have much less muscle strength than the non-injured leg as the muscles have not been working and have shrunk as a result. This is an example of reversibility which means that if training stops or the intensity of training is too low to cause adaptation, the training effects are reversed.

Variation

The principle of variation means you should include a range of training methods and alter your types of training to avoid boredom and maintain enjoyment. By doing this, you are more likely to stay motivated to adhere to your training and that can help you to maximise the benefits of your programme. You can achieve this by adding in some fun and competitive training sessions into the schedule.

Rest and recovery

Recovery time is essential in any training programme so that the body can recover from training and allow adaptations to occur. Without this rest and recovery time, the rate of progression will reduce, and the risk of injury will increase. Examples of rest and recovery include low-intensity activity, sleep and healthy eating.

CHECK MY LEARNING

1   Define the term 'progressive overload'.
2   Explain why you should use the principles of training to design a training programme.

BEST PRACTICE

To get the most out of your training, you need to apply these key principles of training. It helps to maintain motivation and allows goals to be set.

ACTIVITY

Support

Answer true or false to each of the following statements:

- Specificity is making sure that you have enough recovery time in your training programme.
- Variation helps to avoid boredom in training programmes by including a range of activities.
- An adaptation is where the body reacts to a training load and changes to make sure that it can cope with training.
- Progressive overload means that you gradually make things harder so that your body keeps adapting.
- Rest and recovery is wasted time that could be spent training.

Challenge

Write three statements about the principles of training. Two should be true and one false. Ask a partner to read your statements and see if they can correctly identify the true and false statements.

A3: Exercise intensity and how it can be determined 1

Understanding exercise intensity and how it can be measured or worked out is an important part of training correctly. Through the next section, you will learn about the different ways of measuring exercise intensity.

Intensity

Exercise intensity means how much energy is used to carry out the activity. For example, the amount of exercise a participant would use when running 100m or walking 100m. The distance travelled by the participant is the same, but the exercise intensity is different. Running 100m would require the participant to use more energy, the exercise intensity of running 100m is higher than walking 100m.

Measure heart rate

Heart rate (HR) can be used to give a measurement of the intensity of exercise. During exercise, heart rate increases. When we exercise at a higher intensity our heart rate increases.

◻ **Measuring pulse manually**

Heart rate intensity can be used to identify if an athlete is working in their target training zone (aerobic or anaerobic). The sportsperson's selected fitness method could involve working aerobically, to improve aerobic endurance. Their heart rate should be lower than if they were training anaerobically. You can monitor the intensity of an athlete by recording their heart rate. This helps you plan a specific training programme for each athlete.

Training zones

Training zones can be used to work out if the training is effective for the targeted component of fitness.

Training zones are given as the range of heart rate values you should work within for training intensity to result in effective fitness improvement. You can calculate training zones by identifying the sportsperson's heart rate and desired exercise intensity.

Exercise intensity can be identified by applying a sportsperson's maximum heart rate (MHR) to their training. MHR is calculated by using the equation 220 minus your age:

Max HR in bpm = 220 – age

You can then use this to calculate the heart rate required for different training zones.

For example:

A 16-year-old female's MHR is 220 – 16 = 204 beats per minute (bpm)

A 45-year-old male's MHR is 220 – 45 = 175 bpm

Applying MHR to training zones

The **aerobic training zone** is 60–85 per cent of your maximum heart rate (MHR).
The **anaerobic training zone** is 85–95 per cent of your maximum heart rate (MHR).

 Table 3.3: A percentage of MHR is used to calculate how hard you should work your heart to develop aerobic or anaerobic fitness, or for different training zones

50% Max HR	50/100 × Max HR
60% Max HR	60/100 × Max HR
70% Max HR	70/100 × Max HR
80% Max HR	80/100 × Max HR
100%	Max HR

For a 20-year-old female, MHR = 200 bpm

To train in the aerobic zone, their MHR should be between 60 per cent and 85 per cent of 200 bpm.

60 per cent of 200 = 120 bpm

85 per cent of 200 = 170 bpm

Therefore a 20-year-old female's aerobic training zone is a MHR of 120–170 bpm.

For a 20-year-old female to train in the anaerobic zone their MHR should be between 85 per cent and 95 per cent of 200 bpm.

85 per cent of 200 = 170 bpm

95 per cent of 200 = 190 bpm

Therefore a 20-year-old female's anaerobic training zone is a MHR of 170–190 bpm.

ACTIVITY

Support

Work out your maximum heart rate (MHR) using the equation 220 minus your age.

Challenge

Use your MHR to calculate the following:

Your aerobic training zone

Your anaerobic training zone.

CHECK MY LEARNING

1 Give a definition of the term 'exercise intensity'.

2 Describe two different ways of measuring exercise intensity.

3 Why is it important to be able to calculate your training zone?

A3: Exercise intensity and how it can be determined 2

GETTING STARTED

Exercise intensity can be used to measure how hard someone is working during exercise. How can exercise intensity be measured?

The Borg Rating of Perceived Exertion Scale

The Borg Rating of Perceived Exertion (RPE) Scale is a measure of exercise intensity that runs from 6 to 20. A measure of 6 would mean that you are almost at rest, no exertion at all; a measure of 20 would mean you are working your hardest, maximal exertion, you are exhausted.

To use the Borg RPE Scale, a person exercising is shown the scale and they point to a number on the scale to show how hard they think they are working. The number on the scale is then multiplied by 10 to get an estimate of their heart rate during exercise: RPE × 10 = HR (bpm). For example, if the person was working at 16 on the Borg Scale, their heart rate would be calculated as 16 × 10 = 160 bpm.

Sportspeople and sports coaches can use the scale to identify the intensity being worked at during training. This will mean training can be adapted so that the desired intensity is met. This also keeps the athlete safe, as they are monitored throughout their training.

◻ Table 3.4: The Borg RPE Scale can be used to measure how hard somebody is working during exercise

Rating of perceived exertion	Intensity
6	No exertion at all
7	Extremely light
8	
9	Very light
10	
11	
12	
13	Somewhat hard
14	
15	Hard (heavy)
16	
17	Very hard
18	
19	Extremely hard
20	Maximal exertion

Calculating repetition max (RM)

1RM is the maximum amount of weight you can lift in a single repetition. You can use the data to plan your strength training sessions. You would use this value to then plan how much weight you would need to apply as part of a strength training programme.

15RM is the maximum amount of weight you can consistently lift for 15 repetitions. You can use the data to plan your muscular endurance training sessions.

Lifts are known as repetitions or 'reps'. A set is a number of 'reps' completed without a break. Sets are usually repeated after a short break.

For example, if a sportsperson wanted to increase their strength, they would use a weight of 90 per cent of their 1RM and could complete three sets of one to six reps.

To work out the percentage of 1RM, multiply the 1RM by the percentage. For example, if a participant's 1RM is 100 kg, they can work out the weight they should lift to train at 90 per cent intensity:

90 per cent = 90/100 = 0.90

0.90 × 100 = 90 kg

To increase muscular endurance, a sportsperson could use a weight of between 50 per cent and 60 per cent of their 1RM and complete six sets of 15–20 reps.

ACTIVITY

Calculate your own 1RM and 15RM by lifting weights.

Support

Start with a low weight. Remember to carry out an appropriate warm-up before you begin, follow safe lifting practice and always have someone with you to help (spot you).

Challenge

Gradually increase the weight each time.

Technology to measure exercise intensity

- **Heart rate monitors** can be used to measure a person's heart rate accurately. There are different types of monitor, some can be worn during exercise, some are actually built into gym equipment, for example cross trainers, exercise bikes and rowing machines.
- **Smartwatches** would be worn on the wrist, tracking and recording heart rate as the person exercises.
- **Apps** that link to smartwatches can be used to measure exercise intensity. Apps can monitor the distance covered during an activity, the time active and the participant's heart rate to give an indication of the exercise intensity worked at. Apps can be used on tablets, smartphones and computers to analyse the data recorded during activities to measure exercise intensity.

◻ Carrying out a 1RM lift

ACTIVITY

Support

Working with a partner, use a heart rate monitor to measure each other's heart rate.

Challenge

You could use two different types of heart rate monitor and identify the strengths and weaknesses of measuring heart rate with the monitors and their suitability for monitoring heart rate during exercise.

CHECK MY LEARNING

1 What is the Borg Rating of Perceived Exertion?
2 Which different components of fitness can be trained by identifying 1RM and 15RM?
3 Describe how you could benefit from using technology to monitor exercise intensity when you take part in a training session.

Learning outcome A: assessment practice

Explore the importance of fitness for sports performance

How you will be assessed

All of this component is assessed through a written assessment. The written external assessment will contain short and extended questions which cover each Learning outcome in the component. The assessment, an exam, will be set by Pearson. It will contain short and extended questions.

The exam is worth 60 marks and will be carried out under supervised conditions. You will be given 1.5 hours to complete the exam.

For Learning outcome A, you will be expected to demonstrate knowledge of facts, components of fitness, fitness tests, training methods, processes and principles in relation to improving fitness in sport and exercise.

This will include:

- Explaining the importance of fitness for successful participation in sport
- Explaining fitness training principles
- Explaining exercise intensity and how it can be determined.

Below, you will find an example of one typical question from the exam.

CHECKPOINT

Review your learning of this component by answering the following questions. This will help you to prepare for your assessment.

Strengthen

- Outline sports requiring the six different components of fitness.
- Outline sports requiring the five different components of skill-related fitness.
- Describe the principles and additional principles of training.
- Describe exercise intensity and how it can be determined.

Challenge

- Describe why sports and activities require performers to have different amounts of the 11 components of fitness.
- Explain how the principle and additional principles of fitness are applied to fitness training programme design.
- Explain how exercise intensity can be measured or worked out and used to determine a sports performer's target zone.

ASSESSMENT ACTIVITY

Fredrika is a golfer. Golf swings require the performer to remain upright and steady.

(a) Which **one** of the following components of fitness requires the performer to remain upright and steady?

A   Balance

B   Aerobic endurance

C   Muscular strength

D   Flexibility

Fredrika needs coordination to succeed in her sport.

(b) Give a definition of coordination.

To increase her fitness for golf, Fredrika applies an additional principle to her fitness training.

(c) Which **one** of the following is a component of the additional principles of training?

A   Time

B   Type

C   Specificity

D   Frequency

Fredrika is looking to improve the maximum strength in her muscles. To do this she should train at 90 per cent 1RM. Fredrika's 1RM is 60 kg.

(d) Identify the weight Fredrika should use to train for maximum strength. You should show your working.

Fredrika works at 50–60 per cent 1RM and completes 20 reps during a training session.

(e) Identify the component of fitness she is training to improve:

A   Muscular strength

B   Power

C   Speed

D   Muscular endurance

TIPS

- When answering multiple choice questions, take your time to read all of the answers. Eliminate those that you know are incorrect and then try to recall which answer is correct.

- If the question asks for a definition, you need to state what the word or term means. You can give an example to help you describe the word.

B1: Importance of fitness testing and requirements for administration of each fitness test 1

You need to understand the purpose of fitness testing to be able to select the most suitable test for different sports and sports performers. It is important that you can administer fitness tests correctly and are able to collect and interpret the results.

Reasons for fitness testing

Fitness tests should be selected that are appropriate for the type of sport, the sports performer and the component of fitness being tested. When selecting a fitness test there are a number of factors that should be considered.

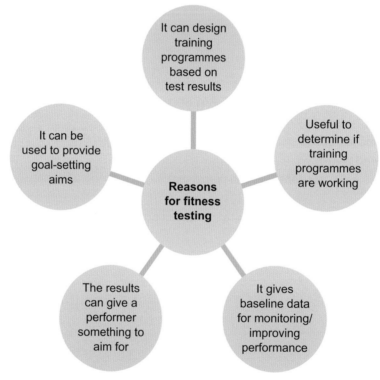

■ Figure 3.1: Reasons for fitness testing

Pre-test procedures

Before fitness tests are carried out, pre-test procedures must be followed. By following pre-test procedures, you can be sure that the fitness test will be accurate and that the sports performer agrees to take part.

Calibrate equipment

It is important to regularly **calibrate** all equipment to make sure that it is working accurately and measuring what it is intended to measure. If a handgrip dynamometer isn't reset to zero before the start of each test, it isn't calibrated and leads to an inaccurate score for the test.

Complete informed consent

Sports performers must complete informed consent before undertaking a fitness test. This means that they need to formally agree to the testing. This is usually done by signing a contract, which is often included as part of a Physical Activity Readiness Questionnaire (PAR-Q).

Complete PAR-Q

Participants are asked to complete a Physical Activity Readiness Questionnaire (PAR-Q) as a pre-test procedure to confirm that they are fit to complete fitness testing and to identify any reasons that would prevent them from completing fitness tests. A PAR-Q is usually a questionnaire that contains questions on personal information about the participant's health, fitness and injury/illness history. PAR-Qs and informed consent must be sought when you join a new gym. This helps keep you safe and supports the instructor in planning sessions.

Complete a pre-fitness check

Prior to exercise participation, sports performers will also be required to complete a participant pre-fitness check. This is another way to check for any areas for concern and reasons that the participant should not carry out fitness testing, for example medical history. The participant pre-fitness test check aims to reduce the risk of injury and to make sure the participant is fit enough to safely carry out testing.

Further requirements for administration of fitness tests

Before testing is carried out you need to ensure that you have knowledge of published standard test methods and equipment to be used for each fitness test. You need to have the ability to safely select appropriate test(s) for given purposes, situations and/ or participants. You will need to choose fitness tests that can be carried out safely by the sports performers, tests that test what you want to measure and tests that are appropriate for the sport or activity the sportsperson participates in.

To be sure that the fitness test results are reliable, you need to make an accurate measurement and recording of test results. It is useful to record fitness test results in a table, this allows you to include all of the information needed; for example, unit of measurement, date, name of participant, fitness test. A results table gives you a visual representation of your data. You can efficiently and quickly compare against normative values and share this data with your performers.

You could use the following list to help you to prepare for a fitness test:

1 Safely select an appropriate fitness test.

2 Find and use the standard test/protocol.

3 Find and use the standard test equipment.

4 Accurately measure the fitness test results or outcomes (for example, record the distance reached in cm in the sit and reach test).

5 Identify normative data for the fitness test.

6 Interpret the test results by comparing to normative data tables.

BEST PRACTICE

Participants must complete a PAR-Q before taking part in physical activity. If you are unsure about any of the participant's answers or need further information, the participant must check with a doctor or seek further information before they can start physical activity.

LINK IT UP

Knowledge of published standard test methods and equipment is explored in Learning outcome B1 of this component.

ACTIVITY

Working in pairs, use the first three points in the list above to find a suitable fitness test, its method and equipment, which can be carried out on a football team looking to measure each individual's muscular endurance.

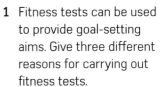

CHECK MY LEARNING

1 Fitness tests can be used to provide goal-setting aims. Give three different reasons for carrying out fitness tests.

2 Explain what is meant by informed consent.

B1: Importance of fitness testing and requirements for administration of each fitness test 2

Reliability of test

Fitness test results need to be reliable. How you measure and record results must be accurate to provide consistency of results. This means that you can be confident the results you recorded are a true representation of what happened. You can use the results to make fair comparisons to other normative data and tests taken on other occasions, both past and future.

The factors affecting **reliability** of fitness test results include:

◻ Table 3.5: Factors affecting reliability of fitness test results

Factors affecting reliability	Action to reduce effect on reliability
Calibration of equipment	All equipment must be checked to ensure that it is working correctly
Intensity of effort	Sports performers should want to take part in the fitness test and try their hardest at all times
Conditions of the testing environment	These should be the same each time the test is carried out, for example inside a sports hall or on a running track on a dry day
Experience of the person administering the test	The person carrying out the test must know how to use the test and have experience of using the test
Compliance with standardised test procedure	The correct procedures must be used for each test

It is important to reduce or, if possible, remove any factors affecting reliability of fitness test results. For example, by calibrating equipment, you can be sure that it is working correctly and making accurate measurements.

Validity of results

For fitness test results to be **valid** and an accurate reflection of the fitness component tested, they must be measured and the results recorded correctly. Following standard procedures and calibrating equipment all help to make the results valid. The tests should be repeatable and environmental conditions should be controlled.

Practicality

The cost of a test can make it impractical for some teams or organisations. If it is too expensive (for example, if it needs lots of staff or equipment) then it means the test would be impractical.

You need to consider the time taken to set up the test, perform the test and analyse the data.

At times, you might only have a small amount of time available to be able to complete your fitness testing. If the test takes a long time to set up, perform, and then analyse the data, this could mean it isn't practical for you to complete it. For example, the multi-stage fitness test requires the CD/track to be played to participants to meet the bleeps each shuttle. However, the 12-minute Cooper run just needs to measure distance around a track. Both tests measure aerobic fitness.

The number of participants that can take part in the test at any time will determine if the test is suitable for the performers you want to test. Sometimes, you might need to test lots of people at once. If you can only test a small number of people at once, it might make the test less practical than you need.

KEY TERM

Practicality refers to how suitable the test is for the given situation, the person administering the test and the people taking part in the test.

ACTIVITY

Support

1 When was the equipment last calibrated? How is it calibrated?

2 How could you motivate a participant before they undertake the test?

3 Where are you doing the test—inside, outside, sports hall, gym, classroom? Can you repeat the test in the same place next time you do this test?

4 Do you know how to carry out the test? Have you administered the test before?

5 Do you have a copy of the test protocols and procedures?

Challenge

With your partner make a list of any factors you have identified that may affect the reliability of fitness test data collected during your chosen test.

CHECK MY LEARNING

1 Describe what is meant by calibrating equipment.

2 Explain what you would do to make sure that the results of a fitness test are valid.

B2: Fitness test methods: aerobic endurance 1

Effective selection of fitness tests for chosen components of fitness is essential for collecting valid and reliable results for different sports performers and their specific sports.

Aerobic endurance

The multistage-fitness test (MSFT), Yo-Yo test, 12-minute Cooper run test and Harvard step test are all methods of testing aerobic endurance. These tests give an indication of the participant's maximum oxygen uptake or VO_2 max. The MSFT is a **maximal test**, which means the participant completes the test until they are exhausted.

Tests for aerobic endurance are suitable for sports people who take part in activities which last more 30 minutes, for example long-distance runners or cyclists, and are often required in team sports such as football, basketball or netball.

Multi-stage fitness test (MSFT)

Also known as the bleep test (20 m distance). There are three versions of this test:

Version 1 is for beginners, the frequency of the bleeps is slower, there is more time between bleeps to run.

Version 2 is the most commonly used version and has faster bleeps than version 1.

Version 3 is called the intermittent Yo-Yo test. The test has short active recovery periods.

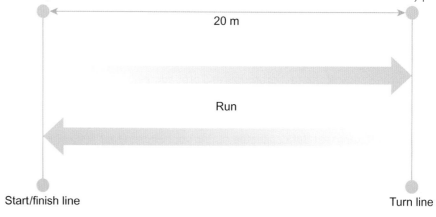

Figure 3.2: How to set up the MSFT

MSFT equipment

Tape measure, MSFT recording or app, speakers or CD player, cones, suitable flooring, such as a sports hall or running track.

MSFT protocol

1 Allow performers to complete a warm-up.

2 Use a tape to measure, place two cones 20 m apart on a flat surface.

3 Performers should line up on the start line.

4 After the triple bleep, the performers should run slowly to the other cone before the next bleep.

5 After the bleep, performers should run back to the other cone. Performers should not get ahead of the bleeps.

6 As the bleeps get closer together, the performers will need to run faster.

7 Performers should keep running until they are physically exhausted or have failed to reach the cone by the time the bleep has sounded three times.

8 Record the level (L) and shuttle (S) reached.

9 Use **normative data** tables to predict VO$_2$ max.

◨ Table 3.6: Normative data results for the MSFT test for adults aged 17–50

	Age	Excellent	Above average	Average	Below average	Poor
Male	17–20	L12; S12	L11; S6	L9; S2	L7; S6	<L7; S3
	21–30	L12; S12	L11; S7	L9; S3	L7; S8	<L7; S5
	31–40	L11; S7	L10; S4	L6; S10	L6; S7	<L6; S4
	41–50	L10; S4	L9; S4	L6; S9	L5; S9	<L5; S2
Female	17–20	L10; S11	L9; S3	L6; S8	L5; S2	<L4; S9
	21–30	L10; S8	L9; S2	L6; S6	L5; S1	<L4; S9
	31–40	L10; S4	L8; S7	L6; S3	L4; S6	<L4; S5
	41–50	L9; S9	L7; S2	L5; S7	L4; S2	<L4; S1

Yo-Yo test equipment

Tape measure, MSFT recording or app, speakers or CD player, cones, suitable flooring, such as a sports hall or running track.

Yo-Yo test protocol

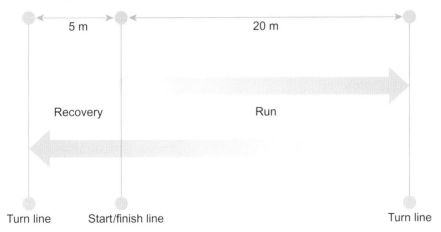

◨ Figure 3.3: Yo-Yo test protocol

1 Allow performers to complete a warm-up.

2 On a flat surface, such as a running track or sports hall, using a tape to measure, place two cones 20 m apart and another cone 5 m after as in the diagram above.

3 Performers should line up on the start line and wait for the test to begin.

4 The test begins with a bleep sound; the performers should run to the opposite cone line and wait for the next bleep sound.

5 The performers should then turn around and run back to the first cone.

6 If the cone/line is reached before the bleep sounds, the performer must wait until the bleep sounds before continuing. If the line is not reached before the bleep sounds, the performer is given a warning and must continue to run to the line.

7 The performer's score is the level and number of shuttles reached before they were eliminated. There is an active recovery period after each 2 × 20 m run.

KEY TERM

Normative data is an indicator of how a participant performed in comparison to the general population.

ACTIVITY

Support

Work with a partner and carry out the MSFT and Yo-Yo test. Take it in turns to be the test administrator and participant so that you both experience these roles.

Produce a table to collect your fitness test results.

Compare your results with your partner and compare them to the normative data.

Discuss your findings.

Which test did you prefer taking part in and why?

Challenge

Analyse why the normative data does not always indicate good performance. Consider age, gender and the participant's sport or activity.

Explain which test you think is more appropriate for a games player and which test you would recommend for a long-distance runner.

CHECK MY LEARNING

Explain the advantage to a coach of having different tests to measure a sportsperson's aerobic endurance.

B2: Fitness test methods: aerobic endurance 2

GETTING STARTED

Tests for aerobic endurance are suitable for sports people who take part in activities that last more 30 minutes. In small groups discuss what tests that measure aerobic endurance all have in common?

Harvard step test

The Harvard step test requires participants to step on and off a bench for a period of time to measure aerobic endurance. The test shows the participant's ability to recover from strenuous exercise and provides an indication of their VO$_2$ max. It is a submaximal test, which means the participant does not have to exercise to exhaustion.

Harvard step test equipment

Metronome, stopwatch, ruler, bench, suitable area such as a sports hall or gym.

■ Table 3.7: Normative data results for the Harvard step test for 16-year-olds

	Male	Female
Excellent	>90.0	>86.0
Above average	80.0–90.0	76.0–86.0
Average	65.0–79.9	61.0–75.9
Below average	55.0–64.9	50.0–60.9
Poor	<55	<50

■ The Harvard step test

Harvard step test protocol

1 Allow performers to complete a warm-up.

2 Start a metronome to provide the stepping pace for stepping onto the bench every two seconds.

3 Give the command 'go' and start the stopwatch.

4 The performer should step up onto the bench and down in time to the metronome.

5 The test is stopped after five minutes, or sooner if the performer is not able to continue for the full test duration.

6 One minute after the test has stopped, record the performer's heart rate – pulse 1.

7 Two minutes after the test has stopped, record the performer's heart rate – pulse 2.

8 Three minutes after the test has stopped record the performer's heart rate – pulse 3.

9 Use the equation to calculate the result: 30,000/(pulse 1 + pulse 2+ pulse 3) = result.

12-minute Cooper run or swim test

The Cooper run or swim test involves running or swimming for 12 minutes. The distance run or swam by the performer is used to measure aerobic endurance. It is a submaximal test, which means the participant does not have to exercise to exhaustion.

12-minute run test equipment

Stopwatch, whistle, cones, tape measure, suitable area, such as a sports hall or running track.

ACTIVITY

Support

Use normative data tables for the MSFT and Harvard step test to identify the fitness test ratings for Otto and Bella.

Otto is 16 years old and male.

Bella is 18 years old and female.

Complete the table below by identifying the fitness test ratings.

Challenge

Explain why the type of sports activity that Otto and Bella take part in and the fitness test used could affect their aerobic endurance result.

Name	Fitness test	Fitness test result	Fitness test rating
Otto	MSFT	11	
Otto	Harvard step test	99	
Bella	MSFT	9	
Bella	Harvard step test	55	

Stretch: Complete the MSFT and Harvard step tests and record your results.

Use normative data to identify your own ratings for both tests. How do your results compare to those of Bella and Otto?

12-minute run test protocol

1 Allow performers to complete a warm-up.
2 The performers should stand at the starting line on the athletics track.
3 Blow a whistle for the performers to start running around the track.
4 At 12 minutes, blow the whistle again for the performers to stop running.
5 Place cones at the point where each performer stopped running.
6 Measure the distance ran by each performer, recorded to the nearest 10 m.
7 Use the normative data table below to interpret the results.

◘ Table 3.8: Normative data table – 12-minute Cooper run for ages 20–29

	Male (m)	Female (m)
Excellent	>2800	>2700
Very good	2400–2800	2200–2700
Good	2200–2399	1800–2199
Average	1600–2199	1500–1799

12-minute swim test equipment

Stopwatch, whistle, cones, tape measure, suitable area, such as a 25 m swimming pool.

12-minute swim test protocol

1 Allow performers to complete a warm-up.
2 The performers should stand at the edge of the swimming pool.
3 Blow a whistle for the performers to dive into the pool and start swimming.
4 At 12 minutes, blow the whistle again for the performers to stop swimming.
5 Place cones at the points where each performer stopped swimming.
6 Measure the distance swam by each performer, recorded to the nearest 10 m.
7 Use the normative data table below to interpret the results.

ACTIVITY

Support

Work with a partner and carry out the 12-minute run test or 12-minute swim test. Take it in turns to be the test administrator and participant so that you both experience these roles.

Produce a table to collect your fitness test results.

Compare your results with your partner and compare them to the normative data.

Discuss your findings.

BEST PRACTICE

The Harvard step test and 12-minute run or 12-minute swim tests are used to measure aerobic endurance. To ensure reliability, validity and practicality of the different tests, you should note the time taken to set up and perform the tests and the number of participants that can take part in the test at any time. This is particularly important if you are planning to undertake the 12-minute swim test.

◘ Table 3.9: Normative data table – 12-minute Cooper swim

	Male (m)	Female (m)
Excellent	>800	>700
Very good	700–799	600–699
Good	600–699	500–599
Average	500–599	400–499
Poor	<500	<400

CHECK MY LEARNING

Explain the difference between the four fitness tests that can be used to measure aerobic endurance.

B2: Fitness test methods: muscular endurance

◻ Performing the one-minute press-up test

Fitness tests can be used to assess muscular endurance. There are different fitness tests which can measure muscular endurance in different areas of the body.

Muscular endurance

Muscular endurance is the ability to contract a muscle or group of muscles against resistance, for example bodyweight or weights, for a period of time. This component of fitness is important for those performers who take part in team sports such as: basketball, netball and individual sports such as martial arts and rowing.

Muscular endurance tests are suitable for sports people who take part in events or sports lasting more 30 minutes, such as rugby and kayaking.

One-minute press-up

The timed press-up test is used to measure localised muscular endurance in the upper body. This is a maximal test, so the participant completes the test until they are exhausted.

One-minute press-up test equipment

Stopwatch, Mat, Suitable flooring, such as a sports hall or gym.

One-minute press-up test protocol

1 Allow performers to complete a warm-up.
2 Performers should start in a full press-up position on a mat, with their arms fully extended.
3 Use a stopwatch to time one minute.
4 The performers should complete as many full press-ups as they can in one minute.
5 A full press-up is one where the elbows are bent to 90 degrees and then fully extended.
6 Use the normative data table below to interpret the results.

◻ Table 3.10: Normative data results for the full press-up test

Rating	Males (rpm)	Females (rpm)
Excellent	>45	>34
Good	35–44	17–35
Average	20–34	6–16
Poor	<19	<5

One-minute sit-up

The timed sit-up test is used to measure localised muscular endurance in the abdominals. This is a maximal test.

One-minute sit-up test equipment

Stopwatch, mat, suitable flooring, such as a sports hall or gym.

◻ Performing the one-minute sit-up test

One-minute sit-up test protocol

1 Allow performers to complete a warm-up.
2 Performers should lay on the mat with their knees bent and feet flat on the floor. Feet can be held by a partner if required.
3 Performers should fold their arms across their body.
4 Use a stopwatch to time them for one minute.
5 Performers must complete as many full sit-ups as they can in one minute.
6 A full sit-up is one where the performer raises their upper body off the floor, up to 90 degrees, and then lowers themselves back to the floor.
7 Use the normative data table below to interpret the results.

Table 3.11: Normative data results for the one-minute sit-up test

Rating	Excellent	Good	Above average	Average	Below average	Poor	Very poor
Males (no of reps)	49–59	43–48	39–42	35–38	31–34	25–30	11–24
Females (no of reps)	42–54	36–41	32–35	28–31	24–27	18–23	3–17

Timed plank test

The timed plank test is used to measure localised muscular endurance in the abdominals. This is a maximal test.

Timed plank test equipment

Stopwatch, mat, suitable flooring, such as a sports hall or gym.

Timed plank test protocol

1 Allow performers to complete a warm-up.
2 Performers should start with the upper body supported on the mat by the elbows and forearms. Their legs and back should be straight, hips lifted off the floor, head looking forwards and toes holding the lower body weight.
3 As soon as the position is assumed, the stopwatch should be started.
4 The performer should remain in this position for as long as possible.
5 The test is stopped when the performer is no longer able to maintain the position.
6 The time the performer held the plank position is the score for the test.
7 Use the normative data table below to interpret the results.

ACTIVITY

Support

Work with a partner and carry out the three different fitness tests for muscular endurance: one minute press-up, one-minute sit-up and plank tests.

Take it in turns to be the test administrator and participant so that you both experience these roles.

Produce a table to collect your fitness test results.

Compare your results with your partner, compare them to the normative data and discuss your findings.

ACTIVITY

Support

Explain the appropriate testing conditions required for the one-minute press-up and sit-up tests to ensure they remain reliable and valid.

Challenge

For a muscular endurance fitness test of your choice, analyse the impact of environmental conditions on the testing environment and test results.

Performing the plank test

Table 3.12: Normative data results for the timed plank test for males and females

Rating	Time
Excellent	>6 minutes
Very good	4–6 minutes
Above average	2–4 minutes
Average	1–2 minutes
Below average	30–60 seconds
Poor	12–30 seconds
Very poor	<15 seconds

CHECK MY LEARNING

1 Why is it important for the performers to carry out a thorough warm-up before participating in a muscular endurance fitness test?
2 What is meant by RPM?

B2: Fitness test methods: flexibility

Fitness tests can be used to assess flexibility. Tests for flexibility are suitable for sportspeople who take part in activities requiring a wide range of movement around a joint for example, gymnastics and martial arts.

Flexibility

Flexibility can be measured at a joint by assessing the range of movement – how far the joint can move. Fitness tests commonly measure flexibility in the lower back and hamstrings, lower leg and shoulder. The test selected will be the one which is most appropriate for the sports performer and the activities/skills they use. For example, measuring flexibility in the lower leg would be suitable for a football player.

Sit and reach test

The sit and reach test measures flexibility in the lower back and hamstrings.

Sit and reach test equipment

Sit and reach box, ruler or tape measure, mat, suitable flooring, such as a sports hall or gym.

□ A sit and reach test

Sit and reach test protocol

1 Allow performers to complete a warm-up.

2 Using a sit and reach box, the performer should remove their shoes and sit with straight legs and feet flat against the sit and reach box.

3 In a slow, steady movement, the performer should stretch forward and reach as far as possible with their hands, sliding them on top of the box and pushing the slider forwards.

4 The performer should hold the slider and keep their knees straight throughout.

5 Record distance reached; this is the result.

6 Use the normative data table below to interpret the results.

□ Table 3.13: Normative data results for the sit and reach test, 16–19 year olds

Rating	Males (cm)	Females (cm)
Excellent	>14	>15
Above average	11.0–14.0	12–15
Average	7.0–10.9	7.0–11.9
Below average	4.0–6.9	4.0–6.9
Poor	<4	<4

Calf muscle flexibility test

The calf muscle flexibility test measures flexibility in the lower back of the leg.

Calf muscle flexibility equipment

Mat, suitable wall, for example the wall of a sports hall or gym.

Calf muscle flexibility test protocol

1 Allow performer to complete a warm-up.

2 The performer should stand a short distance from the wall.

□ The calf flexibility test

3 They should stand with one foot in front of the other, both feet pointing forwards and both heels on the ground.

4 Keeping the heel of the front foot on the ground, the performer should bend their knee so that it touches the wall.

5 The performer should move a little further away from the wall and repeat the process, attempting to touch their knee to the wall.

6 Points 4 and 5 should be repeated until the performer is no longer able to touch their knee to the wall.

7 The distance from the front of the toe to the wall is recorded at the maximum distance the knee could touch the wall, this is the test result.

8 The performer should repeat the test on their other leg.

There are no normative data tables for this test. The test can be used by individuals to compare their own test results to check if a flexibility training programme they are following is increasing the flexibility in their calves.

Shoulder flexibility test

The shoulder flexibility test measures flexibility in the shoulder joints.

Shoulder flexibility test equipment

2 m rope, such as a skipping rope or rock-climbing rope, tape measure, suitable flooring, such as sports hall or gym.

Shoulder flexibility test protocol

1 Allow performers to complete a warm-up.

2 The performer should hold a rope with both hands 10 cm apart.

3 The performer holds both arms out in front of their body, in line with the chest.

4 Then they should rotate the arms so that they move up and over the head and down towards the back.

5 As their arms travel backwards and resistance is felt, the performer should slide their hands further away from each other to allow the movement to continue.

6 The movement should be stopped when the rope touches the performer's back.

7 The performer should return their arms to the starting position whilst not allowing the hands to move along the rope.

8 Measure the distance along the rope between the two thumbs to the nearest cm.

9 Measure the width of the performer's shoulders at the furthest point of each deltoid to the nearest cm.

10 Subtract the shoulder measurement from the rope measurement.

11 Repeat the test three times and record the highest distance achieved in the test.

12 Use the normative data table below to interpret the results.

▣ Table 3.14: Normative data results for the shoulder flexibility test

Rating	Male	Female
Excellent	<7.00	<5.00
Good	11.50–7.00	9.75–5.00
Average	14.50–11.49	13.00–9.74
Fair	19.75–14.49	17.75–12.99
Poor	>19.75	>17.75

B2: Fitness test methods: speed

Speed is the ability to move the body or parts of the body in a short amount of time. The 30 m sprint test and the 30 m flying sprint test are both appropriate methods to measure the physical fitness component of speed.

Speed

The 30 m sprint test and 30 m flying sprint test are both submaximal tests.

These tests are suitable for sports people who take part in activities requiring fast movement, for example forwards in football, tennis players and hurdlers.

30-metre sprint test

30-metre sprint test equipment
- Suitable area, such as a large sports hall or running track
- Cones
- Tape measure
- Stopwatch.

30-metre sprint test protocol

1 Allow performers to complete a warm-up.

2 Measure out a 30 m straight line using a measuring tape.

3 Mark both ends with cones.

4 The performer should place their foot on or behind the starting line, and take up the sprint position.

5 On the timer's command, the performer should sprint to the other cone.

6 The time is recorded from the moment started to the moment the performer crosses the finish line.

7 Repeat the test three times with a three-minute recovery between each test.

8 The fastest of the three times should be used as the test result.

9 Use the normative data table below to interpret the results.

◻ Table 3.15: 30-metre sprint test normative data

Rating	Male (secs)	Female (secs)
Excellent	<4	<4.5
Above average	4.2–4.0	4.6–4.5
Average	4.4–4.3	4.8–4.7
Below average	4.6–4.5	5.0–4.9
Poor	>4.6	>5.0

30-metre flying sprint

30-metre flying sprint test equipment
- Suitable area, such as a large sports hall or running track
- Cones
- Tape measure
- Stopwatch.

◻ Sprinters starting in track and field

30-metre flying sprint protocol

1 Allow performers to complete a warm-up.

2 Measure out 30 m and 60 m in a straight line using a measuring tape.

3 Mark each measurement with a cone.

4 The performer should take up the sprint start position at one end.

5 On the timer's command, the performer should run to the first cone.

6 Start the stopwatch and time how long it takes for the performer to complete the first 30 m and also the full 60 m distance.

7 Conduct the test three times with a three-minute recovery between each test.

8 The fastest of the three times should be used as the test result.

9 Use the normative data table below to interpret the results.

◻ Table 3.16: 30-metre flying sprint test normative data

Rating	Male (secs)	Female (secs)
Excellent	<2.6	<3.0
Above average	2.6–2.9	3.0–3.3
Average	2.9–3.1	3.3–3.5
Below average	3.1–3.3	3.5–3.7
Poor	>3.3	>3.7

ACTIVITY

Work with a partner or in a small group, to carry out the 30-metre sprint and 30-metre flying sprint tests.

Support

Take it in turns to be the test administrator and participant so that you both experience these roles.

Produce a table to collect your fitness test results.

Compare your results with your partner and compare them to the normative data.

Discuss your findings.

Challenge

1 What is the difference between the 30-metre sprint and 30-metre flying sprint tests?

2 Why do you think there is a flying sprint test? Which type of sports participant would benefit from using this test?

CHECK MY LEARNING

1 List reasons why an instructor at a local korfball club may use normative data to compare the athletes' fitness tests.

2 Explain the use of normative data when referring to fitness test results.

3 Explain one strength and one weakness of a speed fitness test for measuring speed of a rower.

B2: Fitness test methods: muscular strength

The component of fitness, muscular strength, can be measured by using a grip dynamometer and carrying out 1RM (repetition maximum) tests.

Muscular strength

Tests which measure muscular strength are **submaximal**.

They are suitable for sports participants who take part in activities that require force, for example throwing events such as discus or javelin, or sports such as weightlifting, boxing, wrestling and American football.

Grip dynamometer

A handgrip dynamometer measures muscular strength in a participant's hand when the participant squeezes the handle.

Grip dynamometer equipment
- Handgrip dynamometer.

Grip dynamometer protocol

1 Allow performers to complete a warm-up.

2 Adjust the handgrip size so the dynamometer is comfortable for the performer.

3 The performer should stand up with their arms by the side of their body.

4 The performer should hold the dynamometer parallel to the side of their body, with the display facing away from them.

5 The performer should squeeze as hard as possible for five seconds, without moving their arm.

6 The test can be repeated three times on each hand, with a one-minute rest between each test.

7 Use the normative data table below to interpret the results.

◻ Grip dynamometer

◻ Table 3.17: Hand grip normative data

Rating	Male (KgW)	Female (KgW)
Excellent	>52	>32
Good	47–51	28–31
Average	44–46	25–27
Below average	39–43	20–24
Poor	<39	<20

One Rep Maximum

The One Rep Maximum test measures muscular strength in targeted muscles or muscle groups. It is a maximal test. Strength is commonly measured in specific muscles by lifting weights appropriate to the muscle group, as shown below:

Type of lift	Muscles targeted
Bench press	Pectorals and triceps
Bicep curl	Biceps
Hamstring curl	Hamstring
Quadricep extension	Quadriceps
Lat pull-down	Latissimus dorsi
Shoulder press	Deltoids

◨ Performing a bicep curl

One Rep Maximum test equipment

- Fixed or free weights
- Suitable area such as a gym.

One Rep Maximum test protocol

1 Allow performers to complete a warm-up.

2 Performers should select a weight lift exercise that targets the muscles or muscle group that are to be tested.

3 The performer should select a weight they can lift and complete one rep of that exercise.

4 After a two-minute rest period the test is repeated with a heavier weight.

5 A spotter should stand in close proximity to the performer, so they are ready to support the weight if the performer is not able to complete the lift.

6 The performer should continue lifting until a maximum weight is successfully lifted. This weight that is lifted is recorded as the One Rep Maximum (1RM).

7 Use the normative data table below to interpret the results.

◨ Table 3.18: One Rep Maximum normative data for the bench press

Rating	Males	Females
Excellent	>1.26	>0.78
Good	1.17–1.25	0.72–0.77
Average	0.97–1.16	0.59–0.71
Fair	0.88–0.96	0.53–0.58
Poor	<0.87	<0.52

ACTIVITY

Support

Work with a partner and carry out the One Rep Maximum test.

Produce a table to collect your fitness test results.

Compare your results with your partner and compare them to the normative data.

Discuss your findings.

Challenge

Explain why the One Rep Maximum is a good test to measure a wide range of different sports performers' muscular strength.

CHECK MY LEARNING ◨◨

1 Why is it important that the test administrator has experience carrying out One Rep Maximum tests for muscular strength?

2 Why should the participant be familiar with the different types of weightlifting techniques before carrying out One Rep Maximum fitness tests for muscular strength?

B2: Fitness test methods: body composition

Body composition is what your body is made of: bone, muscle and fat. Excess body fat increases body weight, which means you would have to carry more load. Extra load can make some sports and physical activities more difficult to complete, which can have a significant effect on a sportsperson's performance.

Body composition

Fitness tests that measure body composition, such as low body fat are suitable for sports participants who take part activities such as gymnastics (require low body fat) and sprinters (require high muscle mass).

Body mass index (BMI)

The body mass index (BMI) measures whether a person's weight is appropriate to their height.

BMI equipment

Weighing scales, tape measure, calculator.

BMI protocol

1 Measure your body weight in kilograms.

2 Measure your height in metres.

3 Use the formula: Body weight (kg)/Height (m) × Height (m) = BMI

◻ Table 3.19: BMI normative data table

Rating	BMI
Underweight	<18.5
Healthy weight	18.5–25
Overweight	25–30
Obese	>30

Weight lbs	90	100	110	120	130	140	150	160	170	180	190	200	210	220	230	240	250	260	270	280	290
kgs	41	45	50	54	59	64	68	73	77	82	86	91	95	100	104	109	113	118	122	127	132
Height ft/in cm																					
4'8" 142.2	20	22	25	27	29	31	34	36	38	40	43	45	47	49	52	54	56	58	61	63	65
4'9" 144.7	19	22	24	26	28	30	32	35	37	39	41	43	45	48	50	52	54	56	58	61	63
4'10" 147.3	19	21	23	25	27	29	31	33	36	38	40	42	44	46	48	50	52	54	56	59	61
4'11" 149.8	18	20	22	24	26	28	30	32	34	36	38	40	42	44	46	48	51	53	55	57	59
5'0" 152.4	18	20	21	23	25	27	29	31	33	35	37	39	41	43	45	47	49	51	53	55	57
5'1" 154.9	17	19	21	23	25	26	28	30	32	34	36	38	40	42	43	45	47	49	51	53	55
5'2" 157.4	16	18	20	22	24	26	27	29	31	33	35	37	38	40	42	44	46	48	49	51	53
5'3" 160.0	16	18	19	21	23	25	27	28	30	32	34	35	37	39	41	43	44	46	48	50	51
5'4" 162.5	15	17	19	21	22	24	26	27	29	31	33	34	36	38	39	41	43	45	46	48	50
5'5" 165.1	15	17	18	20	22	23	25	27	28	30	32	33	35	37	38	40	42	43	45	47	48
5'6" 167.6	15	16	18	19	21	23	24	26	27	29	31	32	34	36	37	39	40	42	44	45	47
5'7" 170.1	14	16	17	19	20	22	24	25	27	28	30	31	33	34	36	38	39	41	42	44	45
5'8" 172.7	14	15	17	18	20	21	23	24	26	27	29	30	32	33	35	36	38	40	41	43	44
5'9" 175.2	13	15	16	18	19	21	22	24	25	27	28	30	31	33	34	35	37	38	40	41	43
5'10" 177.8	13	14	16	17	19	20	22	23	24	26	27	29	30	32	33	34	36	37	39	40	42
5'11" 180.3	13	14	15	17	18	20	21	22	24	25	27	28	29	31	32	33	35	36	38	39	40
6'0" 182.8	12	14	15	16	18	19	20	22	23	24	26	27	28	30	31	33	34	35	37	38	39
6'1" 185.4	12	13	15	16	17	18	20	21	22	24	25	26	28	29	30	32	33	34	36	37	38
6'2" 187.9	12	13	14	15	17	18	19	21	22	23	24	26	27	28	30	31	32	33	35	36	37
6'3" 190.5	11	13	14	15	16	18	19	20	21	23	24	24	26	28	29	30	31	33	34	35	36
6'4" 193.0	11	12	13	15	16	17	18	19	21	22	23	24	26	27	28	29	30	32	33	34	35
6'5" 195.5	11	12	13	14	15	17	18	19	20	21	23	24	25	26	27	28	30	31	32	33	34
6'6" 198.1	10	12	13	14	15	16	17	18	20	21	22	23	24	25	27	28	29	30	31	32	34
6'7" 200.6	10	11	12	14	15	16	17	18	19	20	21	23	24	25	26	27	29	30	32	33	
6'8" 203.2	10	11	12	13	14	15	16	18	19	20	21	22	23	24	25	26	27	29	30	31	32
6'9" 205.7	10	11	12	13	14	15	16	17	18	19	20	21	23	24	25	26	27	28	29	30	31
6'10" 208.2	9	10	12	13	14	15	16	17	18	19	20	21	22	23	24	25	26	27	28	29	30
6'11" 210.8	9	10	11	12	13	14	15	16	17	18	19	20	21	22	23	25	26	27	28	29	30

▢ Underweight   ▢ Healthy   ▢ Overweight   ▢ Obese   ▢ Extremely Obese

◻ Carrying out a waist to hip ratio assessment

◻ The Body Mass Index chart for adults

Bioelectrical impedance analysis (BIA)

Bioelectrical impedance analysis (BIA) measures the resistance encountered by a small electrical current passed through your body.

BIA equipment

BIA machine.

BIA protocol

1 The protocol will be determined by the type of machine used.

2 The machines contain electrodes that come into contact with the skin of the user to send a small electrical current around their body. The skin should be dry so that sweat/water doesn't influence the test results. This will help ensure the rest is reliable.

3 Ensure the performer is properly hydrated, as dehydration can result in a higher body fat reading.

4 Use the normative data table below to interpret the results.

◻ Table 3.20: BIA normative data table

Rating	Males (%)	Females (%)
Essential fat	2–5	10–13
Athletes	6–13	14–20
Fitness	14–17	21–24
Average	18–24	25–31
Obese	>25	>32

ACTIVITY

Why would using BMI testing not be the best way of testing the body composition of a sports performer with low levels of muscle, such as a jockey?

Waist to hip ratio

The waist to hip ratio measures the circumference of the waist and the hips to determine the percentage of a person's body fat.

Waist to hip ratio equipment

- Tape measure.

Waist to hip ratio protocol

1 The performer should stand up straight and breathe out.

2 Measure the circumference of the performer's waist just above the belly button with a tape measure. This should be where the waist is smallest.

3 Measure around the widest part of the hips. Do not pull it too tight.

4 Calculate the waist to hip ratio by dividing the waist circumference by the hip circumference.

5 Use the normative data table below to interpret the results.

CHECK MY LEARNING

1 What makes up a person's body composition?

2 Name three methods to test body composition.

3 Why is it important to be hydrated before carrying out a BIA test?

ACTIVITY

Support

Carry out one or more of the body composition tests. Produce tables to collect your fitness test results.

Compare your results to the normative data.

Challenge

Why do you think the normative data is different for men and women?

◻ Table 3.21: Waist to hip ratio normative data table

Hip ratio Male	Hip ratio Female	Related health risks
0.95 or below	0.80 or below	Low risk
0.96 to 1.0	0.81 to 0.85	Moderate risk
1.0+	0.85+	High risk

BEST PRACTICE

To ensure reliability, validity and practicality of the different body composition tests you should follow the standard procedures and calibrate all equipment to make the results valid. The tests should be repeatable and environmental conditions should be controlled. You must consider the time taken to perform the test, the time taken to set up the test and the time taken to analyse the data from the tests. All of these tests require some data analysis to obtain the test result. For example, to calculate BMI you need to follow the correct equation and make sure that you have the right measurements to complete the equation.

B3: Fitness test methods: agility

Agility is a component of skill-related fitness. Agility is the ability to change direction at speed. Sports and activities that use dodging movements, including gymnastics, badminton and rugby, require high levels of agility.

Illinois agility run test

The Illinois agility run test measures agility. The test requires performers to run forwards and in a circular motion around a series of cones as fast as they can.

Illinois agility run test equipment

Tape measure, cones, stopwatch, suitable floor surface, such as a sports hall or gym.

Illinois agility run test protocol

1 Allow performers to complete a warm-up.

2 Using a flat surface (sports hall floor, running track) measure a course 10 m long by 5 m wide using cones, as in Figure 3.4.

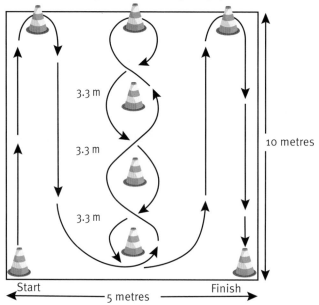

3.3 m

3.3 m

10 metres

3.3 m

Start   Finish
◄———— 5 metres ————►

🔲 Figure 3.4: Illinois agility run test

3 The performer should lie facedown by the start cone.

4 When a whistle is blown, the performer should get up and run around the course, as quickly as possible.

5 Use a stopwatch to record the time taken to complete the course.

6 Use the normative data table below to interpret the results.

🔲 Table 3.22: Illinois agility run test normative data

Rating	Male (secs)	Female (secs)
Excellent	<15.2	<17.0
Above average	15.2–16.1	17.0–17.9
Average	16.2–18.1	18.0–21.7
Below average	18.2–19.3	21.8–23.0
Poor	>19.3	>23.0

T-test

The T-test measures agility. To carry out the test, performers have to run forwards, backwards and sideways as fast as they can.

T-test equipment

Tape measure, cones, stopwatch, suitable floor surface, such as a sports hall or gym.

T-test protocol

1 Allow performers to complete a warm-up.
2 Using cones, set up a T shape, as in the diagram below.

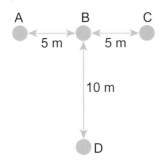

□ Figure 3.5: T-test

3 The performer should start at cone A.
4 The performer should always be facing forwards throughout the test period.
5 The stopwatch is started and the performer sprints to cone B and touches the bottom of the cone with their right hand.
6 They then use side steps to move to cone C and touch the bottom of the cone with their left hand.
7 They then use side steps to move to cone D and touch the bottom of the cone with their right hand.
8 They then run backwards to cone A and the stopwatch is stopped once they are in line with cone A.
9 Use the normative data table below to interpret the results.

□ Table 3.23: Normative data for the T-test

Rating	Males (secs)	Females (secs)
Excellent	<9.5	<10.5
Good	9.5–10.5	10.5–11.5
Average	10.5–11.5	11.5–12.5
Poor	>11.5	>12.5

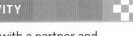
BEST PRACTICE

The Illinois agility run test and the T-test can be used to measure a sports person's agility. To make sure that these tests are reliable, valid and practical, you need to record results consistently, reduce any factors which might affect reliability (calibrate equipment, motivate the participant and follow all standardised test procedures). The tests need to be repeatable, and all environmental conditions should be maintained. For example, if it is raining you could consider delaying the test until the ground is dry.

ACTIVITY

Work with a partner and carry out the T-test. Take it in turns to be the test administrator and participant.

Produce a table to collect your fitness test results.

Compare your results with your partner and compare them to the normative data.

Discuss your findings.

CHECK MY LEARNING

1 How can you ensure that agility tests are reliable?
2 Explain one advantage and one disadvantage of using the T-test to measure the agility of a netball team.

B3: Fitness test methods: balance

 The Stork stand test

Balance is the ability to maintain the body's position without falling. Tests can measure static balance (the ability to remain in an upright position while stationary) or dynamic balance (the ability to remain balanced while in motion).

Balance

Tests that measure balance are suitable for sportspeople who participate in activities that require control of the distribution of weight or to remain upright and steady, for example gymnastics, table tennis and cycling.

Stork stand test

The Stork stand test measures static balance.

The Stork stand test equipment

Stopwatch, mat, suitable floor, such as a sports hall or gym.

The Stork stand test protocol

1 Allow performers to complete a warm-up.

2 The performer should remove their shoes.

3 The performer should place their hands on their hips and stand up straight.

4 One foot should be taken off the floor and placed against the inside knee of the leg that they are standing on.

5 The performer is given one minute to practise holding this position.

6 After one minute the performer should raise their heel off the floor on the leg that they are standing on and balance on the ball of their foot.

7 The stopwatch is started.

8 The performer holds the position on the ball of their foot for as long as they can.

9 The stopwatch is stopped if:
   • the supporting foot moves in any direction
   • the non-supporting foot loses contact with the knee
   • the heel of the supporting foot touches the floor
   • hands are moved away from the hips.

10 The best of three attempts is the final score for this test.

11 Use a normative data table to interpret the results.

◘ Table 3.24: Normative data results for the Stork stand test for males and females aged 16–19

Rating	Score (seconds)
Excellent	>50
Good	40–50
Average	25–39
Fair	10–24
Poor	<10

Y Balance Test

The Y Balance Test measures the ability of a person to balance on one leg whilst moving the other leg in different positions (dynamic balance).

Y Balance Test equipment

Tape measure or ruler, stopwatch, mat, suitable floor, such as sports hall or gym.

Y Balance Test protocol

1 Allow performers to complete a warm-up.

2 The performer should remove their shoes.

3 The performer is permitted a trial run to have a go at performing each move on the Y Balance Test equipment.

4 The performer must stand on the starting position on one foot, the other foot is placed just behind the supporting foot.

5 The non-supporting foot is moved along one of the Y Balance Test locations and the performer pushes the reach indicator as far as possible whilst still maintaining their balance on their supporting leg.

6 They repeat this movement three times and the distance moved by the indicator is measured to the nearest 0.5 cm. The highest score is taken.

7 This foot is then returned to the starting position and is taken along another of the Y Balance Test locations.

8 The test is repeated until the non-supporting foot has completed moving each of the three reach indicators on each section of the Y Balance Test equipment.

9 During the test, the performers must not touch their non-supporting foot down onto the floor or put their foot on top of the reach indicators.

10 Use the normative data table below to interpret the results.

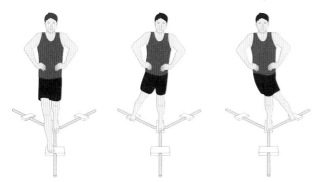

◨ Y Balance Test

The results for the Y Balance Test are specific to the performer because their limb length is a factor in the result. Someone who has longer limbs will be able to score higher than someone with shorter limbs, but this does not mean that they have a higher level of balance.

CHECK MY LEARNING

Why is balance important for a sports performer?

ACTIVITY

Support

Working in a pair or small group, carry out the Y Balance Test. Take it in turns to be the test administrator and participant so that you each experience these roles.

Produce a table to collect your fitness test results.

Compare your results with your partner or group and compare them to the normative data.

Discuss your findings.

Challenge

Explain why limb length can affect the results of the Y Balance Test.

B3: Fitness test methods: coordination

Coordination is the ability to use two or more different body parts at the same time.

Coordination

Tests for coordination are suitable for sportspeople who take part in any activity that requires the movement of two or more body parts, for example gymnastics or high jump. It also includes activities that require the use of sporting equipment, for example hand, eyes and tennis racquet to connect with the tennis ball.

Alternate-hand wall-toss test

The alternate-hand wall-toss test measures hand–eye coordination.

Alternate-hand wall-toss test equipment
- Tennis ball
- Stopwatch
- Tape measure
- Wall such as the wall of a sports hall.

Alternate-hand wall-toss test protocol

1 Allow performers to complete a warm-up.

2 Mark a line two metres distant from a wall.

3 The performer should stand behind this line facing the wall.

4 Start the stopwatch and tell the performer to start.

5 The performer should throw the tennis ball underarm against the wall using their right hand and catch it with their left hand.

6 They then throw the ball with their left hand against the wall and catch it with their right hand.

7 Use a normative data to interpret the results.

▣ Table 3.25: Normative data results for the alternate-hand wall-toss test

Age	Excellent	Above average	Average	Below average	Poor
15–16 years	>35	30–35	25–29	20–24	<20

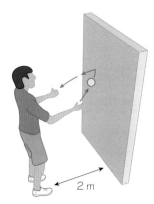

▣ Figure 3.6: Alternate-hand wall-toss test

2 m

Stick flip coordination test

The stick flip coordination test measures hand–eye coordination. The test protocol has two parts, performers have to carry out half flips and full flips with sticks.

The stick flip coordination test equipment
- Sticks: they should be 60 cm long and 2 cm in diameter with tape or paint at one end.

The stick flip coordination test protocol – half flip
1 Allow performers to complete a warm-up.
2 The performer should hold a stick in each hand. Upper arms are held at the side of the body, elbows flexed, and hands held at waist height.
3 The assistant places a third stick across the two sticks held by the performer.
4 The performer must flip the balanced stick so that it rotates and lands back on to the balanced sticks.
5 Five flips should be attempted with each successful attempt recorded. One point per successful flip.
6 If the stick does not rotate or is dropped on the floor this is not counted.

The stick flip coordination test protocol – full flip
1 Start in the same starting position as with the half flip.
2 The performer has to perform a full flip with the balanced stick. This can be shown with the tape at the end of the stick returning to its initial side of the balanced sticks.
3 Five full flips should be attempted.
4 Each full flip is recorded and awarded two points.
5 If the stick does not rotate or is dropped on the floor this is not counted.
6 Add up the scores for the half flip and full flip to arrive at the final result for this test.
7 Use a normative data table to interpret the results.

■ Table 3.26: Normative data results for the stick flip test

Rating	Males	Females
Excellent	14–15	13–15
Very good	11–13	10–12
Fair	5–10	4–9
Poor	3–4	2–3
Very poor	0–2	0–1

CHECK MY LEARNING

1 Which fitness test could you use to test coordination for a large group of people? Why would the test you selected be preferable over another test?
2 Name three sports that would not be suitable for using the stick flip test to measure coordination.

B3: Fitness test methods: reaction time

Reaction time is a component of skill-related fitness. Reaction time is the quickness of a response, for example how quickly a runner can sprint out of the blocks when they hear a starter gun.

Reaction time

Reaction time tests are suitable for sportspeople who participate in any activity where a quick decision or response to a stimulus is needed, for example a 100 m sprinter or in rounders.

Ruler drop test

The ruler drop test measures reaction time by testing how quickly someone can respond to catching a falling ruler.

■ Ruler drop test

Ruler drop test equipment

Metre rule.

Ruler drop test protocol

1 Allow performers to complete a warm-up.

2 The metre rule is held by the person administering the test.

3 The performer should hold their hand out with their index finger and thumb of their preferred hand around the ruler, with the top of their thumb level with the zero line on a one metre rule.

4 The assistant should drop the ruler and the performer has to catch it as soon as possible.

5 The distance between the top of the thumb where the performer caught the ruler and bottom of the ruler should be measured, this is the result.

6 The test should be carried out three times and an average value used for the overall test result.

7 Use the normative data table below to interpret the results.

■ Table 3.27: Normative data for the ruler drop test

Rating	cm
Excellent	<7.5
Above average	7.5–15.9
Average	16.0–20.4
Below average	20.5–28
Poor	>28

ACTIVITY

Support

Work with a partner and carry out the ruler drop test. Take it in turns to be the test administrator and participant so that you both experience these roles.

Produce a table to collect your fitness test results.

Compare your results with your partner and compare them to the normative data.

Discuss your findings.

Challenge

Why is it important that the person carrying out the ruler drop test accurately lines up the bottom of the ruler with the finger and thumb before dropping the ruler?

Online reaction time test

An online reaction time test or reaction test timers can be used to measure reaction time by the performer using a specific computer app or a timing device. The app or timing device requires the performer to respond to a stimulus, such as a noise or a flashing light, as quickly as possible. The app or device will record how long the response takes and provide a reaction time result that can be compared against the app's or device's normative data.

◻ Using an app to measure reaction time

ACTIVITY

Support

Go online and carry out an internet search for an online reaction time test.

Complete the online reaction time test.

Produce a table to collect your fitness test results.

Compare your results to the online test's normative data.

Challenge

What are the benefits and weaknesses of carrying out an online reaction time test?

Which types of sports performer do you think could use online reaction time tests to measure their reaction time?

CHECK MY LEARNING

1 What is meant by reaction time?

2 What is the benefit of high levels of reaction time for a performer who takes part in a raquet sport such as tennis?

3 Explain two pre-test procedures that you need to follow before administering a reaction time test on a sports performer.

B3: Fitness test methods: power

Power is a combination of strength and speed.

Power

Fitness tests that measure power are suitable for sportspeople who take part in activities requiring explosive movements, for example gymnastics and basketball.

Vertical jump test

The vertical jump test measures power in the legs.

Vertical jump test equipment

A vertical jump test board or suitable wall, tape measure.

Vertical jump test protocol

1 Allow performers to complete a warm-up.

2 The performer should stand with their preferred side against a board or wall.

3 With their feet together the performer should reach up as high as possible, an assistant should record the performer's standing reach height.

4 The performer should jump up as high as they can and touch the vertical jump board or wall at the top of their jump.

5 The assistant should measure the distance between the performer's standing reach height and the height reached at the top of the jump, this is the result.

6 The performer can have three attempts with a rest in between each.

7 The best of three attempts is recorded.

8 Use a normative data table to interpret the results.

■ Figure 3.7: Vertical jump test

■ Table 3.28: Normative data results for the vertical jump test, 16–19-year-olds

Sex	Excellent	Above average	Average	Below average	Poor
Male	>65 cm	50–65 cm	40–49 cm	30–39 cm	<30 cm
Female	>58 cm	47–58 cm	36–46 cm	26–35 cm	<26 cm

Standing long/broad jump

The standing long jump, also known as the broad jump, measures power in the legs.

Standing long/broad jump test equipment

A tape measure, suitable flooring to carry out the test, such as a gym or sports hall.

Standing long/broad jump protocol

1 Allow performers to complete a warm-up.

2 The performer should stand behind a take-off line marked on the ground.

3 The performer's feet should be hip-distance apart.

4 The performer must push down on both feet, swing their arms and bend their knees, jumping as far forward as possible.

5 The performer must land on both feet and try not to fall backwards.

6 The distance is measured from the take-off line to the nearest point of contact to the take off line (back of the heels).

7 The test can be repeated three times with a rest period between each attempt.

8 The longest distance recorded is the score recorded.

9 Use the normative data table, right, to interpret the results.

Margaria-Kalamen power test

The Margaria-Kalamen power test provides an overall score of power in a person's legs by considering their weight and height.

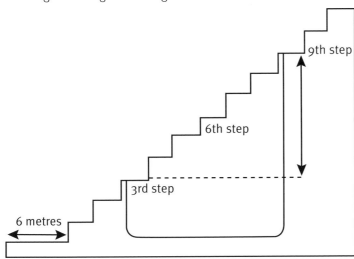

Figure 3.8: Margaria-Kalamen power test

Margaria-Kalamen power test equipment

Tape measure, weighing scales, stopwatch, steps, such as the steps leading up to another level in a building – the steps must not be used by anyone else during the test and should be signposted and closed off.

Margaria-Kalamen power test protocol

1 Allow performers to complete a warm-up.

2 A cone is placed on the 3rd, 6th and 9th steps.

3 The vertical distance is measured between the 3rd and 9th steps in metres.

4 The performer is weighed (kg) and the results recorded.

5 The performer stands 6 m from the first step.

6 An assistant says 'go'.

7 The performer sprints up the stairs, taking three steps at a time landing on the 3rd, 6th and 9th steps.

8 The assistant starts the stopwatch when the participant's foot lands on the 3rd step and stops it when their foot lands on the 9th step.

9 This time is recorded.

There are no normative data tables for this test, however, the test can be used by individuals to compare test results to check if a power training programme they are carrying out is helping to increase the power in their legs.

Power (watts) is calculated by using the following formula:

$$P = (M \times D) \times 9.8/t$$

P = power (watts)

M = athlete's weight (kg)

D = vertical distance (m) from 3rd to 9th step

t = time

Table 3.29: Normative data results for the standing long jump test

Rating	Males (cm)	Females (cm)
Excellent	>244	>191
Above average	229–244	178–191
Average	216–228	163–177
Below average	198–215	150–162
Poor	<198	<150

ACTIVITY

Support

Explain how a performer's motivation affects the reliability of the Margaria-Kalamen power test.

BEST PRACTICE

To ensure reliability, validity and practicality of the different tests, you should consider the time taken to set up and perform the tests and the number of participants that can take part in the test at any time. These tests all require equipment, and the amount of equipment will directly affect the number of people who can be tested at one time. These tests are explosive and require the performer to work at a high intensity, so a thorough warm-up must be completed before the tests are carried out.

CHECK MY LEARNING

1 Give a definition for the term 'power'.

2 Which types of movement are required in sports activities that need high levels of power?

3 Describe one advantage and one disadvantage of using the vertical jump test to measure power for a boxer.

B4: Interpretation of fitness test results

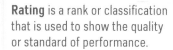

It is important to know how to use normative data tables to interpret fitness test results. By interpreting fitness test data you will be able to provide recommended improvements to a sports performer from their results.

Comparison to normative published data

Normative published data has been collected from hundreds of different people and ranges are set which represent **ratings** for different levels of fitness. Ratings are usually given from excellent to poor. Published data exists in books and online for all of the common fitness tests. Some fitness tests have normative data for specific age groups and sexes (males/females). For some tests there is only one set of data; age and sex do not affect the rating.

Analyse and evaluate test results

By comparing fitness test results to normative data you are analysing the results. When you identify normative ratings for a fitness test result and compare the rating to a performer's previous score or to another sportsperson's score you are starting to evaluate the results. Analysing and evaluating results requires you to compare ratings and make judgments about the results.

You would look to see if the data you have is for the same sports performer, which tests they have completed, the ratings of the data and how often they have taken the tests. You can then begin to make comparisons about the results: does the data show that the sports performer's test results or ratings have improved or got worse, were their tests carried out a long time ago and not comparable?

Recommendations for improvements to fitness performer based on test results

Once you have analysed and evaluated test results, you can provide recommendations for fitness improvements. For example, if a sports performer's flexibility rating was poor and their power rating was excellent, you could recommend that they maintain the training they carry out for power and add more flexibility training.

ACTIVITY

Use the normative data tables below to complete the average results and ratings for William.

Interpret the fitness test results for William to answer the following questions:

1 Which component of fitness did William score the highest rating?

2 Which component of fitness did William score the lowest rating?

3 If William was training to be a gymnast, which components of fitness would you suggest he focuses on developing?

4 If William was training to be a basketball player, which components of fitness would you suggest he focuses on developing?

☐ Table 3.30: Fitness test results

Name:	William Arthur (male)		Height (m):		1.71		
Age:	15		Weight (kg):		75		
Fitness component	Fitness test	Test 1	Test 2	Test 3	Average result	Unit	Rating
Aerobic endurance	12-minute Cooper run	2450	2810	2650		m	
Muscular endurance	One-minute press-up test	36	38	33		No. of reps	
Flexibility	Sit and reach test	8.9	10.11	9.2		cm	
Speed	30 m sprint test	4.4	4.3	4.4		secs	
Muscular strength	Grip dynamometer	48	50	53		kg	

You can use information from the normative data tables for the 12-minute run, the full press-up test, the sit and reach test, 30 m sprint test and hand grip test. All of these are found earlier in this section.

CHECK MY LEARNING

1 Define the term 'normative data' in sport.

2 How is a normative data rating different from a fitness test result?

3 Why is it important be able to interpret fitness test data?

Learning outcome B: assessment practice

Investigate fitness testing to determine fitness levels

How you will be assessed

For Learning outcome B, you will be expected to demonstrate an understanding of facts, components of fitness, fitness tests, training methods, processes and principles in relation to improving fitness in sport and exercise.

This will include:

- explaining the importance of fitness testing and requirements for administration of fitness tests
- explaining fitness test methods for components of physical and skill-related fitness
- interpreting fitness test results.

Below, you will find an example of one typical question from the exam.

CHECKPOINT

Review your learning of this component by answering the following questions. This will help you to prepare for your assessment.

Strengthen

- Outline the importance of fitness testing and requirements for administration of each fitness test.
- Outline fitness test methods for components of fitness.
- Describe fitness test results.

Challenge

- Describe the reasons for and purpose of fitness testing.
- Explain the importance of the requirements and administration for fitness tests.
- Explain the practicality of fitness tests for different sports and for each component of physical fitness. Explain the validity of fitness test results for each component of physical fitness.
- Explain specific fitness test methods for components of fitness.
- Accurately interpret and analyse fitness test data and test results.

ASSESSMENT ACTIVITY

Christophe is a long-distance runner. He uses fitness tests to design training programmes to improve his running performance. Each picture (**A** and **B**) shows a fitness testing method.

(a) Identify the fitness testing method shown in (i) **picture A** and (ii) **picture B**.

Picture A

Picture B

(b) Identify the component of fitness being trained shown in (i) **picture A** and
(ii) **picture B**.

(c) Explain **one** reason why it is important for the participant to be highly motivated before completing a fitness test.

The table below shows some of Christophe's fitness test results.

Fitness test	Rating
T-test	Average
Body mass index	Good
Harvard step test	Below average
30 m sprint test	Good
One-minute press-up test	Excellent

(d) Explain, using the data in the table, one component of fitness Christophe should train to improve his fitness for long-distance running.

(e) (i) Identify **two** pieces of equipment needed to complete the Harvard step test.

(ii) Describe how the Harvard step test should be carried out.

TAKE IT FURTHER

To expand your answer for question (d) you should use the data to identify the component of fitness with the lowest rating and describe why that component is needed for long-distance running.

To expand your answer for question (e), you should think about a time when you participated in the Harvard step test and the protocols you followed.

What equipment was used?

Which protocols were followed?

How was the test measured?

C1: Requirements for each of the following fitness training methods

KEY TERM

Pulse raiser activities are included in a warm-up to gradually increase your heart rate.

To carry out fitness training safely and effectively as part of a training programme you need to know about different types of training methods to develop different components of fitness. You need to understand the requirements of running different training sessions, such as warming up and cooling down.

Probably the most important part of training is knowing how to carry out training sessions safely and effectively. If you can't train safely, you increase your risk of getting injured or ill, both of which will reduce your opportunity to train and any benefits that you gain from training. The key things you need to know about are:

- warm-up
- cool down
- linking fitness training methods to the associated component of fitness
- the application of FITT and other training principles
- the application of appropriate training intensities to fitness training methods.

Warm-up prior to taking part in the fitness training method

Pulse raiser activities

A warm-up includes activities to gradually increase heart rate. These activities are called **pulse raiser activities**. Pulse raiser activities can include going from a fast walk to a slow jog, then to a faster jog, so that blood is pumped around your body at a faster rate. Your breathing rate will also increase to get more oxygen into the body, which is transferred to the blood and taken to the muscles.

To keep things fun and to prepare your body for your sporting activity, you can introduce different aspects of the sport. For example, instead of just jogging around slowly as part of your pulse-raising activities, you could jog with a partner passing a football or rugby ball between each other, to get you prepared for football or rugby.

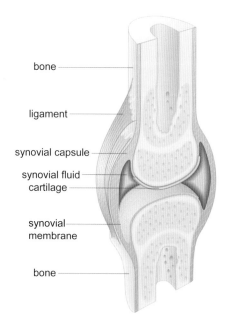

bone

ligament

synovial capsule

synovial fluid
cartilage

synovial
membrane

bone

☐ A synovial joint

Mobility and stretch

The next part of a warm-up is mobility and stretch, this component reduces the risk of injury and helps to prepare the body for exercise. As the muscles contract, they generate heat. This increases the temperature of the blood surrounding the working muscles. As your muscles become warmer, they become more pliable, which reduces the risk of injury and helps prepare your body for exercise. This means they are less likely to tear when they are stretched when taking part in sport or activity.

The warm-up also increases the production of synovial fluid. Synovial fluid is located between the bones of a synovial joint and acts as a lubricant. This means that it helps the bones to slide over each other more easily. During the warm-up phase of an activity session, more synovial fluid is released into the joints, which increases the ability of the joints to move more freely. This helps to reduce the risk of joint injuries.

Cool down after taking part in the fitness training method

After taking part in a sport or activity session, it is important to perform a cool down. A cool down is a set of light activities designed to gradually decrease your pulse and breathing rates back to normal resting levels, to remove **lactic acid**. A cool down should also include stretching, this will help return muscles to their pre-exercise length. During physical activity, movements are due to muscles contracting. When a muscle contracts, it will usually get shorter to produce the force required to move a specific part of the body. To help to reduce this shortening of muscles, the cool down stretch is used to return the working muscles back to their resting length to help to maintain flexibility. If muscles become shorter, they are at greater risk of injury through tearing but the cool down helps to prevent this.

Linking each fitness training method to the associated component of fitness

Throughout this Learning outcome, you will learn about the different training methods and the components of fitness that they can be used to develop. It is important that you always match the appropriate training methods to the components of fitness that you are trying to develop, so that the training is effective.

Application of the basic (FITT) and additional principles of training to each fitness training method

For each of the training methods you look to use as part of a training programme, you should make sure that you apply each of the different principles of training. Doing so will make sure that your training is effective and that you reduce the risk of injury.

Application of appropriate training intensities to fitness training methods

You need to be able to apply the correct training intensities for a sports performer when designing training programmes. These training intensities includes percentage of maximum heart rate or a percentage of the amount of weight that you can lift. You should use the correct training intensity to meet the needs of the individual to make sure that training is both safe and effective.

KEY TERM

Lactic acid is a waste product or by product that builds up during activity.

LINK IT UP

You can find more information about the basic and advanced principles of training in Learning outcome A of this component.

ACTIVITY

Support

1 Ask a partner to find your pulse on your wrist or neck.

2 Use a stopwatch to time 60 seconds and ask your partner to record your pulse rate for 60 seconds. At the same time you should count your breaths (how many times you breath in and out).

3 Now take part in a five-minute pulse-raising activity, such as walking then progressing into different speeds of jogging.

4 Use a stopwatch to time 60 seconds and ask your partner to record your pulse rate for 60 seconds. At the same time you should count your breaths.

Challenge

5 What is the difference between your pulse rate before and after your pulse-raising activity?

6 What is the difference in your heart rate before and after your pulse-raising activity?

CHECK MY LEARNING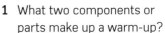

1 What two components or parts make up a warm-up?

2 What is the purpose of a cool down?

C2: Fitness training methods: aerobic endurance 1

GETTING STARTED

In small groups discuss why you think it is helpful to have different methods to enhance aerobic endurance. Think about the different sports and activities people participate in.

Aerobic endurance has several different fitness training methods. Sports and activities that require high levels of aerobic endurance require the body to work for long periods of time. Fitness training methods to improve this component of fitness need to work the body for similarly long periods of time.

Aerobic endurance

There are four main training methods that you can use to develop aerobic endurance.

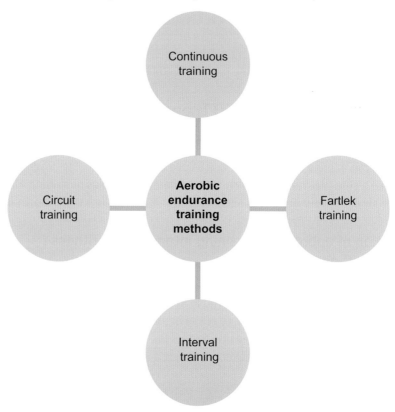

Figure 3.9: Aerobic endurance training methods

Continuous training

Continuous training involves working the body at a constant steady pace and moderate intensity for an extended period, usually over 30 minutes. For example, jogging, cycling or swimming for at least 30 minutes. Usually, the work intensity is between 60 per cent and 80 per cent of maximum heart rate.

LINK IT UP

Look back at Component 2, Learning outcome A1 to remind yourself about the components of fitness.

ACTIVITY

Support

Calculate 60–80 per cent of your maximum heart rate (MHR), to work out your heart rate range for continuous training.

MHR is calculated by using the equation 220 minus your age.

Challenge

Calculate 60–80 per cent maximum heart rate (MHR) for a man who is aged 39 and for a woman who is aged 25.

Fartlek training

Fartlek training mixes periods of low intensity work with higher intensity to push the body. The intensity can be varied by travelling at different speeds, for example alternating between walking, jogging, running and sprinting, or over different terrain, such as up and down hills. The training is continuous with no rest periods. Equipment such as a harness, running with weights or running with a weighted backpack can also be used in Fartlek training to increase the intensity. Fartlek training can have many different benefits as a training method, including the opportunity to vary the training to make it more specific for individual needs. This is useful in sports such as football.

KEY TERM

Fartlek means 'speed play' in Swedish. It combines continuous training with interval training.

◘ Fartlek training

CHECK MY LEARNING

1 How can you identify exercise intensity?

2 What level of intensity should a sports performer work at to improve aerobic endurance?

C2: Fitness training methods: aerobic endurance 2

Interval training

Interval training involves a period of work followed by a period of rest or recovery, before completing another work period.

When designing interval training sessions, you need to consider:

- the number of intervals (rest and work periods)
- the intensity of the work interval
- the duration of the work interval
- the duration of the rest interval
- the intensity of the rest interval.

An example of an interval training for aerobic endurance could be one set of three repetitions of five-minute runs interspersed with 150 seconds of rest. The exercise intervals will be at an **intensity** of around 60–80 per cent of a person's maximum heart rate. To increase aerobic endurance, you would decrease the number of rest periods, and your work intensity when compared to speed training.

◨ Interval training on a treadmill

Circuit training

Circuit training to develop aerobic endurance involves completing a number of different stations or exercises in succession with minimal rest periods in between. The stations or exercises are organised so that the performer completing the circuit uses different muscle groups at each station to avoid fatigue. Circuit training aimed at developing aerobic endurance might include activities such as running, cycling or other repetitive movements.

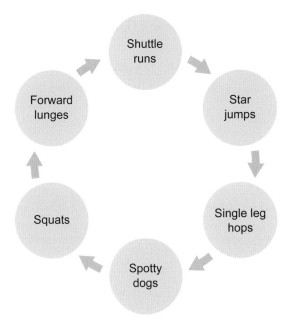

◻ Figure 3.10: Example of an aerobic endurance circuit

All stations or exercises should be completed for 30 seconds.

There should be a 30-second rest period in between each station or exercise.

The circuit should be repeated three times.

A warm-up should be carried out before and a cool down after the circuit.

ACTIVITY

Support

Design a circuit for a long-distance runner who wants to improve their aerobic endurance. The circuit can be completed in a sports hall and should have at least five different stations or exercises.

Challenge

How could you adapt your circuit and make it sport specific for a basketball player who wants to improve their aerobic endurance?

CHECK MY LEARNING

1 Name four different training methods for aerobic endurance.
2 Which aerobic endurance training method would be most suitable for a:
   a long-distance swimmer
   b rugby player?

C2: Fitness training methods: flexibility

Flexibility is a component of fitness that people might miss out to concentrate on other components of fitness. However, being flexible is directly linked to success in almost every sport.

Flexibility

Think about your own training. How much time do you spend working on flexibility?

Flexibility training involves different types of stretching. There are three main types:
- static active
- static passive
- proprioceptive neuromuscular facilitation (PNF).

Static active

Static active stretching, often known as active stretching, involves you applying internal force to stretch and lengthen the muscle. In this type of stretching the stretch or end position is held for a period of time. For example, standing tall and stretching your arms straight up and holding this position for 20 seconds, will help to stretch the muscles in your shoulder joints and spine.

□ Static active stretching

Static passive

Static passive stretching involves you using another person or an object (such as a wall) to apply external force and cause the muscle to stretch. In this type of stretching you remain relaxed and keep still with the range of movement being used at the joint being stretched. For example, sitting down and reaching towards your toes with your arms straight forward, a partner stands behind you and gently pushes your back forwards. The position can be held for 30 seconds and will help to stretch the muscles in your lower back, hips and hamstrings.

□ Static passive stretching

Proprioceptive neuromuscular facilitation (PNF) technique

PNF is an advanced form of flexibility training, which involves the targeted stretching and contracting of the muscle group. It increases the range of movement at a joint by increasing the length of the muscle and its elasticity.

You need a partner to be able to perform this type of stretching and it usually involves three steps:

1 Stretch the targeted muscle group as far as it can go.

2 Whilst in that position, **isometrically contract** the muscle group against a partner for six seconds.

3 Relax the muscle group and allow your partner to stretch it again. You should find you can stretch further now.

□ Proprioceptive neuromuscular facilitation

C2: Fitness training methods: muscular endurance

Muscular endurance is the ability of a muscle or muscle groups to be able to contract repeatedly for long periods of time, which is important for successful performance in a range of sports.

Muscular endurance

A competitive triathlete would need high levels of muscular endurance to be able to perform well across all the different events within their triathlon competition (swimming, running and cycling). Training for muscular endurance should include exercises with a high number of repetitions and use a low resistance or load.

Free weights

The most common method of improving muscular endurance is resistance training, using either free weights or fixed resistance machines. A **free weight** is one that is not attached to machinery, such as **barbells** and **dumbbells**. A barbell is a long bar with weights at both ends, which you lift using both hands. Dumbbells have a shorter bar with weights at both ends, which are used one in each hand. Free weights are used to perform exercises to develop specific muscle groups, such as using tricep extensions to develop your triceps, bicep curls are used to improve the biceps, or a chest press is used to improve your pectoral muscles.

◻ Weightlifting using free weights

Fixed resistance machines

Fixed resistance machines use stacks of weights attached to pulleys or air pressure to provide resistance. This type of strength training equipment provides exercises that only permit specific movements.

To improve muscular endurance, you should use high repetitions and low loads. A repetition is how many times you repeat the exercise or lift the weight. The load is the amount of weight you lift, for example a 10 kg dumbbell. To improve muscular strength, you also use repetitions and load, but you would use low repetitions and high loads.

Think about the types of sports and activities that require muscular endurance. Can you summarise the types of training a sports performer would need to carry out to increase their level of muscle endurance? Consider intensity and time.

BEST PRACTICE

Where muscular endurance is an important component of fitness for your sport, you should focus on the muscles/muscle groups that are relevant to your sport when conducting muscular endurance training. Two main ways that you could complete this type of training are resistance training (free weights and resistance machines) and circuit training.

KEY TERMS

Free weight is not attached to machinery, such as barbells or dumbbells.

Barbell is a long bar with weights at both ends, which you lift using both hands.

Dumbbell is a shorter bar with weights at both ends, and you lift one in each hand.

Fixed resistance machines use stacks of weights attached to pulleys or air pressure to provide resistance.

Circuit training

Circuit training for muscular endurance involves working at **exercise stations** that are muscular-endurance based. As with aerobic endurance circuits, you exercise for a specific period followed by a short rest period. For muscular endurance, this might be 45 seconds of work and 15 seconds of rest. The stations or exercises are organised so that the individual going around the circuit uses different muscle groups at each station to avoid fatigue. You don't always need additional equipment; you can use body weight as a form of resistance for circuit-training exercise stations by using exercises such as press-ups and different types of squats. A successful circuit for muscular endurance can use body resistance exercises or weights with low loads and high repetitions.

KEY TERM

Exercise station is the place in a circuit training session where you perform your exercises.

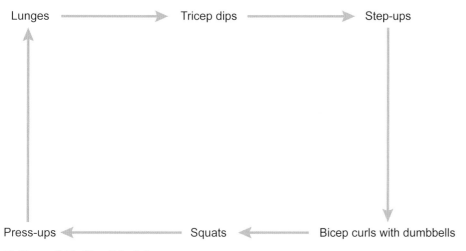

■ Figure 3.11: Circuit training

BEST PRACTICE

When designing circuit-training sessions, you should include a variety of exercise stations that can help you work towards your session goals and stay interested.

ACTIVITY

Imagine that you are a circuit-training instructor, working in your local village, running community-based circuit-training classes for people over 50 years of age who are new to circuit training.

Support

Plan a muscular endurance circuit-training class for a group of 10 people.

Challenge

Which exercises would you include and why?

CHECK MY LEARNING

Explain which type of muscular strength training would be the most appropriate for a rugby team that has access to a sports field.

C2: Fitness training methods: muscular strength

To increase muscular strength you need to use a fitness training method that aims to overload your muscle tissue causing **muscular hypertrophy**.

Muscular strength training

Free weights and fixed resistance machines

Similar to training muscular endurance, the most common method of improving muscular strength is resistance training, using either free weights or fixed resistance machines. To improve muscular strength, you need to use exercises that have a low number of repetitions and use high loads. To start, the sports performer should find their 1RM. They would usually use weights that are 70–80 per cent of their 1RM.

Lifts are known as repetitions or 'reps'. A set is a number of 'reps' completed without a break. Sets are usually repeated after a short break. For example, if a sportsperson wants to increase their strength, they would use a weight of 90 per cent of their 1RM and could complete three sets of one to six reps. To increase muscular endurance, a sportsperson could use a weight of between 50 per cent and 60 per cent of their 1RM and complete six sets of 15–20 reps.

▣ Figure 3.12: Training for different goals

Fixed resistance machines use stacks of weights attached to pulleys or air pressure to provide resistance. This type of strength-training equipment provides sets of exercises that only permit movement for a specific exercise. For example, a fixed resistance machine for completing hamstring curls only permits the hamstring curl movement exercise to be completed; it cannot be used for any other exercises.

Weight-training exercises should not be carried out alone, you should always have a partner or spotter to help you to lift safely. To decrease the likelihood of injury, you should also make sure that you are free from injury and not fatigued before carrying out weight training with free weights or resistance machines.

▣ Free weights session

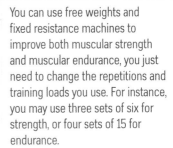

ACTIVITY

Support

1 Make a list of the advantages and disadvantages of using free weights to improve muscular strength.

2 Make a list of the advantages and disadvantages of using fixed resistance machines to improve muscular strength.

Challenge

3 Explain which type of muscular strength training you would recommend for a beginner.

DID YOU KNOW

You can use free weights and fixed resistance machines to improve both muscular strength and muscular endurance, you just need to change the repetitions and training loads you use. For instance, you may use three sets of six for strength, or four sets of 15 for endurance.

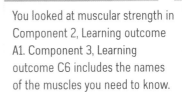

LINK IT UP

You looked at muscular strength in Component 2, Learning outcome A1. Component 3, Learning outcome C6 includes the names of the muscles you need to know.

Muscular strength training can be made more specific to the sports performer's sport or activity by working on the major muscles and muscle groups used in the skills and techniques. For example, a horse rider needs muscular strength in their legs, in the hamstrings, quadriceps and gluteal muscles. They would benefit from hamstring curls, leg raises and single-leg deadlifts.

 Table 3.31: Examples of muscular strength training for muscles and muscle groups using free weights and fixed weight machines

Strength training exercise	Muscle or muscle group	Location
Hamstring curls	Hamstrings	Upper leg
Leg raises	Quadriceps and hip flexors	Upper leg
Side plank	Obliques, abdominals	Core
Bench press	Triceps	Upper arm
Dumbbell curl	Biceps	Upper arm
Deadlifts	Gluteus maximus, erector spinae	Core
Calf raises	Gastrocnemius	Lower leg

Dumbbells can be used to perform dynamic exercises to strengthen different muscle groups. For example, bicep curls are used to strengthen the biceps, a chest press is used to strengthen the chest muscles.

CHECK MY LEARNING

1 Name three different sports or activities that would benefit from muscular strength training.

2 Use the terms 'number of repetitions' and 'loads' to describe how to improve muscular strength using free weights or resistance machines.

C2: Fitness training methods: speed

As with other components of fitness, you can increase your speed using lots of different training methods. Three main methods are acceleration sprints, interval training and resistance drills.

Speed

Speed is the ability to cover a set distance as quickly as possible. Events such as a 100-metre sprint are all about getting to the finish line faster than the other athletes. However, speed is also important in many different types of sports and activities, and it can be important to be able to perform repeated bouts of speed-dependent activities in a game. Being able to sprint to the ball before an opponent in football or sprinting to intercept a ball thrown by an opposing team in basketball both require lots of speed.

Acceleration sprints

Acceleration sprints involve you gradually increasing your pace as you go through the sprint activity. You would start from a standing or rolling start, progress to striding out, and then move to a maximal sprint.

◻ Sprinter leaving the starting blocks

Acceleration sprints replicate the type of sprinting that takes place in many different sports, such as netball when a player is jogging to receive a pass and then increases their speed to sprint with the ball to run past defenders. Speed is gradually increased from a standing or rolling start to jogging, then to striding, and then to a maximal sprint. Rest intervals of jogging or walking are used between each repetition.

Acceleration sprints are also a good form of aerobic exercise, so can be used as a combination training method. They require no equipment or training facility, and several sports performers can train at the same time. The risk of injury is minimised in this training method because the intensity and speed are increased gradually. However, acceleration sprints are only suited to sports and activities that require sprinting in one direction.

GETTING STARTED

Make a list of different sports and activities that require speed. Try to give an example of how speed is used in each of these sports and activities; for example, speed is needed in netball for a player to be able to intercept the ball.

KEY TERM

Acceleration is an increase in the rate of velocity with time. Something that has velocity is moving with speed and direction. Something that accelerates moves in a direction and gets faster as it moves. To accelerate, the movement needs momentum to change speed and not just move.

DID YOU KNOW

Sprinters accelerate during 100 m races and don't reach their top running speed until approximately 60 m.

◻ Acceleration sprints on the track

ACTIVITY

Support

Explain how completing acceleration sprint training can benefit the race times of a 100 m sprinter.

Challenge

Analyse the use of acceleration sprint training for a 100 m sprinter and a team player who plays in an attacking position, such as a hockey or rugby wing.

Interval training

You learned about Interval training earlier in this component. Using interval training to improve speed still involves you going through a period of work followed by a period of rest, before completing another work period.

When designing interval training sessions, you should think about:
- the number of intervals (rest and work periods)
- the intensity of the work interval
- the duration of the work interval
- the duration of the rest interval
- the intensity of the rest interval.

However, when using interval training to increase speed, you would increase the number of rest periods and increase your work intensity when compared to speed training. Interval training to build speed uses very short, high-intensity work periods followed by a rest or recovery period.

Speed is improved by increasing the work intensity and decreasing the number of rest periods. The interval rest periods should vary to meet the needs of the individual sports performer and their goals. This type of training suits sports and activities that involve different intensities with recovery periods, for example football, hockey, tennis.

Resistance drills

Resistance drills involve you using equipment to hold you back and provide extra load as you sprint. As you are sprinting while being resisted by an extra load, this helps to target the muscles used to complete the sprinting so that they become stronger. The most common types of resistance drills are hill runs, parachutes, sleds, bungee ropes and resistance bands.

Resistance drills can be used to increase the load the participant has to sprint against. This overloads the muscles to make them stronger. This increases the intensity of the sprinting, overloading the sprinting muscles. Assisted sprinting, such as running downhill, makes sprinting easier and helps the muscles get used to the process of moving at speed.

Resistance drills are best suited to sports and activities that involve travelling at speed, for example netball and football, sports where you sprint in a straight line. The equipment used to add resistance is specialist and can be expensive. There is a risk of injury if the sports performer does not complete a thorough warm-up before training.

ACTIVITY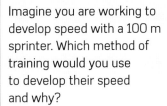

Imagine you are working to develop speed with a 100 m sprinter. Which method of training would you use to develop their speed and why?

LINK IT UP

You can find out how to test a sports performer's speed in Learning outcome B2 of this component.

KEY TERM

Resistance is a force that opposes the movement of an object, slowing it down.

BEST PRACTICE

If you are using resistance equipment, you should make sure that you check it regularly and especially before each time you use it in training to make sure that it is safe and in good working order.

CHECK MY LEARNING

1 What is meant by the term 'acceleration'?
2 How does using interval training to increase speed differ from increased aerobic endurance? Your answer should include reference to the number of rest periods and intensity.
3 Name a resistance exercise that could help a hockey player improve their speed.

◻ Parachute running

C3: Fitness training methods: agility

The most common fitness training method for improving agility is speed, agility and quickness training (SAQ). SAQ drills help to develop a sports performer's physical ability and motor skills.

Agility

Agility is needed in sports where you need to be able to change direction at speed, whilst maintaining control of your body. You can probably think of lots of examples from netball, football and hockey where this would be important for successful performance. This is where training agility becomes very important.

Speed, agility and quickness training (SAQ)

To train agility, you need to take part in sport-specific training which includes speed, agility and quickness (**SAQ**) **training** principles. This can be tailored to the needs of different sports but generally involves you sprinting and then changing direction over a set course. In hockey this could be dribbling the ball while sprinting around cones set up on the pitch or having teammates act as opponents and dribbling at speed around them while keeping control of the ball and keeping the ball away from them. This represents the type of speed that is specific to the sport and includes sport-specific skills such as sprinting while dribbling the ball.

◻ Footballers running through a ladder drill

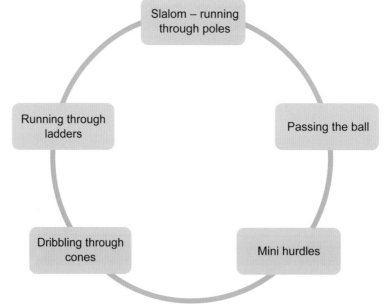

Slalom – running through poles

Passing the ball

Mini hurdles

Dribbling through cones

Running through ladders

◻ Figure 3.13: Example of SAQ drills for a football player

- Equipment – slalom poles, training ladders, footballs, cones, mini hurdles.
- Warm-up – An appropriate warm-up should be completed before taking part in SAQ drills.
- Time – Each drill should be performed for 30–50 seconds with a 20-second rest in between.

Support

Design a sport-specific SAQ training session that includes at least five different drills to help a handball player improve their agility.

Challenge

How could you amend your SAQ training session, and the five different drills, to make it suitable for a hurdler who wants to improve their agility?

SAQ drills can be made sport specific and are appropriate for all ages and abilities. These drills are good for sports and activities where there is a change of direction when sprinting. The equipment needed is cheap and easy to use and very little time is needed to set it up. Performers need to have a good level of fitness to complete SAQ drills because, if they become tired, injury can occur due to poor technique.

◻ Table 3.32: Drills for different types of agility training

Type of agility training	SAQ drills
Sport-related advantages	Good for activities requiring quick changes of direction
Examples of related sports	Dodging the opposition in a team game such as football or netball, freestyle skiing, gymnastics
Equipment-related advantages	This training can take place outside or inside so the weather will not affect the ability to take part The equipment needed is cheap and easy to use and very little time is needed to set it up
Other advantages	Can be carried out by an individual at times that fit in with their other commitments
Sport-related disadvantages	Very few sports are carried out at the same intensity and duration
Equipment-related disadvantages	Takes time to set up the equipment before the drills can start
Other disadvantages	Can lead to an injury if a thorough warm-up is not completed before training Performers need to have a good level of fitness to complete SAQ drills because if they become tired, injury can occur due to poor technique

1 Give a definition of the term 'agility'.

2 Explain the advantages and disadvantages of using SAQ training to improve agility for a tennis player.

C3: Fitness training methods: power

GETTING STARTED

In small groups, discuss the use of power in different sports and activities and identify training methods to improve power.

Power can be improved by using plyometrics, a fitness training method that uses explosive movements which cause rapid muscle contractions. Power training movements use a lighter weight compared with strength training but one that allows the person to perform a high number of repetitions to simulate repeated use of power in competition.

Plyometrics

Think of your muscle as an elastic band – the elastic band will fire further if you stretch it further back before letting it go. Plyometric training takes the muscle through an **eccentric muscle** action that lengthens and stretches the muscle before a powerful **concentric muscle** action. The shorter the time between the stretching phase and shortening, the more power can be generated. Plyometric training is any exercise that enables a muscle to reach maximum force in the fastest possible time. This sort of training is usually carried out by jumping on and off benches and steps, but you can include lunging, bounding, incline press-ups, and barrier hopping and jumping. Over time, this makes the body create a faster rate of contraction, which will improve power.

KEY TERMS

Eccentric muscle contraction is where the muscle lengthens when it contracts.

Concentric muscle contraction is where the muscle shortens when it contracts.

◘ Figure 3.14: Plyometric training is often carried out by jumping on and off benches or steps

DID YOU KNOW

Plyometric training is also known as plyos, plyo box training and jump training.

Adapting plyometric exercises

Plyometrics can be made sport specific by replicating some of the movements used in the sport or activity, for example hopping and jumping. It uses movements which cause muscles to lengthen and then immediately shorten to develop power in the legs. By reducing the time between the muscle lengthening and shortening, more power is produced. The sports performer can change the intensity they work at by increasing the number of repetitions of the exercise.

Plyometric training is high intensity and can cause injury to performers who have not sufficiently warmed up. Plyometric exercises can be selected to improve the muscle groups that require power.

◻ Table 3.33: Examples of plyometric exercises that could be used to develop power for specific sports activities

Sport examples	Type of activity	Plyometric exercise
Gymnastics	Jumping on the spot	Tuck jumps
Basketball	Jumping forward from standing	Hops and bounds
Netball	One-leg jumps from a standing start	One-leg hops onto a box
Long jump	Two-leg jumps from standing	Two-leg jumps over hurdles

LINK IT UP

Remind yourself about the components of skill-related fitness by looking at Component 2, Learning outcome A2.

Equipment

Plyometric exercises should be done on a surface that will absorb some of the force produced by the explosive movement.

The equipment used is often boxes or benches, which are easily accessible and easy to set up. These exercises can be carried out at any time, as long as the equipment is set out.

Suitability

When choosing a training method, you need to consider the suitability for participants of different ages and abilities. Plyometric training is high intensity and can cause injury to performers who have not sufficiently warmed up.

Plyometric training can lead to injury because the muscles go through high levels of stress. As such, this type of training is not suitable for beginners or young athletes.

ACTIVITY

Support

Describe three different plyometric exercises that would be suitable for an experienced high jump athlete to use to improve their power.

Challenge

Select two different sports to complete the activity above, for example describe plyometric exercises that would be suitable for a boxer to use to improve their power.

CHECK MY LEARNING

1 Write a definition of the term 'plyometrics'.

2 Give two advantages and two disadvantages of using plyometric training.

3 Which groups of sports performers should not use plyometric training?

C3: Fitness training methods: balance, coordination and reaction time

You need to be able to suggest and justify appropriate skill-related fitness training methods for specific sports performers that are different ages and of different sporting abilities.

Balance

There are two main types of balance: static and dynamic.

- **Static balance:** static balance is the ability to remain upright when stationary. Training to improve static balance will usually involve balancing on a reduced size base of support, for example using a balance or wobble board standing on one foot.
- **Dynamic balance:** dynamic balance is the ability to remain upright whilst moving. Training to improve dynamic balance uses movements whilst holding a balanced position. For example, standing on one leg and flexing and extending the support knee to move the body down and upwards, or running with the ball in football, whilst under pressure.

Balance training is suitable for all ages and abilities, though there can be a risk for older people as it can cause loss of balance and falls. Several performers can participate at the same time, as long as there is enough equipment, and this training can be carried out anywhere. Sometimes specialist equipment, such as wobble boards, is required for balance training.

Having good core strength can also help with balance. The core muscles, back and abdominal muscles help to maintain posture and allow body parts to stay fixed when others are moving. For example, your core muscles help to keep you standing upright when you lift one foot off the floor.

🔲 Training for static balance

ACTIVITY

Support

1 Explain why completing a balance training programme would help to improve the sporting performance of a gymnast.

2 How would you adapt a balance training programme to meet the needs of:

   A 16-year-old gymnast

   A 45-year-old weightlifter?

Challenge

3 Why is it important to carry out a thorough warm-up before taking part in balance training?

Coordination

Coordination is the ability to use two or more parts of the body smoothly and efficiently at the same time. Training methods to improve coordination involve specific exercises that use two or more body parts together. For most sports and activities coordination training will be specific to the types of movement required in that sport, for example a high jump athlete could practise their jumping technique over a lower bar and increase the height as they improve.

Sports that require hand–eye coordination, for example a badminton player, would also replicate the movements used in the sport. They could practise using their arm to move a racquet at the right time to hit a shuttlecock.

◻ **Curling requires hand–eye coordination**

Coordination training requires motor skills and is best performed when the person is not tired, as it requires a lot of concentration. It can be made sport specific and does not require any specialised equipment. Injury can be caused if the person loses concentration and a thorough warm-up should be performed before training to minimise the risk of injury and increase the performer's alertness. Traffic cones could be used, for example using different colour cones for stop, go and slow down.

Reaction time

Reaction time is the ability of a person to respond quickly to an external **stimulus**. Training to improve reaction time is often made sport or activity specific, and requires the performer to respond quickly to an external stimulus. For example, a cricket player needs to be able to respond quickly to the ball being bowled at their bat. Reaction time training for a cricketer could involve reacting to balls being bowled at different speeds and from different directions.

Reaction time training does not require any specialist equipment and can be adapted to suit the specific needs of a sports performer. To minimise the risk of injury from this type of training, a thorough warm-up and cool down should be completed.

KEY TERM

Stimulus is something that produces a reaction. For example, a loud bang will make you look to see what made the noise. The noise is the stimulus.

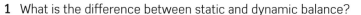

CHECK MY LEARNING

1 What is the difference between static and dynamic balance?

2 What type of exercises could a netball player perform to improve their coordination?

3 What is meant by a stimulus?

4 How can reaction time training be adapted to meet the needs of a tennis player?

C4: Additional requirements for each fitness training method 1

Each of the different types of fitness training has its advantages and disadvantages. You will need to take these into account when you are looking at the different training methods you want to use.

When designing a fitness training programme for a sportsperson you need to consider additional requirements for each training method. You must also assess the advantages and disadvantages of the training method to be able to select the most appropriate methods of training for the individual or group, their sport or activity and the provision of facilities and equipment available to them.

- Number of people that can take part
- Cost of equipment
- Ease of set up
- Access to venue/location
- Risk of injury to the performer, if performed incorrectly
- Effectiveness of training for the sports performer

◻ Figure 3.15: The additional requirements for each fitness training method

Number of participants

Sports and activities require different numbers of participants. Individual activities have only one performer, but they often form a group and may train with others and not always alone. Team sports require more than one person to take part. Teams perform together and usually train together. It is important to understand the number of people who can complete the training method at one time.

For training methods that require the use of expensive equipment, such as resistance machines to develop muscular strength, the number of people who can take part is limited by the number of machines. If the training is carried out for a short period of time, for example short sets of heavy loads, performers can work in pairs or small groups and share the equipment. When using weights, performers should always work in pairs so that one can spot the other. Equipment that is expensive to buy, or not easily available, limits the number of people. However, if there is more equipment, such as cones or ladders for SAQ training for agility, more people can participate.

If the training method requires no equipment but does need a large space, the number of people participating is limited by the space available. For example, an aerobic training method such as the MSFT or bleep test, requires a running space of 20 m length with extra space at either end for turning.

Cost of equipment

If the equipment needed to carry out a training method is very expensive it will prevent a lot of performers or clubs being able to afford it. This limits the availability of the equipment and access to those training methods, for example fixed weight resistance machines, used to train muscular strength. Types of sports and activities that have more funding will have more access to the latest equipment. For instance, the average cost of a treadmill is currently £1500.

Ease of set up

Complicated training equipment may need a trained person to set it up; this can prevent performers from using it regularly. There is a reliance on the trainer to set it up and be prepared for the training session, this removes any spontaneity and requires careful prior planning.

It could be that the training method requires large pieces of equipment, which might need several people to assist with its preparation. Storage could be an issue. Where is the equipment kept, can it be accessed easily, at all times, or rarely? Equipment that is difficult to set up or hard to move is less likely to be used regularly. There is a high risk of injury if equipment is not checked and set up incorrectly.

◘ Footballer using a training ladder

CHECK MY LEARNING

1 What is meant by additional requirements for training methods?
2 Explain how ease of set up could affect the selection of a training method for an individual athlete.

C4: Additional requirements for each fitness training method 2

GETTING STARTED

Fitness training methods have additional requirements, these are considerations which affect the ability to successfully use the method. In small groups discuss training methods you have used. Were you on your own, part of a small team, part of a large team (more than 15 people)? Was the training method carried out inside, outside, did it require special equipment?

ACTIVITY

Support

Explain how access to a sports facility could affect the type of fitness training a sportsperson can participate in.

Challenge

Analyse the time restrictions of leisure facilities. Consider closing time, staggering requirement and the availability of 24/7 gyms.

Access to venue/location of training

You need to know where the training will take place before you can plan a training session. Where is the facility? Where is it located? Is there a bus route, car park, is it within walking distance, is it near the club's own facility? These factors need to be considered to make sure sports performers can access the training venue.

It is also important to consider any time restrictions. Does the facility shut at a specific time, is it somewhere that requires staff and relies upon them to open the facility? A facility that opens during set times can be planned into the training timetable, if the opening times are ad hoc, it is more difficult to plan when you can gain access.

Risk of injury to the performer if performed incorrectly

Performers who are new to the sport and have a lower level of skill and fitness or who are recovering from an injury are at a higher risk of injury. Performers need to have learned the correct technique before increasing the intensity used when carrying out the training method. For example, plyometric training to increase power requires explosive movement. Performers need to know how to correctly perform the movements, or they may injure themselves. Performers may need to decrease their training level while the correct technique is being learned, this could lead to fitness in that component decreasing temporarily.

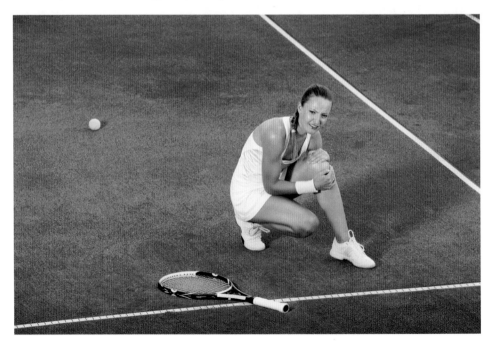

◘ Injured tennis player

Effectiveness of training for given sports performer

Before selecting a training method, you need to consider whether the training method is appropriate for the individual sports performer's needs. Will the method of training meet the need to improve that component of fitness? Some training methods are more effective than others. You need to know if the performer has previous experience with the method: do they know how to do it, do they like it, is it interesting for them? It is also useful to know if the training method can be carried out with a friend or group. Preventing boredom is an important factor. Being able to train in a method you like, are familiar with and alongside someone else, can build motivation and help prevent boredom.

KEY TERMS

Specificity in a training programme means training in a way that is appropriate in order to produce the desired outcome.

Replicating is copying, reproducing or remaking the same thing.

Specificity to component of fitness

Each component of fitness has specific training methods. You need to make sure that the training method is suitable for improving the component of fitness. For example, a sports performer who wishes to improve their flexibility should carry out flexibility training. PNF would be an appropriate training method, as it helps to improve the range of movement around a joint, increasing flexibility. It would not be useful for the same athlete to carry out Fartlek training as this helps to develop aerobic endurance and not flexibility.

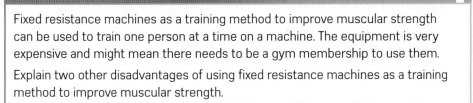

ACTIVITY

Fixed resistance machines as a training method to improve muscular strength can be used to train one person at a time on a machine. The equipment is very expensive and might mean there needs to be a gym membership to use them.

Explain two other disadvantages of using fixed resistance machines as a training method to improve muscular strength.

Replicating demands of the sport

For a training method to be the most effective it needs to mimic or copy the demands of the sport or activity. For example, a rock climber would benefit from strength training that replicates the movements they use during their climbs. This could be done by using their own bodyweight when climbing or adding additional weight to a belt to increase the load. Using bodyweight as the resistance, the load is a good way to mimic sporting activities and be able to increase specific components of fitness.

CHECK MY LEARNING

1 What is meant by access to venue/location of training when referring to a training method?

2 How could access to venue/location of training affect a training method's suitability for training an individual or a team?

C4: Additional requirements for each fitness training method 3a

The tables provided below and on the following pages include information about additional requirements for each training method. These requirements help identify what needs to be considered before the training method can be selected, and whether a training method is suitable and practical for individuals or teams to carry out.

▣ Table 3.34: Requirements for aerobic endurance training

Type of aerobic endurance training	Continuous training	Fartlek training	Interval training	Circuit training
Number of people that can take part	These types of training can be carried out by individuals or large groups			
Cost of equipment	No equipment is required for these types of training			Equipment is not always needed for this type of training
Ease of set up	These types of training require very little set up			Circuits can be set up very quickly and easily
Access to venue/location	These training types do not require specific venues, they can be carried out in a local park, sports hall, gym or running track			
Risk of injury to the performer, if performed incorrectly	Low risk of injury as training is carried out at a low intensity			
Effectiveness of training for the sports performer	Suitable for sports participants who take part in activities that last more 30 minutes			

▣ Table 3.35: Requirements for muscular endurance training

Type of muscular endurance training	Free weights and fixed resistance machines	Circuit training
Number of people that can take part	Restricted by the number of weights and machines available	Circuits can be carried out by individuals or large groups
Cost of equipment	Free weights and resistance machines can be very expensive	Equipment is not always needed for this type of training
Ease of set up	Fixed resistance machines require no set up after the manufacturer has installed them. Free weights require checking and a spotter	Circuits can be set up very quickly and easily
Access to venue/location	Training can only be completed when the free weights or fixed resistance machines are available	Circuits do not require a specific venue, they can be carried out in a local park, sports hall, gym or running track
Risk of injury to the performer, if performed incorrectly	The participants must carry out a thorough warm-up to reduce the chance of injury	Low risk of injury as training is carried out at a low intensity
Effectiveness of training for the sports performer	Suitable for sports participants who take part in activities that last more 30 minutes	

▣ Table 3.36: Requirements for muscular strength training

Type of muscular strength training	Free weights and fixed resistance machines
Number of people that can take part	Restricted by the number of weights and machines available
Cost of equipment	Free weights and resistance machines can be very expensive
Ease of set up	Fixed resistance machines require no set up after the manufacturer has installed them. Free weights require checking and a spotter
Access to venue/location	Training can only be completed when the free weights or fixed resistance machines are available
Risk of injury to the performer, if performed incorrectly	The participants must carry out a thorough warm-up to reduce the chance of injury
Effectiveness of training for the sports performer	Suitable for sports participants who take part in activities that require force, e.g. throwing events

◻ Table 3.37: Requirements for speed training

Type of speed training	Acceleration sprints	Interval training	Resistance drills
Number of people that can take part	These types of training can be carried out by individuals or large groups		Restricted by the amount of equipment available, e.g. parachutes, sleds, bungee ropes, resistance bands
Cost of equipment	Equipment is not always needed for this type of training		The cost of parachutes, sleds, bungee ropes, resistance bands can be expensive
Ease of set up	These types of training require very little set up		You need to follow the manufacturer's instructions for using parachutes, sleds, bungee ropes and resistance bands
Access to venue/location	These training types do not require specific venues, they can be carried out in a local park, sports hall or running track		
Risk of injury to the performer, if performed incorrectly	The participants must carry out a thorough warm-up to reduce the chance of injury		To reduce the risk of injury the manufacturer's guidance must be followed when using: parachutes, sleds, bungee ropes and resistance bands
Effectiveness of training for the sports performer	Suitable for sports participants who take part in activities that require fast movement, for example sprinting		

◻ Table 3.38: Requirements for flexibility training

Type of flexibility training	Static active	Static passive	Proprioceptive neuromuscular facilitation (PNF) technique
Number of people that can take part	These types of training can be carried out by people working in a pair or large groups		
Cost of equipment	These types of training can be carried out without any equipment		
Ease of set up	These types of training require very little set up		
Access to venue/location	These training types do not require a specific venue, they can be carried out in a local park, sports hall or gym		
Risk of injury to the performer, if performed incorrectly	The participants must carry out a thorough warm-up to reduce the chance of injury		
Effectiveness of training for the sports performer	Suitable for sports participants who take part in activities that require a wide range of movement around a joint, for example gymnastics, martial arts		

CHECK MY LEARNING

1 For a fitness training method of your choice, describe what is meant by additional requirements.

2 Explain why cost is an additional requirement for the fitness training method you selected in question 1.

C4: Additional requirements for each fitness training method 3b

◼ Table 3.39: Requirements for power training

Type of power training	Plyometrics
Number of people that can take part	This type of training can be carried out by individuals or large groups. If equipment, such as a bench, is used, training will be limited by the amount of equipment. However, training is carried out for a short period of time so participants would not need to wait long for their turn if sharing equipment
Cost of equipment	This type of training can be carried out with minimal equipment. Often a bench or a training ladder is used
Ease of set up	This type of training requires very little set up
Access to venue/location	This training type does not require a specific venue, it can be carried out in a local park, sports hall or gym
Risk of injury to the performer, if performed incorrectly	There is a high risk of injury. Participants must complete a thorough warm-up before training. The correct technique must be followed, participants may need to lower the intensity of training while they learn the correct technique to prevent injury
Effectiveness of training for the sports performer	Suitable for sports participants who take part in activities that require explosive movements such as lunging, bounding, incline press-ups, barrier hopping and jumping, for example gymnastics, basketball

◼ Table 3.40: Requirements for agility training

Type of agility training	Speed, agility and quickness training (SAQ)
Number of people that can take part	This type of training can be carried out by individuals or large groups
Cost of equipment	Equipment is not always needed for this type of training, sometimes ladders, cones and poles are used – these are not expensive to buy
Ease of set up	SAQ drills can be set up quickly and easily
Access to venue/location	This training type does not require a specific venue, it can be carried out in a local park, sports hall or gym
Risk of injury to the performer, if performed incorrectly	There is a risk of injury. Participants must complete a thorough warm-up before training. The correct technique must be followed, participants may need to lower the intensity of training while they learn the correct technique to prevent injury
Effectiveness of training for the sports performer	Suitable for sports participants who take part in activities that require quick changes of direction, for example dodging the opposition in a team game, freestyle skiing

◼ Table 3.41: Requirements for reaction time training

Type of reaction time training	Specific training exercises to practise quick responses to an external stimulus
Number of people that can take part	This type of training can be carried out by individuals or large groups, depending on the training exercises used
Cost of equipment	It depends on the training exercise used, a ball hopper used to fire tennis or cricket balls can be expensive
Ease of set up	It depends on the training exercise used, a tennis or cricket ball hopper does not take long to set up
Access to venue/location	It depends on the training exercise used, a tennis or cricket ball hopper is usually available at a sports centre, tennis or cricket club. Access to the equipment is dependent on the facility being open
Risk of injury to the performer, if performed incorrectly	The participants must carry out a thorough warm-up to reduce the chance of injury
Effectiveness of training for the sports performer	Suitable for sports participants who take part in activities where a quick decision or response to a stimulus is needed

◻ Table 3.42: Requirements for balance training

Type of balance training	Specific training exercises that require balancing on a reduced size base of support
Number of people that can take part	This type of training can be carried out by individuals or large groups, depending on the training exercises used
Cost of equipment	It depends on the training exercise used, a balance or wobble board is not very expensive
Ease of set up	No preparation is needed to set up a balance or wobble board
Access to venue/location	This training type does not require a specific venue, it can be carried out in a local park, sports hall or gym
Risk of injury to the performer, if performed incorrectly	The participants must carry out a thorough warm-up to reduce the chance of injury
Effectiveness of training for the sports performer	Suitable for sports participants who take part in activities requiring the control of the distribution of weight or to remain upright and steady

◻ Table 3.43: Requirements for coordination training

Type of coordination training	Specific training exercises using two or more body parts together
Number of people that can take part	This type of training can be carried out by individuals or large groups, depending on the training exercises used, for example practising serving a tennis ball into a plastic hoop would rely on the number of hoops available
Cost of equipment	It depends on the training exercise used, a plastic hoop is not very expensive
Ease of set up	Very little time is needed to set up a hoop to practise serving tennis balls
Access to venue/location	This training type does not require a specific venue, it can be carried out in a local park, sports hall or gym
Risk of injury to the performer, if performed incorrectly	The participants must carry out a thorough warm-up to reduce the chance of injury
Effectiveness of training for the sports performer	Suitable for sports participants who take part in any activity requiring the movement of two or more body parts and can include the use of sporting equipment, for example hand, eyes and tennis racquet to connect with the tennis ball

CHECK MY LEARNING

Analyse why the additional requirements for fitness training methods must be considered before including a fitness training method in your training programme.

C5: Provision for taking part in fitness training methods

GETTING STARTED

Think of a sports facility in your local area. What **provision** does it have for types of equipment, availability, cost and other support available?

You need to be aware of the providers of fitness training so that you can select fitness training methods appropriately. You need to know how their **provision** varies in relation to types of equipment available, cost, other support available and access, so that sports performers have the provision they require to train.

Public provision

Organisations with a role to benefit the general public are subsidised by local government and often run at a loss. These organisations do not aim to make a profit but to make sport and activities available to everyone. Examples include local swimming pools, leisure centres and parks.

KEY TERM

Provision is something that has been provided or supplied, for example a football pitch that is available to use.

LINK IT UP

You looked at different provision for sport and physical activities in Component 1, Learning outcome A1.

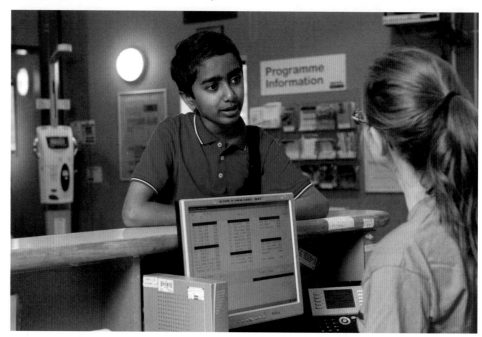

◘ Local swimming pools provide fitness opportunities at a subsidised cost

Private provision

Businesses and private clubs that undertake business for profit for the owners of the business or the benefit of the business and its members. For example, golf clubs and private gyms. People have to pay a membership fee and subscriptions to be a member. Only members can use all of the club's facilities and equipment, sometimes non-members can pay for a day's membership.

Voluntary provision

People or groups that undertake activities for no payment. Local sports clubs are often run by volunteers, for example grassroots football clubs.

DID YOU KNOW

There are more than 2700 public leisure facilities in the UK.

Advantages and disadvantages of public, private and voluntary provision

 Table 3.44: Some of the advantages and disadvantages of each type of provision

Provision	Public	Private	Voluntary
Equipment	Good range of equipment for most sports and activities High availability	Excellent range of high-spec equipment	Good range of equipment for most sports and activities Good range of equipment, often donated
Availability	There are many facilities with a wide range of equipment for most sports and activities Provision is available in most villages, all towns and cities	There are many facilities around the UK with a wide range of equipment for all sports and activities	Provision is available in most villages, all towns and cities Provision for specific sports and activities will differ, depending on the location and the volunteers available to run activities
Cost	The prices are subsidised to make it more affordable for everyone There are often membership plans that can allow you to save money if you pay for more sessions in advance There are discounts for people on lower incomes	Membership can be very expensive There is usually a monthly subscription fee	You normally pay a minimal yearly subscription fee You might pay a small amount to attend each session Each organisation will structure its own payment plan
Other support available	The provider will have links to other facilities available in the local area It may have links with national governing bodies There will be disability access into the facility for most sports and activities	The facility or club will have links with its sport's national governing body There will be disability access into the facility for most sports and activities	The organisation will have links with national governing bodies Where possible there will be disability access into the facility for some of the sports and activities Each organisation will have its own disability arrangements

 Volunteers are an important part of fitness provision, especially for children

CHECK MY LEARNING

1 What is meant by provision?

2 Which type of provision is available to everyone?

3 Which type of provision requires membership or a fee to use?

4 Explain how provision can affect a sports performer's ability to follow a fitness training programme.

5 Analyse the advantages and disadvantages of the provision of the three different types, public, private and voluntary, in the UK for a sport of your choice.

C6: The effects of long-term fitness training on the body: aerobic endurance training 1

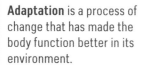

KEY TERMS

Adaptation is a process of change that has made the body function better in its environment.

Cardiac hypertrophy is an increase in the size and strength of the heart muscle.

You need to be aware of how training methods affect the different body systems, which can lead to adaptations to improve specific components of fitness.

Adaptations to the cardiovascular systems

Aerobic endurance training creates a number of changes or **adaptations** to your cardiovascular system. Each of these changes has benefits for your overall health and sports performance.

The structures of the cardiovascular system include the heart and blood vessels. The heart consists of two separate pumps, the right side of the heart pumps blood to the lungs and the left side pumps blood to the rest of the body, including the working muscles and the brain.

The function of the cardiovascular system is to supply the body with sufficient blood. During exercise the demand for blood in the working muscles increases, so the speed of blood flowing through the heart and lungs increases.

When blood reaches your working muscles, it can release oxygen, which is used by muscle cells to make energy aerobically (with oxygen). The deoxygenated (anaerobic) blood then returns back to the heart where it is pumped to the lungs to collect more oxygen.

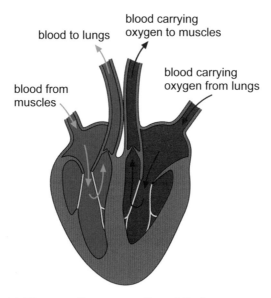

◻ Diagram of a cross section of the heart

Cardiac hypertrophy

The heart is a muscle and when your heart muscle is exercised it will increase in size (see Figure 3.16). This is known as **cardiac hypertrophy**. If you were to dissect the heart of a top aerobic endurance athlete, you would find that the walls of the left ventricle are a lot thicker than those of a person who did not perform regular aerobic exercise. This increase in the size and strength of the walls of the heart means that you can pump more blood per beat and transport more oxygen around the body as a result.

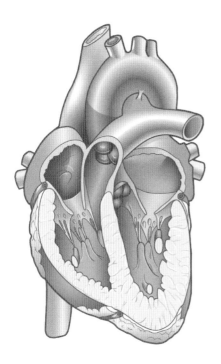 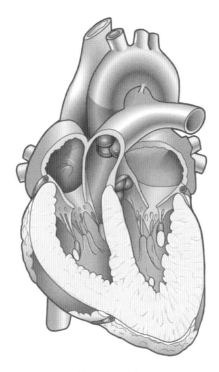

Normal   Hypertrophic

Figure 3.16: Cardiac hypertrophy, where the walls of the left ventrical are thicker in the hypertrophic heart

Decreased resting heart rate

Because the heart increases in size, it can pump out more blood each time it beats. The amount of blood the heart can pump per beat is called the **stroke volume.** As the stroke volume is increased, the heart no longer needs to beat as often to get the same amount of blood around the body. This results in a decrease in resting heart rate. You will find that the fitter a sports person is, the lower their resting heart rate. Cardiac output is the amount of blood that needs to be circulated when at rest for the body to function at optimal levels. It is calculated by multiplying heart rate by stroke volume:

Cardiac output = Heart rate (HR) x Stroke volume (SV)

CHECK MY LEARNING

1 What is meant by adaptation?

2 Which structures make up the cardiorespiratory system?

3 Explain why long-term aerobic endurance adaptations to the cardiovascular system would be beneficial to an international triathlete.

C6: The effects of long-term fitness training on the body: aerobic endurance training 2

The muscles in the respiratory system contract so that we can breathe when at rest and during exercise.

Adaptations to the respiratory system

Aerobic endurance training creates a number of changes or adaptations to your respiratory system. Each of these changes has benefits for your overall health and sports performance.

The function of the respiratory system is to bring fresh air into the lungs and remove waste gases. Air is breathed in through the nose or mouth, it travels down the trachea and into the lungs. Gaseous exchange occurs in the lungs as oxygen is absorbed into the blood through the thin layer of cells in the lining of the lungs and carbon dioxide moves across from the blood into the lungs to be breathed out.

The structures of the respiratory system include the nose, mouth, trachea or windpipe, and lungs. The intercostal muscles and diaphragm make up the respiratory muscles. When you breathe in, the diaphragm contracts and flattens, it produces a vacuum inside the chest and air is sucked into the lungs. When you breathe out, the diaphragm relaxes and moves upwards forcing air out of the lungs.

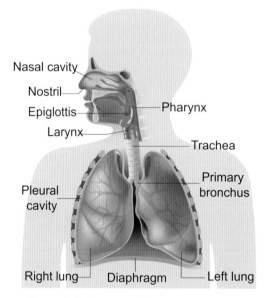

Nasal cavity
Nostril
Epiglottis
Larynx
Pharynx
Trachea
Primary bronchus
Pleural cavity
Right lung — Diaphragm — Left lung

■ Figure 3.17: Diagram of a cross section of the respiratory system

Increased strength of respiratory muscles

Through regular aerobic endurance training, you can increase the strength of your respiratory muscles. These are the muscles around the ribs that allow the ribs to move up and down during breathing. The intercostal muscles allow you to breathe in and out. Having stronger respiratory muscles can improve the inhalation and exhalation of your lungs and more oxygen breathed in can be used to supply energy through the aerobic energy system for muscle contraction. This can help to improve your **vital capacity**, which is the amount of air that can be forced out of the lungs following a **maximal inspiration**.

Sports scientists can analyse the amount of carbon dioxide and oxygen in the air to assess how much of each gas the sports performer has used or produced.

Types of blood vessels

There are three main types of blood vessels in the body: veins, arteries and capillaries. The function of blood vessels is to transport blood around the body. Veins carry deoxygenated blood to the heart. Arteries carry oxygenated blood away from the heart, capillaries can carry oxygenated or deoxygenated blood. Capillaries are the smallest blood vessel; their walls are only one cell thick. This means they can transfer gases and nutrients through their walls, this process is called diffusion.

◻ An athlete exercising whilst the air he breathes is analysed

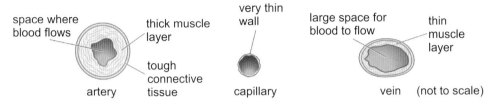

◻ Cross section of the different types of blood vessels

Increased capillarisation around the alveoli

When you regularly take part in sport or physical activity, this increases the **capillarisation** around the **alveoli** in your lungs and in your muscle tissues. The increase in capillaries helps to increase the rate of **gaseous exchange** and, therefore, increase the amount of oxygen entering the blood and the amount of carbon dioxide leaving the blood. This improves the oxygen flow to the working muscles and the removal of waste products, so that you can keep exercising for longer. Figure 3.18 shows the process of gaseous exchange.

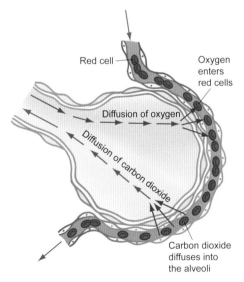

◻ Figure 3.18: The process of gaseous exchange

CHECK MY LEARNING

1 State the function of the respiratory system.

2 Explain why long-term aerobic endurance adaptations to the respiratory system would be beneficial to an international triathlete.

C6: The effects of long-term fitness training on the body: flexibility training

GETTING STARTED

Think about what happens to your body when you exercise. Then consider what happens to your flexibility as you exercise and move around more. Compare your own flexibility to a gymnast. What are differences and similarities?

LINK IT UP

There is more information about the function and structure of muscular and skeletal systems on pages 206–211.

Adaptations to the body need to occur to improve a component of fitness. Flexibility training will cause changes in the muscular and skeletal systems, allowing the body to become more flexible.

Adaptations to the muscular and skeletal systems

The main function of the muscular system is to produce movements. The function of the skeletal system is to allow movement, support the body, protect internal organs and store minerals.

Flexibility causes several adaptations to these body systems. The range of movement at joints is increased, ligaments and tendons become stronger, and muscle length increases.

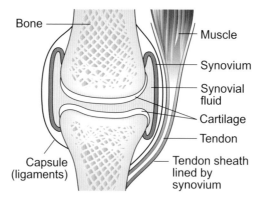

Bone — Muscle — Synovium — Synovial fluid — Cartilage — Tendon — Capsule (ligaments) — Tendon sheath lined by synovium

◘ The structures within a synovial joint

Increased range of movement permitted at a joint

The range of movement at a joint is affected by the structures within it. A synovial joint has synovial fluid, this is like oil and helps lubricate the joint. This fluid helps the joint to move easily, and flexibility training can help to produce synovial fluid and keep the joint moving smoothly. Other structures in the joints include tendons and ligaments. They are made up of fibres like elastic bands and help to keep the bones fixed within the joint. If the tendons and ligaments are inflexible, the range of movement at the joint will be decreased.

DID YOU KNOW

Ligaments connect bones to bones, and tendons connect muscles to bones. They are both made of strong collagen fibres.

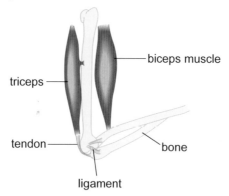

triceps — biceps muscle — tendon — bone — ligament

◘ The elbow joint

Increased flexibility of ligaments and tendons

Flexibility training can help to increase the flexibility of ligaments and tendons, which can increase their ability to stretch and increase the range of movement at the joint.

ACTIVITY

Find some Plasticine or Blu Tack. Put it in the fridge for a few minutes or leave it somewhere cold. With the cold Plasticine or Blu Tack, pull it and stretch it quickly to see how long you can stretch it. Now squash and pull gently, stretching the Plasticine or Blu Tack for a minute, try to warm it up! Then pull it and stretch it quickly to see how long you can make it. What do you notice happens? What is the difference to the stretchiness of the Plasticine or Blu Tack when it is cold and when it is warm?

Increased muscle length

Muscles are made up of muscle fibres. These fibres have the ability to stretch and contract. These muscle contractions are what happens when we move body parts. Muscles work in pairs, one contracts and shortens and the other contracts whilst lengthening. The muscles pull on bones and produce movement at joints. If the muscle fibres are short and close together the movement produced will be less than if the muscle fibres are longer and further apart. Flexibility training aims to lengthen muscles, which then increases the range of movement possible at joints. Sports performers, such as gymnasts, benefit from longer (more elastic) muscles so that they can perform stretches and skills that require their joints to work in an extreme range of movement.

◘ **Rhythmic gymnasts need excellent flexibility**

CHECK MY LEARNING

1 What is the function of the muscular system?

2 What is the function of the skeletal system?

3 Describe two adaptations of flexibility on the musculoskeletal systems.

4 Why is it useful for a basketball player to be more flexible?

C6: The effects of long-term fitness training on the body: muscular endurance training

The long-term effects of participating in regular muscular endurance fitness training on the body include adaptations to the muscular system.

Adaptations to the muscular system

Muscular endurance training involves regularly participating in activities such as weight training, for a minimum of six weeks. The principles of training must be applied to ensure that overload is achieved, so that the muscles adapt to the training method.

Capillarisation around muscle tissues

Muscle tissue is made up of bundles of muscle fibres. Capillaries deliver and remove oxygenated and deoxygenated blood to and from the muscle tissue. Blood contains oxygen nutrients that are needed for exercise. Waste products such as carbon dioxide are produced during exercise. These are dissolved in the blood and taken away by capillaries. An increase in the number of capillaries surrounding muscle tissue means that more blood and nutrients can be delivered, and more waste products can be removed. This will allow the muscle to use oxygen more quickly, this means the muscle can continue to contract and work for longer.

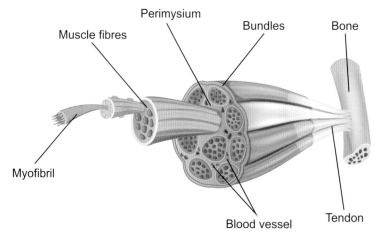

◻ Muscle fibres

◘ Completing a muscular endurance circuit training session

Increased muscle tone

Muscle tone means the tension in your muscles that help to maintain your posture. Muscle tone can be seen in the definition of muscles on a person's body. The muscles that help you remain upright and not fall over are also valuable in sports activities. Muscular endurance training helps to increase muscle tone, this improves posture and the muscles which stabilise joints during movement. Joint stability helps to reduce the risk of injury to muscles and joints and also allows the correct technique to be used, which will better improve muscular endurance.

Muscle endurance is the ability of muscles to keep contracting for long periods of time. Developing muscular endurance helps to promote greater efficiency of movement, this will allow the muscles to continue working for longer. Increased muscular endurance will also delay fatigue, meaning that sports performers can continue to work for longer before the effects of tiredness prevent them from continuing.

CHECK MY LEARNING

1 Identify three different sports or activity performers who would benefit positively form the long-term effects of muscular fitness training.

2 Explain how increased muscle tone can help to prevent injuries.

C6: The effects of long-term fitness training on the body: muscular strength and power training

Long-term muscular strength and power training cause adaptations to the body's muscular and skeletal systems. These adaptations allow a sports performer to perform better in all activities that require muscular strength and power, for example weightlifting, boxing or swimming.

These training methods cause adaptations to the muscular and skeletal systems, which result in improving the sports performer's ability in sports that require high levels of these components of fitness.

Adaptations to the muscular and skeletal systems

Muscular strength and power training causes the body to adapt by increasing muscular hypertrophy, **tendon** and **ligament** strength and bone density.

The muscular system is responsible for producing movement. Muscles also have an important role in protecting organs, helping with digestion and blood flow. In sport, the most relevant function of the muscular system is the ability to produce movement by controlling skeletal muscles and regulating blood flow to be able to deliver oxygenated blood to working muscles, as well as removing blood containing waste products.

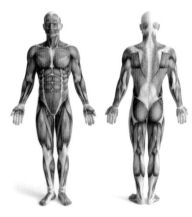

■ Skeletal muscles

The main structures that make up the muscular system are three different types of muscles:
- Cardiac muscle, found in the heart, is responsible for producing each heartbeat or contraction.
- Smooth muscle, found in the digestive system, helps move food around the different organs.
- Skeletal muscles are attached to bones and allow us to move. Movement is produced when ligaments and tendons pull on the bones and movement is produced at the joints.

The skeletal system has four main functions:
- The bones act as levers and allow us to produce movement. Bones provide support and protection for the organs within the body.
- The skeleton allows movement of the body as a whole and its individual parts. The bones act as levers and also form joints that allow muscles to pull on them and produce joint movements.
- Some bones contain marrow, which produces red blood cells, white blood cells and platelets.
- Bones are also able to store minerals.

The structures of the skeletal system include 206 bones, cartilage, **ligaments** and **tendons**. Ligaments and tendons are both made of strong collagen fibres. These structures work together to allow us to move our body in different directions, and to remain upright and stable in difficult positions. For example, an ice skater needs to be able to move their body into different positions while keeping their balance.

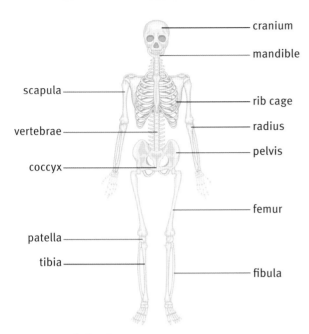

cranium

mandible

scapula

rib cage

radius

vertebrae

pelvis

coccyx

femur

patella

tibia

fibula

◪ Human skeletal system

Muscle hypertrophy

Muscle hypertrophy happens when a muscle is stressed through lifting heavy weights. Your muscle tissue experiences very small tears called **micro-tears**. These stimulate the muscle tissue to rebuild so that it is bigger and therefore stronger than before. If this process is repeated, the muscle tissue will continue to increase in size and strength.

Increased tendon and ligament strength

A joint is where two bones meet. Ligaments hold bones together; therefore, the stronger the ligaments holding the two bones together, the stronger the joint is going to be. Strong tendons are also beneficial as they help to prevent sports injuries as well as contributing to a person's overall strength. When you regularly participate in strength and power training, this will increase the strength of your tendons and ligaments.

Increased bone density

Bones are continually being remodelled, where old bone cells are removed and new bone cells are laid down. Minerals are used in the remodelling process and are used when new bone cells are formed to make the bones stronger and denser – this means they will be less likely to break on impact, such as when a football player is tackled or if a volleyball player dives on court. Taking part in regular muscle strength and power training increases the rate of bone remodelling and increases the amount of minerals laid down in the process, which increases bone **density**.

◪ Why are strong ligaments and tendons important for rugby players?

DID YOU KNOW

The tendons in your wrist allow you to grip, and most people have a hand grip strength of around 25 kg. A trained athlete might have a grip strength of 75 kilos! The average for a 16–17-year-old male performing in top end sports is 32.6–52.4 kg.

KEY TERM

Density is how compact something is or its consistency.

CHECK MY LEARNING

1 What is the function of ligaments and tendons?

2 What is meant by bone density?

3 Explain how the long-term effects of muscular strength and power training can help improve the performance of a boxer.

◪ Why is monitoring bone density important for boxers?

C6: The effects of fitness training on the body: speed training

Participating in long-term speed training aims to make the body adapt to lactic acid by tolerating higher levels of this waste product. Speed training effects can benefit sports performers who take part in speed sports such as sprinting, but also sports and activities that have skills or techniques that require speed, such as netball when a player sprints into a space on the court to receive a pass.

Speed training aims to increase a sports performer's speed: their ability to get from one place to another more quickly. It requires a performer to move their joints through a range of movement more quickly, which also increases flexibility. Because the muscles are being worked in speed training, the muscle fibres repeatedly contracting quickly helps to improve balance.

ACTIVITY

Working with a partner or small group, take it in turns to administer and take part in a speed test, for example the 30-metre sprint test. Protocols for this test can be found on page 150.

Before you take part in the speed test, make a note or have a discussion with your partner about how your muscles and legs are feeling. For example, are the muscles relaxed, tight, sore?

Carry out the speed test.

Straight after the test, make another note or have a discussion with your partner about how your muscles and legs are feeling now. For example, are the muscles relaxed, tight, sore?

You could complete the test again after a three-minute break.

Support

Have a discussion with your partner or group about the effects of the speed test on the muscles in your legs. Make comparisons between how your legs felt before the test and straight after you had finished.

Challenge

Analyse why you think your legs felt different after completing the speed test.

Consider lactic acid and the effects of lactic acid on muscles.

Adaptations to the muscular system

Primarily, the long-term effect of speed training is the adaptation to the muscular system caused by an increased **tolerance** to lactic acid. Speed training, such as sprinting, is a high-intensity activity that requires a lot of energy to be produced quickly. To do this, the body uses the lactic acid energy system. The waste product from this energy system is lactic acid.

◘ Speed training is important in rugby training

Increased tolerance to lactic acid

Lactic acid is produced when the body makes energy from glucose. It causes the blood to become acidic and an increase in acid in the blood will prevent muscles from working efficiently. A build-up of lactic acid causes fatigue and will prevent a participant from continuing to perform. Speed training increases muscle tolerance to lactic acid. If your body has an increased ability to tolerate or cope with lactic acid, it will be able to work at a higher level for longer.

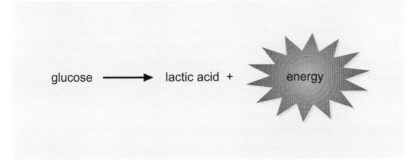

glucose ⟶ lactic acid + energy

◘ The body uses glucose to make energy and this process produces lactic acid

ACTIVITY

Support

What is lactic acid?

Challenge

Explain why it is beneficial for a sports performer, such as a 100 m sprinter, to have an increased tolerance to lactic acid.

DID YOU KNOW

Usain Bolt was the world's fastest man. He competed in 100 m sprints and would run at a top speed of 47.2 kph, that is almost 30 miles per hour!

CHECK MY LEARNING

1 Identify three different sports or activities that require high levels of speed to be successful.

2 Explain two benefits to the performer of regular speed training for one of the sports or activities you identified in question 1.

Learning outcome C: assessment practice

Investigate different fitness training methods

How you will be assessed

For Learning outcome C, you will be expected to apply an understanding of facts, components of fitness, fitness tests, training methods, processes and principles in relation to improving fitness in sport and exercise.

This will include:

- Explaining the requirements for fitness training methods
- Explaining fitness training methods for physical and skill-related components of fitness
- Explaining the additional requirements for fitness training methods
- Explaining the provision for taking part in fitness training methods
- Explaining the effects of long-term fitness training on the body systems.

CHECKPOINT

Review your learning of this component by answering the following questions. This will help you to prepare for your assessment.

Strengthen

- Outline how to carry out fitness training safely and effectively as part of a training programme.
- Suggest fitness training methods for specific sports participants.
- Describe the advantages and disadvantages of training methods.
- Describe providers of fitness training.
- Describe how training methods affect the different body systems.

Challenge

- Justify appropriate fitness training methods that could be used for specific sports participants for different ages and different sporting abilities.
- Explain the advantages and disadvantages of training methods.
- Analyse the provision of fitness training and how this varies in relation to types of equipment available, cost, other support available and access.
- Analyse how training methods affect the different body systems, which can lead to adaptations to improve specific components of fitness.

ASSESSMENT ACTIVITY

Lola is a tennis player. She is looking to join a tennis club in her local area. Lola has to decide whether to join a private provision club or a voluntary provision fitness club.

(i) State **one** advantage of voluntary provision for Lola.

(ii) State **one** disadvantage of voluntary provision for Lola.

Lola completes a warm-up before every training session.

(b) Explain **two** reasons for warming up before a training session.

Lola takes part in some fitness tests to assess her fitness for tennis.

(c) Explain **one** reason why Lola would use the ruler drop test to assess her fitness for tennis.

(d) Explain **one** advantage and **one** disadvantage of using the ruler drop test to assess fitness for a tennis player.

TAKE IT FURTHER

To expand your answer for question (d) you could include examples from your experience of performing the ruler drop test. You could also think about the advantages and disadvantages of other fitness tests and consider common advantages and disadvantages of fitness testing. For example, the number of participants, cost, equipment needed.

TIPS

In your answers, make sure you include information that is linked to the sport, the component of fitness and the question.

If there are two marks available for an answer, make sure you write two different statements or give two different facts.

Make sure you answer the question with what is asked; for example, if the questions asks you to 'describe' ensure that your answer contains a description.

D1: Personal information to aid training fitness programme design

Before writing a fitness training programme you need to identify the sports performer's aims and objectives and collect personal information. This will allow you to design a safe and effective programme specifically to meet their personal needs.

Aims and objectives

Aims and objectives give a clear indication of the purpose of the training programme. Aims are the details of what a sports performer would like to achieve for their selected sport. For example, a high jumper might aim to improve the height of their jump. Objectives identify how they intend to meet their aims using an appropriate component of fitness and method of training. For example, a high jumper could include different types of speed training in their programme.

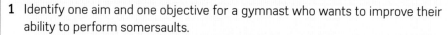

ACTIVITY

Support

1 Identify one aim and one objective for a gymnast who wants to improve their ability to perform somersaults.

2 Identify one aim and one objective for a hockey player who wants to improve their ability to keep running around the pitch during a game.

Challenge

Why is it important for the gymnast and hockey player to have aims and objectives for their training programmes?

Lifestyle and physical activity history

To make a safe and effective training programme, you must collect personal information from the sports performer. This information can be collected through the use of questionnaires or data sheets. The types of information needed include:

- Medical history
- Physical activity
- Lifestyle.

Medical history

It is important to be aware of any existing and previous illnesses and injuries, this will help to ensure the performer is fit and able to complete the training programme. Medical screening or medical history questionnaires commonly collect information about heart conditions, blood pressure, diabetes, asthma and pregnancy.

Physical activity

Before designing a training programme you need to know the performer's current level of fitness and all physical activities they regularly participate in. This can be done by asking the performer to complete fitness tests and a questionnaire.

Lifestyle

Lifestyle factors include things that can affect the performer's ability to train and perform in their sport or activity. These include drinking alcohol, smoking and sleep. Lifestyle information can be collected by interviewing the performer or asking them to complete a lifestyle questionnaire.

Attitudes, the mind, and personal motivation for training

To be able to design a training programme that the performer wants to complete, you need to identify their current level of **motivation** and any factors that will affect training, both positively or negatively. For example, negative experiences may make them not want to try that exercise again. If someone took part in a plyometrics training session and they didn't warm up correctly and injured their ankle, they might be scared to try it again. Using positive experiences, such as types of training they enjoy, will help the performer remain motivated and want to complete the training programme.

A performer's **attitude** towards training and their motivation will affect the success of the programme. If someone has a positive attitude and is highly motivated, they will want to carry out the training programme, they will want to meet their aims and objectives and improve their sports performance. You can identify a performer's attitudes and motivation by completing questionnaires or carrying out interviews.

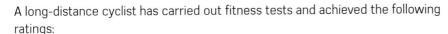

CHECK MY LEARNING

A long-distance cyclist has carried out fitness tests and achieved the following ratings:

Aerobic endurance – average

Muscular endurance – average

Muscular strength – above average

1   Identify one aim for the cyclist to use to design their training programme.

2   Identify one objective the cyclist can use to design their training programme.

3   Explain the importance of collecting personal information before designing a training programme.

4   Analyse the impact of the cyclist's attitude and motivation on training programme design.

ACTIVITY

Support

Find examples of medical history and lifestyle questionnaires online. Use these to design your own medical history and lifestyle questionnaires.

Challenge

Analyse the use of medical history and lifestyle questionnaires for assessing a participant's readiness for exercise.

KEY TERMS

Motivation is the internal mechanisms and external stimuli that arouse and direct behaviour. Motivation is a need or drive that makes us want to achieve something.

Attitude is the way of feeling or thinking about something or someone that affects behaviour towards the thing or person.

LINK IT UP

You can find out more about the influence of goal setting on motivation in Learning outcome D3 of this component.

D2: Fitness programme design 1

Once you have collected personal information and agreed aims and objectives with the sports performer, you can begin to design their safe and effective training programme.

Use personal information to aid training programme design

Training needs to be specific to the individual sports performer. To do this you need to collect and use personal information. Medical and lifestyle information about the sports performer allows you to make safe and effective choices when selecting which components of fitness to focus on and training methods to be used.

The medical history questionnaire example in Table 3.45 shows the type of information you can collect from a sports performer. This information is personal and must be kept confidential. You do not share it with anyone else and it must be stored securely. The sports performer must give their consent to provide you their personal information.

◻ **Table 3.45: Medical history questionnaire example**

	YES	NO
Do you have a heart condition?		X
Do you have any breathing problems?		X
Do you suffer from diabetes?		X
Do you have any joint or bone problems?	X	
Are you pregnant?		X
Have you had any operations or been admitted to hospital in the last two years? Please state any operations or hospital admissions in the any other information box below.	X	
Do you take any regular medication? Please list any medications in the any other information box below.		X
Are you aware of any reason that would prevent you from participating in regular exercise?		X
Any other information: I had knee surgery to repair a torn ligament in my left knee one year ago.		
Name: Olivia Wright		
Signature: O wright		Date: 1.2.22

ACTIVITY

The information in the medical history questionnaire example for Olivia shows that she has had a joint injury and an operation to repair her knee a year ago. Recent surgery is a contraindication for exercise.

1 Why is it important to check for any **contraindications** before designing a training programme?

2 What should you do before you design a training programme for someone with a contraindication for exercise?

The lifestyle screening questionnaire example below shows the type of information you can collect from a sports performer. This information can help you to select appropriate aims and objectives for them.

◻ Table 3.46: Lifestyle screening questionnaire example

	YES	NO
Do you smoke?	X	
If yes, how many a day?	10	
Do you regularly drink alcohol?		X
If yes, how many units a week?		
How many hours do you usually sleep most nights?	8	
Do you have any allergies?	X Milk	
If so, what are you allergic to?		
What is your occupation?	Student	
How much physical activity do you take part in per week?	6 hours	
Do you feel stressed?	X	
Blood pressure	120/80	
Height (cm)	169	
Weight (kg)	65	
BMI	22.7	
Age	16	
Sex	Female	

Any other information:
I am feeling stressed about my exams and worried about managing my time. I want to play sports and go to training but have to revise for my exams as well.

Name: Olivia Wright

Signature: *O Wright*   Date: 1.2.22

ACTIVITY

Use the information in the lifestyle screening questionnaire example for Olivia to answer the following questions:

1 Identify three lifestyle factors that could affect the design of Olivia's training programme.

2 Explain how stress could impact Olivia's ability to follow her training programme.

3 Explain why it is useful to know the person's occupation before designing a training programme.

CHECK MY LEARNING

1 What is meant by the term 'contraindication'?

2 Identify two methods you can use to collect medical and lifestyle information.

LINK IT UP

You can find information about lifestyle and physical activity history, attitudes and the mind, and personal motivation in Learning outcome D1 of this component.

D2: Fitness programme design 2

The FITT principles are used to plan training programmes designed to improve fitness of participants and positively affect their participation in sport and activity.

Selection of appropriate training method or activity

The purpose of a fitness training programme is to maintain any strengths and improve any weaknesses. The selection of appropriate training methods or activities to improve or maintain the selected components of fitness needs to be specific to the individual sports performer. Fitness testing data will give an indication of the sports performer's current level of fitness and will identify which components of fitness need to be maintained or improved.

ACTIVITY

Use the information in the tables below to answer the questions:

Name: Lola	Sport/activity: Tennis
Component of fitness	**Fitness test rating**
Muscular strength	Average
Muscular endurance	Above average
Power	Average
Aerobic endurance	Above average

Name: Hugo	Sport/activity: Football
Component of fitness	**Fitness test rating**
Speed	Above average
Flexibility	Poor
Aerobic endurance	Average
Power	Average

1 Who should focus their training programme on improving flexibility?
2 Which component of fitness should Lola maintain?
3 Which component of fitness was Lola's weakest?
4 Which component of fitness is most important for Lola to focus on for the sport she takes part in?
5 Which component of fitness is most important for Hugo to focus on for the sport he takes part in?

Application of the FITT principles and additional principles of training

When you design a training programme you need to follow the principles of training. These principles make sure that the programme is designed to meet the needs of the sports performer. The frequency, intensity and duration of training all need to be at the right level for the sports performer to gain fitness improvements. The training programme needs to be at a level that allows the performer's body to adapt to training and improve fitness without causing injury.

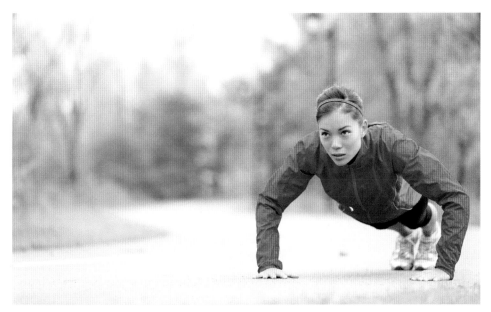

◪ An athlete performing a press-up as part of her specific training method

The FITT principles of training

- **Frequency** – the number of training sessions completed over a period of time. Aim for three to five sessions per week.
- **Intensity** – how hard an individual will train. This can be set using the performer's heart rate and RPE (rate of perceived exertion).
- **Time** – how long an individual will train for. Aim for 15–60 minutes of activity, depending on the intensity. Someone with a low level of fitness should work for longer at a lower intensity.
- **Type** – how an individual will train by selecting a training method to improve a specific component of fitness. For example, to train for aerobic endurance you could train in a way that links to your sport such as cycling or swimming.

The additional principles of training

- **Progressive overload and adaptation** – in order to progress, training needs to be demanding enough to cause the body to adapt, improving performance.
- **Specificity** – training should meet the needs of the sport or physical/skill-related fitness goals to be developed.
- **Individual differences** – training should meet the needs of an individual, their aims and goals.
- **Reversibility** – if training stops or the intensity of training is lowered, fitness gains from training are reversed and lost.
- **Variation** – altering types of training to avoid boredom and maintain motivation to train. There needs to be sufficient time between training sessions to allow the body to adapt and recover.
- **Rest and recovery** – to allow the body to recover and adapt.

CHECK MY LEARNING

1 What does FITT stand for?
2 Explain why it is important to follow the FITT principles of training when designing a training programme.

D3: Motivational techniques for fitness programming 1

Motivational techniques should be used when designing fitness training programmes. Motivation is linked to performance and overall success in a sport or activity. If a person's motivation is high, they are much more likely to train regularly and perform better.

Motivation for a sports performer is what makes them want to train, compete and win in their sport or activity. Motivation is what makes them go outside to train on a cold and wet day, it is what makes them keep trying to learn new skills and improve techniques.

Types of motivation

There are two main types of motivation: intrinsic and extrinsic.
- **Intrinsic motivation** is when a sports performer takes part in sports and activities because they want to. Their motivation is that they enjoy participating, they gain pleasure from the activity and the accomplishments they feel from playing. Intrinsic motivation can help a sports performer push themself to succeed because they want to and they enjoy achieving goals.
- **Extrinsic motivation** comes from external rewards, such as prize money, a trophy, status or celebrity status. This type of motivation can be more difficult to maintain. If the sports performer fails to meet a goal, they might lose their motivation and not want to train or perform regularly. For example, if a footballer plays in a losing cup match, they might not continue to train as they are not motivated to train for their sport, their motivation was to win the cup.

ACTIVITY

1   What is the difference between intrinsic and extrinsic motivation?

2   Complete the table below, identifying if the reason to participate is an example of intrinsic or extrinsic motivation:

Reason for participating in sports activities	Intrinsic or extrinsic motivation
Takes part in cricket because they love the sport	
They train to improve their skills so they can be the best 100 m sprinter in their club	
They enjoy being part of a team, working together with others and winning as a team	
They want to win the prize money	

Benefits of motivation on the sports performer

Motivation has a positive impact on a sports performer and their performance in their sport or activity. Being highly motivated can help a sports performer to.
- **Increase participation** – if you are motivated you want to train and participate in your sport or activity.
- **Maintain training and intensity** – someone who is motivated will want to complete their training programme and will be keen to work at the intensity selected for them.

- **Increase fitness** – people who are motivated have increased levels of participation, maintain their training and are happy to train at a high level of intensity. These factors will all lead to achieving an increased level of fitness.
- **Improve performance** – being motivated, wanting to participate, training regularly and increasing fitness levels will all lead to a sports performer improving their overall sports performance.

 Individual motivation can make a big difference to team performance

Motivational techniques

Motivational techniques aim to improve a sports performer's motivation level. Someone who is more motivated performs better in their sport or activity. Motivation can come from several different people: sports coaches, teammates, supporters, family and friends.

Motivational techniques include:

- **Making it fun** – if the sports performers enjoy what they are doing they will want to participate, play harder and continue to train.
- **Introducing competition** – an element of competition can motivate people to succeed and want to train and perform.
- **Celebrate wins and ignore losses** – giving praise and identifying strengths of a performer will boost their motivation and make them feel better about losing when it happens.
- **Setting goals** – goals allow sports performers to know exactly what they are working towards and when they have completed their aim.

CHECK MY LEARNING

1 Identify three benefits of motivation for a sports performer.
2 What is the purpose of motivational techniques?

D3: Motivational techniques for fitness programming 2

Motivational techniques can be used to help a sports performer follow their fitness programming by wanting to train and meet their goals.

Principles of setting goals to increase and direct motivation

Setting goals is an important part of designing a training programme. You need to be clear about the training goals, discuss and agree them with the sports performer before designing the programme. Goals need to be exciting and something to aim for, but also realistic.

SMARTER personal goals

Goals should be SMARTER. SMARTER goals allow you to design a training programme that is specific to meet the needs of an individual.

S – the goal must be **specific** to what the participant wants to achieve, for example improve explosive power when sprinting

M – Goals must be **measurable**, for example 'I want to complete a 100m sprint in under 11 seconds'

A – the participant must be able to **access** the training and have the time to take part

R – the participant must be able to actually **reach** the goal and not aim for improvements beyond what can be achieved in the time frame or beyond their fitness/ability level

T – there must be a specific **timescale** or deadline for the goal, so that the participant can review their achievement

E – the goal should be something the person finds **exciting** and really wants to achieve. This will have an impact on their sports performance, so that they are motivated to train regularly and work hard to achieve the goal

R – the results should be clearly **recorded** so that the participant can see their progress towards achieving their goal

Short-term and long-term goals

Goals should have a time period; they can be short- or long-term goals.

- Short-term goals are usually set over a short period of time, between one day and one month. This might be what a performer wants to achieve in one session or over a few weeks.
- Long-term goals allow a performer to achieve in the long term, this could be over a season, a period of months or even years.

Short-term goals can be used to help work up to long-term goals and can offer motivation to keep going.

Goals can be selected to meet an outcome or to learn a process. Outcome goals, or performance goals, have a clear outcome; for example, winning a race or setting a personal best. Process goals are performance related and often involve improving techniques. For example, a swimmer may aim to improve their tumble turns.

ACTIVITY

Christie is a rugby player who wants to improve two components of fitness: aerobic endurance and power.

Use the SMARTER principle to set goals for Christie. The first one, specific, has been completed for you.

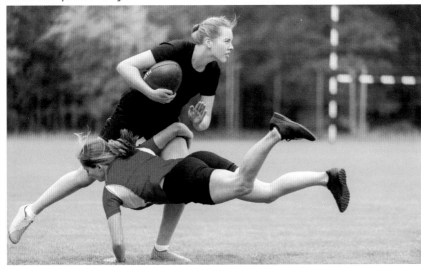

Specific	To be able to keep a steady running pace throughout the whole game and have more power to kick the ball further.
Measurable	
Achievable	
Realistic	
Time related	
Exciting	
Recorded	

Influence of goal setting on motivation

Effective goal setting can increase motivation and concentration. It can provide direction for behaviour and maintain focus on the task in hand. Goal setting can make it easier to tackle large or complex tasks by breaking them down into smaller ones. Goals can help you achieve more in less time, which can help to maintain motivation.

Goal setting is linked to performance and can improve motivation. Someone who is more motivated will follow their training programme, they will want to achieve their goals. This will lead to an increase in skills and fitness and an improvement in overall sports performance. Setting goals and making sure they are appropriate for the individual is a critical part of training programme design.

CHECK MY LEARNING

1 Give a definition for the term 'motivation'.
2 Describe how SMARTER goals can be used to help design a training programme.
3 Explain how SMARTER goals can help a sports performer maintain motivation.

LINK IT UP

You can find information about attitudes, the mind and personal motivation for training earlier in this component.

Learning outcome D: Assessment practice

Investigate fitness programming to improve fitness and sports

How you will be assessed

This component builds on knowledge, understanding and skills acquired and developed in Components 1 and 2 and includes a synoptic assessment. You will need to apply your knowledge and understanding of the body's reaction to participants taking part in physical activity and the components required to develop fitness.

For Learning outcome D, you will be expected to make connections with concepts, facts, components of fitness, fitness tests, training methods, processes and principles in relation to improving fitness in sport and exercise.

This will include:
- Explaining the use of personal information to aid training programme design
- Explaining fitness programme design
- Explaining motivational techniques for training programme design.

CHECKPOINT

Review your learning of this component by answering the following questions. This will help you to prepare for your assessment.

Strengthen
- Outline the use of personal information to aid training programme design.
- Outline fitness training programme design.
- Describe motivational techniques for training programme design.

Challenge
- Analyse the importance of using personal information to aid training programme design.
- Explain fitness programme design.
- Analyse motivational techniques for training programme design.

ASSESSMENT ACTIVITY

1. Michele is training to improve her aerobic endurance and flexibility. Table 1 shows two weeks of Michele's training programme.

Table 1

Week	Mon	Tues	Wed	Thurs	Fri	Sat	Sun
1	Yoga session – 1 hour	Rest day	Fartlek training – 45 min				Rest day
2	Fartlek training – 50 min	Rest day		Yoga session – 1 hour		Rest day	

Explain **two** principles of training that Michele is applying in her training programme.

2. Johan is a rugby player. He uses the SMARTER principles of goal setting for his training programme.

The picture shows Johan tackling in a game of rugby.

(a) Complete Table 2 by stating:

(i) the name of the principle of goal setting represented by each letter.

(ii) why this principle will increase Johan's motivation to train.

Table 2

	Name of principle of goal setting represented by letter	Why this principle will increase Johan's motivation to train
S		
E		

▫ Joanne playing rugby

Joanne has high levels of speed and power.

(b) Assess the importance of high levels of **speed** and **power** when tackling during a game of rugby.

TAKE IT FURTHER

To achieve a higher mark you need to demonstrate accurate and detailed knowledge and understanding of the importance of high levels of speed and power when tackling during a game of rugby.

The points you make need to be relevant to the question.

You need to provide well-developed and logical assessment that clearly considers the factors or events and their relative importance, leading to supported judgments.

TIPS

- Question (a) is a synoptic question, it draws upon knowledge from Components 1, 2 and 3.

- In your answers, make sure you include what you have learned about the components of fitness and sports performance.

Glossary

A sports coach is a person involved in the direction, instruction and training of a sports team or athlete.

Acceleration is an increase in the rate of velocity with time. Something that has velocity is moving with speed and direction. Something that accelerates moves in a direction and gets faster as it moves. To accelerate, the movement needs momentum to change speed and not just move.

Adaptation is a process of change that has made the body function better in its environment.

Aerobic endurance is your ability to exercise at moderate intensity for extended periods of time. Exercise intensity is a measure of how hard a physical activity feels while you're doing it.

Aerobic training zone is 60–85 per cent of your maximum heart rate.

Agility is the ability to rapidly change body direction, accelerate, or decelerate.

Alveoli (also known as air sacs) are the smallest structures in the respiratory system. They have very thin walls which allow carbon dioxide and oxygen to pass through them.

Anaerobic training zone is 85–95 per cent of your maximum heart rate

Attitude is the way of feeling or thinking about something or someone that affects behaviour towards the thing or person.

Balance is the ability to control your body's position and not fall over.

Barbell is a long bar with weights at both ends, which you lift using both hands.

Body composition refers to the relative ratio of fat mass to fat-free mass in the body.

Calibration is a process or action which checks something (equipment, an instrument, a device) for accuracy.

Capillarisation is the process where new capillaries are formed at the alveoli in the lungs.

Cardiac hypertrophy is an increase in the size and strength of the heart muscle.

Concentric muscle contraction is where the muscle shortens when it contracts.

Conditioned practice takes the rules of the game and alters them so that practice can still take part in a game situation but focuses on a particular skill.

Contraindication is a factor that could be harmful to health. For example, a person recovering from surgery should not exercise until their doctor says it is safe for them to do so. The contraindication is recent surgery.

Coordination is the ability to combine multiple movements from more than one part of the body into a single movement that is smooth and efficient.

Density is how compact something is or its consistency.

Direct violations directly affect play or a player.

Drills are a repetitive training activity with the purpose of learning or developing a particular skill or technique.

Dumbbell is a shorter bar with weights at both ends, and you lift one in each hand.

Dynamic stretching means performing movements while performing the stretch.

Eccentric muscle contraction is where the muscle lengthens when it contracts.

Exercise station is the place in a circuit training session where you perform your exercises.

Extrinsic motivation is when a person is motivated by external rewards (such as a trophy or prize money) for taking part or for doing well.

Fartlek means 'speed play' in Swedish. It combines continuous training with interval training.

Fitness means being physically strong and healthy.

Fixed resistance machines use stacks of weights attached to pulleys or air pressure to provide resistance.

Flexibility is the range of motion available at the joints of the body. It includes the ability of a person to move a joint fluidly through its complete range of movement.

Foul is inappropriate or unfair behaviour by a player, usually due to a violation of the rules of the game.

Free weight is not attached to machinery, such as barbells or dumbbells.

Gaseous exchange is the process of oxygen moving or diffusing into or out of the bloodstream and carbon dioxide moving into or out of the bloodstream.

GPS tracks a player's health and fitness as well as distance covered and position during the game.

Hypertension means high blood pressure.

Hyperthermia is a result of overexertion in hot temperatures, when the body absorbs or generates more heat than it releases.

Hypothermia is a drop in body temperature below 35°C.

Indirect violations do not occur in the direct line of play.

Individual sports are sports that a participant can play on their own against an opponent. An example of an individual sport is tennis.

Indoor sport facilities are buildings available to play indoor sports.

Intensity is the amount of work, force or exertion.

Intrinsic motivation is when a person is motivated by internal factors, not external rewards.

Isolated practices are a type of practice where the situation does not change, the equipment stays the same and the routine is repeated until it becomes automatic. There are no opponents and players have no environmental factors to respond to so no decisions to make.

Isometric contractions is when a muscle or group of muscles contract without changing length, the attached joints also remain still.

Lactic acid is a waste product or by product that builds up during activity.

Ligaments connect bones to bones.

Maximal inspiration is the highest amount of air that you can breathe in during a breath.

Maximal test the participant completes the test until they are exhausted.

Micro-tears are tiny tears in your muscles that result from exercise and are necessary for muscle hypertrophy to take place.

Moderate intensity exercise means the activity will raise your heart rate, and make you breathe faster and feel warmer.

Motivation is the internal mechanisms and external stimuli that arouse and direct behaviour. Motivation is a need or drive that makes us want to achieve something.

Muscular endurance is where a muscle can continue contracting over a period of time against a light to moderate fixed resistance or load.

Muscular hypertrophy is an increase in muscle size.

Muscular strength is the maximum force (in kg or N) that can be generated by a muscle or muscle group.

National governing bodies (NGBs) are organisations that govern and regulate sports.

National parks are outdoor facilities offering outdoor and adventure activities.

Normative data is an indicator of how a participant performed in comparison to the general population.

Office for National Statistics (ONS) is a non-ministerial government department that collects, analyses and shares statistics about the UK's economy, society and population.

Officials control how a sports match is played and administer the rules.

Overload is training at a higher intensity than previously to create adaptations to training.

Power is the ability to perform strength-based movements quickly.

Practicality refers to how suitable the test is for the given situation, the person administering the test and the people taking part in the test.

Progressive overload is continuing to increase the intensity of exercise over time to make continued fitness gains.

Provision is something that has been provided or supplied, for example a football pitch that is available to use.

Pulse raiser activities are included in a warm-up to gradually increase your heart rate.

Rating is a rank or classification that is used to show the quality or standard of performance.

Reaction time describes how fast an athlete is able to respond to an external signal or stimulus.

Reliability is the ability to repeatedly carry out the same test and achieve comparable results each time.

Replicating is copying, reproducing or remaking the same thing.

Reps per minute (RPM) is the number of repetitions completed in one minute.

Resistance is a force that opposes the movement of an object, slowing it down.

SAQ training is a mixture of dynamic movements that aim to increase a performer's speed and agility.

Skills are the expertise or talent that is needed to perform a sport or physical activity.

Smartwatch features technology to monitor heart rate and other vital signs.

Specificity in a training programme means training in a way that is appropriate in order to produce the desired outcome.

Speed is when a person travels very fast over a short distance, calculated as distance covered divided by the time taken to cover the distance.

Static stretching means holding a stretch for a period of time in a static (still) position. The muscle or muscle group should be extended to its furthest point. Unlike dynamic stretching, this stretch should be held for 10–15 seconds.

Stimulus is something that produces a reaction. For example, a loud bang will make you look to see what made the noise. The noise is the stimulus.

Strategy involves the use of tactics and decision-making to achieve a long-term or overall aim.

Stroke volume is the amount of blood pumped per beat.

Submaximal means less than maximum exertion. The intensity put in by the sports performer is high, but not the highest they could exert.

Tactics are the smaller specific steps that are taken to achieve the overall aim.

Teaching points are information about a skill or technique that needs to be conveyed to and understood by the athlete for the skill to be learned and replicated. They are the key aspects that need to be highlighted to ensure the correct and safe way to perform the technique.

Team sports are sports which can only be played as a team, they cannot be played individually. An example of a team sport is football.

Tendons connect muscles to bones.

Tolerance is the ability to endure something.

Training threshold is the safe and effective intensity to work at to undergo adaptation.

Training zone is the correct intensity at which you should exercise to experience fitness improvement.

Validity is how accurate a set of results are. Do the results measure what we want them to?

Vigorous intensity exercise means the activity will make you breathe hard and fast.

Vital capacity is the amount of air that can be forced out of the lungs (expelled) following a maximal inspiration.

Answers

Component 1

P4 Activity

Learner group discussion.

p5 Activity

NGB choice of learner.

p5 Check my learning

1 Choice of learner.

2 NGBs are important – use the link to discover why: http://www.sportni.net/performance/governing-bodies/what-is-a-governing-body/

3 Role of an NGB is to govern and administer a sport on a national basis.

p7 Activity

Answer from own experience or video.

p7 Check my Learning

1 Improved fitness, development of leadership skills, building resilience and self-confidence, meeting new people.

2 Meeting people with similar interests, improves self-esteem, learning a new skill, offers an opportunity to experience a positive risk-taking activity.

3 Physical health benefits each element of fitness: heart will strengthen, making blood pump more effectively around the body. Muscles and bones will be stronger, improved bone density. Flexibility will be improved, reducing the risk of musculoskeletal impacts.

p8 Activity

The case study should include benefits of the chosen physical activity.

p9 Check my learning

1 Any bodily movement produced by the skeletal muscles that requires energy expenditure.

2 Three from: meeting new people, improved fitness, improved confidence, improved body confidence, improved physical health.

3 Choice of learner.

p10 Activity

Examples to represent public, private & voluntary organisations within the local area.

p11 Activity

Local area information needed.

p11 Check my learning

1 Public facility = Park football pitch, leisure centre. Private facility = private gym, outdoor activity centre. Voluntary facility = local amateur rugby club, local amateur hockey club.

2 Differences in characteristics:

Public = to provide provision in local communities with a low cost to encourage participation, funded by taxes and the national lottery, purposeful and safe.

Private = to make a profit, meeting the demand of current trends in sports participation, investors fund the facilities, members pay a yearly/monthly fee, the quality will be high.

Voluntary = to empower local people to come together and be more active, funded from membership subs, fundraising and sponsorship, the facility will be purposeful and safe (often use public facilities), available in most communities.

3

Public	Private	Voluntary
Advantage = cost	Advantage = high quality	Advantage = within local communities
Disadvantage = availability of all sports	Disadvantage = membership fees	Disadvantage = local people train the teams

p13 Activity

1 Kian is 16 yrs old and is recommended to participate in sport and physical activity for 60 minutes per day

2 Choice of learner.

3 Choice of learner.

p13 Check my learning

1 Government recommendation for sport and physical activity participation:

Children (5–11 years) and adolescents (12–17 years): 60 minutes of moderate or vigorous activity per day.

Children and young people with a disability: 120–180 minutes per week moderate to vigorous intensity.

Adults (18–49 years): 150 minutes of moderate or 75 minutes of vigorous activity per week.

Older adults (50+ years): 150 minutes of moderate or 75 minutes of vigorous activity or a combination of both per week.

Adults with a disability: 150 minutes of moderate to vigorous exercise per week with no less than 10 minutes for each session.

p15 Activity:

Challenge: Role models. Choice of learner.

Learner's own response. For example, footballer Marcus Rashford campaigns against both child hunger and racism in football. He was awarded an MBE in 2021 for his campaign to end child food poverty.

p15 Check my learning

1 Cost is a barrier as some people may not be able to afford private gym membership.

2 Accessibility: Reason 1: Location of the activity might be a distance from the individual's home. Reason 2: Public transport may be limited.

3 Time may be a barrier as college, a part-time job and family commitments may impact time to participate in sport and physical activity.

4 Personal reasons could include worries about body image, lack of self-confidence and self-esteem or feeling unfit to participate in sport or physical activity.

5 Culture may be a barrier to participation due to any of: limited access to single-sex sessions; limited access to appropriate sports clothing; limited role models; limited access to male-dominated sports for women from some cultural backgrounds.

p16: Activity

Own research.

P17 Activity

Learner's own research

p17 Check my learning

1 Offer discounted sessions, offer free equipment hire, offer free parking at the venue.

2 For example: concerns about body image, low self-confidence, parental or guardian influence, limited previous participation, low fitness levels, extended time off from previous participation, concerns that taking part in sport or physical activity may make existing health conditions worse.

3 Research from own area.

P21 Activity

Learner's own research.

p21 Check my learning

1 Clothing and footwear for rugby: rugby shirt, shorts, football socks, studded boots. Clothing and footwear for badminton: sports top, shorts, socks, trainers. Clothing and footwear for hiking: thermoregulated top, walking trousers or shorts, walking socks, gloves, hat and walking shoes/boots.

2 The importance of waterproof clothing is to reduce the barrier of weather as an impact on participation.

3 The importance of studded boots is to reduce the risk of slipping resulting in an injury.

p23 Activity

History of the mouth guard: The first mouth guard was created in 1890 by a London dentist, Woolf Krause. It was called a gum shield and it was specifically designed to be worn by boxers to prevent them getting lip lacerations, which were a common injury of this sport at the time.

Benefit of a mouth guard in sport and physical activity: protects teeth and lips from impact.

Concussion in rugby: https://www.drakefoundation.org/rugby-concussions/

p23 Check my learning

1 Spinning class: spinning bike. Aqua aerobic class: weighted ankle and wrist weights.

2 Hockey: hockey stick, goals and a hockey ball. Racketball: racket, ball.

3 Ice hockey: mouth guard, helmet, body pads, shin guards, padded shoes.

4 Importance of ice packs is to decrease inflammation and numb pain in the area. Importance of bandages is to control bleeding and reduce the risk of infection.

p25 Activity

1 Assistive technology is often used to describe products or systems that support and assist individuals with disabilities, restricted mobility or other impairments to perform functions that might otherwise be difficult or impossible.

2 Assistive technologies to support those with a hearing impairment: hearing aid, hearing loop and Bluetooth systems.

Assistive technologies to support those with a visual impairment: long cane, magnifying glass, optoelectronic reading system, audio books and touch watch.

3 Learner's own research.

p25 Check my learning

1 Wheelchair sports: rugby, tennis, basketball, boccia, cycling, athletics, fencing, sailing and dancing.

2 Hearing aid and talking watch.

3 The impact of prosthetics is that amputee athletes can have improved flexibility, balance and strength.

p27 Activity

Learner's own research.

p27 Check my learning

1 Indoor facilities: sports hall, gym, dance studio. Outdoor facilities: mountain, river and football/rugby pitch.

2 To officiate netball, the official will need a whistle and notebook.

3 Performance analysis is important as it allows a participant to improve their performance enabling motivation and commitment to increase.

p29 Activity

Sport	Material used in footwear	Has the grip helped performance?	Does the footwear have rebound?
Netball	Synthetic	✓	✓
Ice hockey	Thermo-formed composite material	✓	✗
Basketball	Leather	✓	✓
Mountain biking	Leather	✓	✓
Wind surfing	Neoprene	✓	✗

Learner's own response

p29 Check my learning

1 Thermoregulation is defined as the maintenance of a stable core body temperature.

2 Hypothermia is a drop in body temperature below 35°C. Hyperthermia is a result of overexertion in hot temperatures, when the body absorbs or generates more heat than it releases.

3 The purpose of aerodynamic clothing is to reduce forces of air moving past.

4 The benefit of compression clothing is to increase blood flow to the area covered by the clothing.

p31 Check my learning

1 Graphite and titanium squash rackets are lighter, helping to improve the swing and absorb vibration.

2

Fact file on golf drivers
• New drivers come with a titanium club face
• The club face is either inserted or welded to the club frame
• Drivers come in varying thicknesses to increase the springiness
• Drivers come with internal support behind the face to increase strength
• The crown (top section of the driver) is made from titanium or carbon, making it the lightest section of the club

p33 Check my learning

1 A personally fitted mouth guard is important because it is less likely to fall out and then the force of the impact can be distributed more evenly.

2 The purpose of protective equipment is to protect participants from impacts.

3 Protective equipment for a field sport and weight training could be non-slip gloves.

p35 Check my learning

1 Prosthetics are defined as artificial body parts.

2 Example of prosthetics for a sport could be blades for a runner or the Eagle for a golfer.

3 Equipment can be adapted in a gym to allow a seat for non-disabled participants and the chair removed for a wheelchair user.

4 Sport wheelchairs are non-folding and have pronounced angled wheels.

p37 Activity

1 VAR is used in football as a 'video assistant referee'. It allows a qualified referee who watches the match via a number of screens to view slow-motion replays. It was developed to enable the on-field referee to be advised and supported.

2 Learner's own views.

p37 Check my learning

1 The benefit of a sprung floor is to absorb some of the impact experienced by high-impact sports and physical activities.

2 The benefit of a 3G pitch is that it is available for sport and physical activity at all times which is hard wearing, durable and resilient.

3 VAR is used in football to support the on-field referee with their application of the rules.

p39 Activity

Integrated sensors are electronic devices that connect to the participant's body and communicate information.

The impact is that participants can measure performance and physical health during and after a performance.

p39 Check my learning

1 The purpose of an action camera is to provide footage of the participant's view when taking part in an activity. A coach can also use the footage to analyse performance.

2 It can be used by a coach to record an individual so that their performance can be analysed, and enabling skills and techniques to be reflected upon.

3 GPS can detect fatigue, which could indicate an injury, and provides information on appropriate intensity during athletic performance, which is vital in changing training routines to enhance success in the sport or physical activity.

p41 Check my learning

1 Time is a limitation as technology takes time to set up and upload the data.

2 Learner's own research.

3 Impact of inaccurate data is that players' performance is affected and fans' opinions distorted.

4 Usability is an issue as sports need appropriate people with understanding of the technology to set up, use and feedback the data.

p45 Check my learning

1 A warm-up is important as it increases the blood flow to deliver oxygen to the exercising muscle groups. The warm-up increases body temperature, reducing the risk of injury to the muscles and tendons.

2 Pulse raiser is a section of the warm-up designed to increase the participant's heart rate and body temperature.

3 Pulse raiser for a climbing activity: race another person to a point on the wall. Pulse raiser for a game of table tennis: split into teams on both sides of the table, participants serve then run to the other side of the table, continuous play should happen. Pulse raiser for a swimming session: instructor places floats in the water and participants must gather the floats one at a time and make a pile on the side.

p47 Check my learning

1 Four responses of the cardiorespiratory system:

1 Heart rate will increase as the body moves faster from rest, so when performing a pulse raiser, the participant will begin to run, which will increase their heart rate.

2 Breathing rate and depth of breathing will increase as we take in more air, as when the pulse raiser is performed, the body asks for more air, so the rate at which you breathe increases.

3 The working muscles will have an increase to the supply of oxygen they receive as the heart is pumping blood around the body faster, getting to the muscles and increasing their supply of oxygen.

4 As a result, an increase in the removal of carbon dioxide will occur as we breathe out faster.

2 Three responses of the musculoskeletal system:

1 Increasing the temperature of the muscles, which allows the muscle to increase its elasticity.

2 Increasing the pliability of the muscles, allowing muscles to move to make the movements for the sport or physical activity.

3 Reducing the risk of muscle strain due to increased blood flow and lessen the risk of injury.

p49 Activity

Activities for Rose – 65 years old and enjoys chair aerobics.

Area	Suggested Mobiliser Exercise
Spine	Roll forward whilst sitting in the chair towards the toes
Hips	Stand up and hold the back of the chair, perform hip circles
Knees	Stand up and hold the back of the chair, perform squats
Ankles	Perform ankle circles

p49 Check my learning

p51 Check my learning

1 A preparation stretch uses the main muscles that will be used in the sport or physical activity going to be performed.

2 A static stretch means putting a muscle or muscle group in a position where the muscle can be extended for a period of time to its furthest point.

3 A dynamic stretch means performing movements whilst performing the stretch.

p53 Check my learning

1 Response of the cardiorespiratory system when performing preparation stretches:

• slight drop in heart rate

• slight drop in breathing rate

• maintained elevated heart and breathing rate for dynamic stretches.

2 Response of the musculoskeletal system when performing preparation stretches:

• extending muscles so that they are fully stretched so less likely to tear during sport or physical activity.

p55 Check my learning

1 Moderate intensity exercise means the activity will raise your heart rate, and make you breathe faster and feel warmer.

2 Vigorous intensity exercise means the activity will make you breathe hard and fast.

3 Four low-impact activities: walking, swimming, cycling and dancing. Four high-impact activities: aerobics, boxing, martial arts and rugby.

4 All activities can be adapted to allow individuals with a disability to participate. For example, swimming can be adapted to use a hydro pool or weighted floats and rugby can be adapted to wheelchair rugby.

p57 Check my learning

1 A sport-specific warm-up is designed for the needs of the participants as well as for the requirements of the sport or physical activity. It focuses the body by stretching the correct muscles, as well as the mind by mentally preparing the participant for the performance they are going to take part in.

2 A pulse raiser for hockey could be relay races with hockey challenges.

3 A mobiliser for trampolining could be a squat on a mini trampoline.

4 A preparation stretch for a climber could be a high knee bend.

p59 Check my learning

1 A warm-up session should consist of a pulse raiser, a mobiliser and preparation stretch.

2 Your position is vital when delivering the warm-up so that you can see all your participants so that advice can be given and demonstrations can be seen.

p61 Activity

A potential pulse raiser could be 'stuck in the mud' where children run around an area whilst two are 'on' and then others have to crawl under their legs to free the tagged person. A way to support the participants would be to share the instructions, offer a demonstration on how to 'tag' and how to free someone. You should then wander around the game to offer advice to each participant.

p61 Check my learning

1 Four ways to support participants during a warm-up:

1 Offer clear instructions.

2 Use diagrams when explaining complex activities.

3 Use demonstrations to clarify teaching points.

4 Give time for questions from the participants.

2 Benefits of observing participants are that as an instructor you can clarify the exercises and offer teaching points to individuals on their performance.

Component 2

p67 Activity: Aerobic endurance

Support

Sports requiring high levels of aerobic endurance: hockey, netball, swimming 1600 metres, football, basketball, ironman triathlon.

Challenge

The ironman triathlon is one of the ultimate endurance events. It requires athletes to complete a 3.9 km swim, 180.2 km bicycle ride and a marathon 42.2 km run, in that order. Due to the distance required and the time it takes, on average 12 hours and 35 minutes, a very high level of aerobic endurance is needed. The cardiovascular system needs to work efficiently and effectively to keep supplying the body with the oxygen and nutrients to keep moving and remove the waste products produced.

p67 Activity: Muscular endurance

Support

Other examples of when muscular endurance might be needed in everyday life include gardening, vacuuming and walking around the supermarket.

p67 Check my learning

1 The six components of physical fitness are:
- aerobic endurance
- muscular endurance
- muscular strength
- speed
- flexibility
- body composition.

2 For sports that require sustained physical activity, such as football, rowing and tennis, a good level of aerobic endurance is needed to keep the muscles supplied with oxygen and nutrients and therefore able to perform the movements needed to play. Without aerobic endurance, the body will become tired and will no longer be able to keep moving.

3 a Muscular endurance is needed in the sport of kayaking in the arms, shoulders, back and core. The shoulder and back muscles are fundamental to effective strong paddle strokes, a strong core is needed to maintain balance and stroke rotation, and endurance in the arm muscles is needed for the push/pull motion of the paddle strokes.

  b Rock climbing requires muscular endurance in the core for the balance and strength to hold your body close to the wall, upper back muscles which work with your core to keep you stable on the wall, leg muscles to provide the push force needed to move up the wall and arms to provide the pull force needed to move up the wall when the legs can't provide enough push power.

p68 Activity

Support

Individual sports that require high levels of strength	Team sports that require high levels of strength
e.g. Wrestling, boxing, powerlifting	e.g. American football, rowing, rugby

Challenge

A high level of muscular strength is needed in wrestling as a lot of the time is spent pushing and pulling the opponent, either on the mat or standing upright, therefore wrestlers need to have the muscle strength to accomplish the task.

American football involves short bursts of powerful play and short periods of recovery. Athletes need muscular strength to resist fatigue, avoid injury, and last longer in the game.

p69 Activity

Support and Challenge

For example:

Sport	Team or individual	Why speed is required
Swimming	Individual	Speed is needed to be able to cover the distance in the shortest amount of time and beat your opponents. Speed is needed in starts, turns, and stroke rate
Rowing	Team	Speed is very important in short-distance rowing as the quicker the stroke rate the faster the distance will be covered in

Challenge

High speed is important in sports that require short bursts of intense muscle work, it involves the ability to move all or part of the body as quickly as possible.

p69 Check my learning:

1 a Surfing is a complete physical sport. Paddling for a wave requires strength in the shoulders, upper back and core. To 'pop up' from lying on the board requires strength in the chest, shoulders and back. Once on the wave, strength is needed in the quads and glutes.

  b Football requires strength in the glutes, quadriceps and hamstrings to provide the force behind many football movements. The glutes and hamstrings drive your legs back behind you, and the quadriceps extend your knees, as needed for kicking.

2

Individual sports	Team sports
Swimming	Football
Cycling	Ice hockey
100 m sprint	Baseball

p70 Activity

Support

1 Golf requires flexibility in the shoulder in order to be able to swing the club.

2 Whole body flexibility is required in diving to be able to perform many of the movements well, and to prevent injury.

3 Flexibility is important for figure skaters to reach and maintain different body positions. If the body isn't used to moving that way, there is a greater risk of injury.

4 Learner's choice.

5 Learner's choice.

p71 Activity

Support

Mark Cavendish (Tour de France cyclist) has a physique that consists of a slight and skinny upper body and large muscular thighs. This is perfect for cycling as the muscle mass in his legs will help produce the power and force needed, and he carries very little other body fat or muscle mass and so, he does not need to work harder than necessary to move his body.

Dina Asher-Smith (track and field athlete) has an all-over toned and muscular physique. As a sprinter her low body fat will ensure she is not carrying excess fat mass which can negatively impact speed, and her large muscles will produce the power and speed required.

Owen Farrell (rugby player) has a large build with lots of muscle mass. Rugby is a physically demanding sport that requires players to have high levels of muscle mass and relatively low body fat levels. This is so they can run or sprint, as well as tackle and scrum.

p71 Check my learning

1 E.g. I have flexible hips and hamstrings. This is because I practise yoga regularly, which is known to increase flexibility, but also I weight train, with exercises such as the Romanian deadlift stretching the hamstrings when under load.

2 Body composition can greatly affect sporting performance. Strength and power are directly

related to muscle mass (size) because a bigger muscle is able to contract with more force, which can improve your acceleration and maximum speed. Lower body fat can have a beneficial effect on your endurance and agility as any additional weight will create more resistance during exercise, meaning that your muscles have to work harder to maintain a certain level of performance.

p73 Activity

Support

Sport/ activity	The components of fitness that are most important for performance
Volleyball	Speed
	Muscular endurance
Tennis	Aerobic endurance
	Flexibility
Rock climbing	Muscular strength
	Muscular endurance
Crossfit	Aerobic endurance
	Muscular endurance

Challenge

E.g. The aim of Crossfit has been to develop broad, general and functional fitness. It is a form of high intensity interval training, with Crossfit workouts focusing on strength and conditioning and being made up of functional movements performed at a high intensity level. This will require, and develop, aerobic endurance and muscular endurance.

p73 Check my learning

1 Physical fitness means being physically strong and healthy, and able to carry out the tasks and movements required by your everyday life.

2 E.g. In swimming, aerobic and muscular endurance are the most important components of physical fitness and will have a direct impact on performance. When swimming a particular stroke such as backstroke, the same arm and leg action is repeated, therefore a high level of muscular endurance is required to avoid fatigue, which will lead to stroke deterioration. A high level of aerobic endurance is needed to keep supplying oxygen to the muscles for a sustained period. Without this constant supply, the muscles will not have enough oxygen to meet the demands of the activity and performance will decrease.

p75 Activity

Support

E.g. The long jump requires quick, explosive leg power. Long jumpers need to be able to run fast and use their hip strength to pull their body up on take-off and forward during the landing.

p75 Check my learning

1 Skill-related fitness is the aspect of sport that is needed to be able to successfully perform the more technical aspects of many sports and activities.

2 Power is a combination of strength and speed. It is the ability to use strength at speed, whereas muscular strength is the amount of force a muscle can exert against a resistance. The main difference is that strength refers to the ability to overcome resistance, while power refers to the ability to overcome resistance in the shortest period of time.

p76 Activity

Support

- Basketball – agility is important in basketball as it is not played in a straight line, but instead requires constant changes of direction.

- Skiing – agility is needed in skiing to constantly adapt to terrain changes, and snow conditions while staying balanced.

- Table tennis – table tennis is not a static sport. It requires you to make rapid movements and reactions to get into position, change direction and react to the ball.

- Ice hockey – players must have agility to move and change direction quickly and control and pass the ball, all while staying balanced.

Challenge

Being able to move quickly also relies on cognitive functions. If an athlete can interpret what they are seeing quickly then they will be able to respond to it more quickly and ensure they are in the right position. For example, in badminton, being able to interpret how the opponent is holding their raquet will give information on the type of shot that is coming their way and the athlete can position themself best to return it.

p77 Activity

Support

E.g. Fencing requires quick reaction times. Points are scored by touching or hitting the opponent; therefore it is important to be able to react quickly and defensively to move away from an opponent's attacking movements but also react quickly to take advantage of an opportunity for an offensive move.

E.g. Reaction times in netball are important as being able to react quickly can mean intercepting the ball from the opposition and taking control of play.

p77 Check my learning

1 Judo players need good agility to perform complicated sequences of moves such as combinations and counters. Good agility will

also allow them to link other defensive and offensive techniques.

Footballers require agility to be able to change direction with the ball in order to keep the defence from getting possession of the ball. Being able to stop, start and change direction quickly gives players a greater chance of keeping possession of the ball and completing plays.

2 Reaction time is important for good performance and success in many sports. For example, a hockey goalkeeper only has a split second to react to a shot. If they have a slow reaction time then the goal can have already been scored, whereas by improving their reaction time they will have a greater chance of saving the ball.

p79 Activity: Balance

Support

Sports and activities that involve static balance	Sports and activities that involve dynamic balance
Gymnastics, yoga, snooker	Gymnastics, football, surfing, equestrian

Challenge

Static balance is needed in yoga to be able to maintain a pose or position for an amount of time.

Dynamic balance is needed in surfing to be able to stay on the board whilst changing foot and body position to manoeuvre along the wave.

p79 Activity: Coordination

Support

Learner's own test result.

Challenge

An easy way to improve hand-eye coordination is to play catch with yourself by throwing a tennis ball against a wall and practising catching it with one hand, and then the other. This drill will improve your ability to react quickly and accurately to what you're seeing.

p79 Check my learning

1	Hand-eye coordination sports	Hand-foot coordination sports
	Tennis, badminton, volleyball	Football, mountain biking, trail running

2 Balance is the ability to maintain control of your body and keep upright, whereas coordination is the ability to move two or more body parts at the same time in a controlled way.

p83 Activity

Support

Activity	Skills needed
Diving	Strength, flexibility, coordination, timing
Rugby	Passing, catching, running, tackling, kicking, teamwork, positioning
Golf	Grip, aim, set up, club selection, pivot, swing, judging distance and conditions

Challenge

Activity	Skills needed	Basic or complex	Open or closed	Self-paced or externally paced
Diving	Strength	Basic	Closed	Self
	Flexibility	Basic	Closed	Self
	Coordination	Complex	Closed	Self
	Timing	Complex	Open	External
Rugby	Passing	Basic	Open	External
	Catching	Basic	Open	External
	Running	Basic	Closed	Self
	Tackling	Complex	Open	External
	Kicking	Basic	Open	External
	Teamwork	Complex	Open	External
	Positioning	Complex	Open	External
Golf	Grip	Basic	Closed	Self
	Aim	Complex	Closed	Self
	Set up	Complex	Closed	Self
	Club selection	Basic	Open	Self
	Pivot	Complex	Closed	Self
	Swing	Complex	Closed	Self
	Judging distance and conditions	Complex	Open	External

p83 Check my learning

1 A skill is the expertise or talent needed to perform a sport or movement.

2 Describe the factors that make up a skill: basic or complex, open or closed, self-paced or externally paced.

- **Basic or complex:** The number of parts to the skills that need to be mastered, the more complex a skill the longer it will take to become proficient.

- **Open or closed:** Whether the environment in which the skill is performed is stable or variable. If it varies then athletes will have to adapt their skills to a changing or unpredictable environment.

- **Self-paced or externally paced:** Whether the timing of the performance of the skill is determined by the athlete or factors external to the athlete, such as the start of a race or the presence of an opponent.

p85 Activity

Support

E.g. One of the main 'game changer' strategy aims of England Football (the FA) is to win a major tournament as international tournament success will transform English football and be inspirational for millions of boys and girls.

Challenge

A strategy is a long-term or overall aim, whereas tactics are the smaller specific steps that are taken to achieve the overall aim. The main difference is the size of the goal and how long it may take to achieve; tactics are simpler and shorter term.

p85 Check my learning

1 A strategy is a long-term or overall aim. Tactics are the smaller specific steps that are taken to achieve the overall aim.

2 Many factors may influence the strategy or tactics a tennis player could adopt at a tournament and affect the style of play they choose to implement. These could include the type of court they are playing on, grass, clay or indoor, the weather conditions, any injuries they may have or have recently had, the number of players and rounds in the tournament, and who their strongest opponents are and when they might meet them in the tournament.

p87 Activity

Support

Sport	Example of an isolated practice
Swimming	Catch up pull practice
Badminton	Forehand smash with recovery
Netball	Shooting from around the circle
American football	Ball throw and catch practice

Challenge

A hurdler preparing for a competition would want to perfect their technique to ensure they are moving as efficiently as possible. They may want to focus on isolated practices on skills such as their start or hurdle take off.

p87 Check my learning

1 An isolated practice involves performing a skill or technique in the same conditions with the same equipment until it becomes automatic. An example from a team sport would be a rugby scrum, and an example from an individual sport would be block starts in swimming.

2 The advantages of isolated practices are that as the situation and environment are controlled, players do not have to worry about an opponent and so can focus on the skill and practice without the complexity of a game situation. They are also an easy way to introduce a sport to new players, and can be used when space is restricted, or can be practised individually, so do not need lots of players.

The disadvantages of isolated practices are that it is not a realistic game-like situation, which means that other skills that are needed in games, such as judgment, interpretation and decision-making, are not practised. Also, due to the repeated practising of one skill, isolated practices can become boring to players.

p89 Activity

Support

Sport	Competition situation practice or drill
Hockey	Attacking the circle drills with defenders
Football	Corner set plays
Rowing	Set up a 'friendly' or mock competition race

Challenge

E.g. The ways that a hockey practice could be made more competition-like are:

1 Invite an audience or supporters to watch. This will increase the pressure felt by the players.

2 Tell players their performance will be being analysed and assessed. This will increase pressure and anxiety as the athletes will know they are being watched and judged.

3 Set up a competition, increase the stakes and have a prize for the winners.

p89 Check my learning

1 Competition situation practices aim to replicate the conditions of real a match and therefore help athletes to learn how to perform as well in a competition as they do in practice.

2 Competition situation practices are a useful training tool as athletes not only need to be technically proficient and skilled at their sport, but also need to be able to apply and perform these skills in competition conditions to win. These types of practices aim to make practices

as match-like as possible such as the number of players, introducing opponents, using the full area of play and having the presence of an official.

p93 Activity

Support

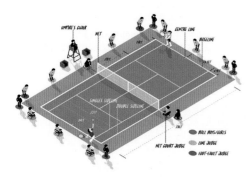

Challenge

Without an official, there would be no neutral or unbiased person overseeing the football game and enforcing the rules. The rules of the game would be managed by the teams and players themselves and may lead to intentional or unintentional cheating. For example, a player may score a goal by touching the ball with their hand but deny that this happened – in this scenario who would decide if the goal was allowed or not? Officials are needed to enforce the prescriptive rules of the game to ensure fairness.

p93 Check my learning

1   A sports official is someone who manages the play of a competition and ensures the rules and laws of the sport are followed correctly.

2   The role of a referee or umpire is to ensure that all of the rules (or laws) of the game are followed by the players. They have to make decisions on whether an act is legal or not, according to the sporting rules and set the appropriate penalty.

It is the responsibility of a referee or umpire to be knowledgeable on the rules, confident in their ability and decisive at applying the rules. They need to be able to stay calm, communicate well and not allow players to question their decisions.

p95 Activity

Support

E.g. In cricket there are the following officials:

- there are two on-field umpires. One umpire is positioned behind the stumps at the bowler's end of the pitch – they make decisions on leg before wicket (LBW) appeals, no balls, wides and leg byes. The second umpire stands at the square leg position and makes decisions on stumpings and run outs

- matches which have television cameras at the ground have a third umpire

- timekeeper

- scorer, in professional games there are two scorers.

Challenge

Sport played at an amateur or grassroots level does not have the funding or sponsorship of high-end top-level sport, therefore it is not always possible to have dedicated scorers, timekeepers or video reviewers. In these instances, other officials will take on the additional duties, such as the umpire or referee taking on score keeping.

p95 Check my learning

1   The role of the timekeeper is to measure the duration of the game, the intervals of play, the rest periods, and start and stop the clock at various stages, ensuring accurate time is kept.

2   The role of the video review official is to view the video replay and advise the referee or umpire on what occurred. The main benefit is that it gives referees a second chance to look at an incident before deciding on the appropriate course of action, or it can ensure unfair decisions are ruled out.

p97 Activity

Support

	Football	Boxing
1 What must the referee/ umpire/ judge wear?	FIFA allows referees to wear shirts in one of five specified colours (black, red, yellow, green or blue). Must also wear black shorts, black socks (with white stripes in some cases), and black shoes	White button shirt with black bow tie, black trousers (not jeans) and black flat-soled shoes
2 What level of fitness is required?	FIFA has two fitness tests for men and women that referees must pass at least once a year	None specified
3 What equipment is needed by officials to carry out their role?	Whistle, watch, penalty cards, data wallet with pen and paper, and a coin	None specified

Challenge

The fitness requirements for officials will vary depending on the sport, this is because it is not as important in some sports for officials to be as physically fit as it is in others. For example, a netball umpire needs to be able to run along the side lines and keep up with play, whereas a tennis referee can view all play from their stationary elevated position.

p97 Check my learning

1   To be an effective and respected official, there are certain responsibilities that must be fulfilled such as appearance, fitness and equipment. By meeting the requirements the official is showing that they take their role seriously and demonstrating their commitment to their position.

p99 Activity

Support

E.g. Prior to a match, hockey umpires have a responsibility to carry out pre-match checks including checking the pitch, the state of goals and nets, and the playing surface.

Challenge

Carrying out checks on uniform, equipment and facilities are vital to ensuring the safe play of a sport. Officials need to verify that safety rules are being complied with and ensure there is no risk of injury to sports players or spectators. For example, if there is debris on the playing area there is a risk of injury to players.

p99 Check my learning

1.   Sports officials have a responsibility to ensure that every event is carried out safely in order to protect players, spectators, coaches and all officials. Carrying out pre-match health and safety checks is one way of ensuring this.

2.   The best referees and umpires are those who are able to communicate effectively with players. It can be difficult to make decisions in a fast-paced match and not everyone will agree with them, but ensuring they are communicated in a calm and clear manner will ensure control is maintained.

p101 Activity

Support

Sports that play a fixed amount of time	Sports that are played until a certain number of points
Netball, football, rugby, basketball	Tennis, badminton, snooker, volleyball

Challenge

In team sports, substitutions may be used to replace a player who has become tired or injured, or one who is performing poorly, or for tactical reasons. Substitutions are not allowed in individual or paired sports as these are testing the skill and performance of one person and so would not be appropriate.

p101 Check my learning

1 Rolling substitutions allow players to enter and leave the game for other players an unlimited number of times during the course of the game, as allowed in ice hockey. In sports that use set substitutions, a fixed number is allowed during a game and only at certain times, such as after an interval or when play has stopped.

2 Some sports matches are played for a fixed amount of time, and the winner will be the person who has performed the best within that set period, for example netball or hockey. Other sports matches are played until a player or team reaches the number of points required to win, such as tennis or snooker.

p103 Activity

Support

Sport	Size of playing area
Basketball	28 m long × 15 m wide
Karate	8 m × 8 m, with 2 m on all sides as a safety area
Squash	9.75 m long × 6.4 m wide
Volleyball	18 m long × 9 m wide
Beach volleyball	16 m long × 8 m wide, with additional clearance of 5-6 m on all sides
Rounders	Senior principal play area 20 m × 12 m. Overall area required 100 m × 60 m

Challenge

E.g. In netball, if a game is tied at the end of the fourth quarter in a play-off or placing match, extra time of two seven-minute halves will be played. If a tie still remains at the end of extra time, then play will continue until one team leads by two goals.

In cricket, a tie occurs when both teams end on equal scores at the end of a game. A draw is also possible, which happens when one or both teams have not completed their innings by the scheduled end of play.

p103 Check my learning

1 In some games, players need to gain an advantage to target a specific goal, for example the goal in hockey.

In other games, the distance equipment is moved will determine the number of points achieved by the performer, for example how high a high jumper jumps.

Some sports have clear-cut and objective methods of scoring, such as when a net is scored in basketball.

Other sports are subjective, and judges assess performance to award points. For example, in figure skating.

2 Learner's choice.

It is important to check the size of the playing areas according to each sport's regulations as otherwise scores and results may not count if games are not played on the correct size playing area.

p105 Activity

Support

E.g. Rules on equipment in netball	E.g. Rules on equipment in rugby
Size 5 netballs are the official size used by players over the age of 10 years Children aged under 10 should use a size 4 netball	World Rugby requires that size 5 balls are used by men's and women's teams in senior international competitions. The ball must be oval and made of four panels that are leather or a suitable synthetic material Balls must have a length in line between 280–300 millimetres, an end-to-end circumference of 740–770 millimetres, and width circumference of 580–620 millimetres In senior rugby, players may choose to wear headguards shoulder pads, and mouth guards but it is not mandatory

Challenge

Some sports do not have mandatory rules for protective equipment but state that additional protective equipment may be worn by players if they wish. Players may choose to wear additional protective equipment to reduce the risk of injury.

p105 Check my learning

1 In sports that involve equipment such as balls and sticks there are often strict rules on the protective equipment that must be worn by players. This is to protect them from injury. For example, boxers must wear a gum shield. These sports may also set out optional

protective equipment that players can wear if they wish to further protect themselves, for example a head guard in adult male boxing is optional.

2 In netball, play is restarted after a foul with a free or penalty pass or shot, depending on what the infringement was and where it happened. Play is restarted after a goal is scored by returning to a centre pass. These alternate between teams regardless of who scored last.

p107 Activity

Support

Sport	Position of officials
E.g. Volleyball	The 'first' referee is positioned in an elevated position in line with the net The 'second' referee is on the other side of the net opposite the first referee and officiates from the ground
E.g. Surfing	The judging panel are based on the beach in a quiet and private judging area with a clear view of the competition area
E.g. Water polo	Ideally, water polo games have two referees, one for each side of the pool

Challenge

The best position for officials is one where they can see clearly and make the correct decision. For example, in surfing competitions, being based on the beach will mean the panel can see the surfer in front of the wave and will have a clear view of all of their movements.

p107 Check my learning

1 Rule violations can be accidental or intentional, direct or indirect. The way in which rule violations are dealt with varies across sports, and may include possession being awarded to the opponent, a free kick/ pass, being booked or a player being sent off.

For example, in netball a defender who is less than 1 metre (3 ft) away from a player making a shot will have a penalty pass or shot awarded against them. Or in football, a player who intentionally performs a late tackle will be issued a yellow or red card.

2 The use of hand signals assists officials in communicating their decisions and means all competitors and spectators receive a clear message about how the regulations are being applied to play.

p111 Activity

Support

Whole drill	Part drill
Triangle passing drill – a simple passing and receiving drill that focuses on the basics of a good first touch and positive 10-yard pass	The stepover – a skill of quick feet where a player feints a change of direction by throwing a foot over the ball, then quickly shifts the ball in the opposite direction and accelerates away from the defender
Cones set up in a triangle	
A total of eight players are needed with two groups of three and a group of two on each cone	Initial practice – go through the motions while standing still with the ball
After each pass, the player follows the ball to join the back of the group	
Change direction every minute or less	

Challenge

E.g. Rugby passing four-stage drill:

Stage 1 – players are positioned along a straight line approx. 2 m apart. They stay still and pass the ball along the line to the next player, who then passes it on until it gets to the end.

Stage 2 – players practise lateral passing whilst travelling at varying speeds, walking/jogging/running.

Stage 3 – a few passive opponents are introduced. They walk towards the line but do not interfere. The line of players must pass the ball around the opponents.

Stage 4 – the opponents become active and will try to intercept the ball. The line must successfully pass the ball from one end of the line to the other without it being intercepted.

p111 Check my learning

1 The aim of isolated drills is that through focusing practice on a particular area the athlete will progress through the stages of skill acquisition towards autonomous skill mastery.

2 A passive opposition is an opponent that is not actively involved in play but their presence adds an element of pressure. An active opposition is one that is fully engaged in play and making their own decisions.

p113 Activity

Support

A football example of a conditioned practice focused on ball handling would be a three-player vs three-player mini game. Each team has one goal to defend and one goal to attack. The ball is not allowed to stop or go over head height. By passing and dribbling the ball players must try to score three goals. The first team to score three goals wins.

Challenge

The three-player vs three-player conditioned practice will develop players' passing and dribbling skills. They will have a much smaller space to work within and so need to be accurate with their passing so as not to be intercepted.

p113 Check my learning

1 A conditioned practice alters the rules of the game so that a practice can still take part in a game situation but focus on one particular skill.

2 E.g. Allows players to practise skills in a game context; players can practise solving problems under match-like conditions; allows players to develop confidence in transferring skills into real game situations.

p115 Activity

Support

Learner's choice.

Challenge

Learner's choice.

p115 Check my learning

1 Skill demonstration increase a player's understanding of a skill by providing an accurate model that they need to replicate. It allows them to see what the skill looks like and how it is performed.

2 E.g. Make sure the correct form is used; demonstrate the skill several times; slow the skill down so athletes can see every movement involved in performing the skill.

p117 Activity

Support

Swimming, freestyle catch-up drill.

Teaching points:

- keep one arm extended
- wait to start your next arm stroke until your other arm taps the extended arm
- stay in a streamlined position
- focus on keeping body position high
- make sure your hands stay directly in front of the shoulder
- drill is to practise patience and balance.

Challenge

When giving teaching points, coaches should use short sentences and highlight the key points in order of priority to ensure the information being given is easily understood.

p117 Check my learning

1 Not all athletes will learn best by watching, which is why it is importnt to use verbal teaching points as well demonstrations.

2 Teaching points should be short and concise so that they are easily understood. They should just contain the key aspects in order of priority that need to be highlighted to ensure the correct and safe performing of a technique or skill.

p119 Activity

Support

Sport: netball.

Limited space drill: end zone game, can be played in any marked-out area with any number of players. Court markings and posts are not needed. Players have to pass the ball to their shooter who is stood inside the 'end zone' (a channel at the end of the marked area) without having the ball intercepted by the other team.

Limited equipment drill: agility drill if no netball court/balls/posts available. Set up a course in which players have to practise different footwork, for example run forwards to first marker, side shuffle to next marker, run zig zag between next markers, sprint to next marker, etc.

Limited players drill: defensive rebound drill. Two players and two defenders around the area of the post. Player takes a shot; the shot is missed in order for the defender to jump and collect the rebound.

Challenge

If drills are not adapted to the space, equipment and number of players available, then it is likely that practices will be disorganised and ineffective, and players will not be motivated. For example, if a higher-than-normal number of players attended for a rugby practice but the drills that had been planned only involved using a small number of players at a time, then this will mean many of the players will be left doing nothing and they will become bored.

p119 Check my learning

Drills and practices are used to improve participants' sporting techniques. To be effective, it is important to know how to organise and demonstrate them. Therefore, coaches need to consider the space, equipment and participants available and plan appropriate drills to match these factors.

p121 Activity

Support

Learner's choice.

Challenge

Learner's choice.

p121 Check my learning

1 The timing of practices is important to make sure that players maintain motivation and interest. If a particular drill is performed for too long then players may become fatigued in one area. Coaches need to ensure that their sessions are focused and developing the range of skills needed for the sport.

p123 Activity

Support

Learner's choice.

Challenge

Learner's choice.

p123 Check my learning

1 A sports coach is a person involved in the direction, instruction and training of a sports team or athlete. Their role is to help athletes work towards achieving their full potential. They do this by observing participants, giving instructions, highlighting teaching points and providing feedback.

Component 3

p129 Activity

Learner's own response.

p129 Check my learning

1 A component of fitness is a part of fitness or a way to split fitness into different parts. Components of fitness are important for sport performance. Sports and activities require different amounts of different components of fitness for the performer to be successful.

2 Physical components of fitness are the basic elements of fitness: aerobic endurance, muscular endurance, flexibility, speed, muscular strength and body composition. Skill-related components of fitness involve movements that allow you to complete an activity or skill.: agility, balance, coordination, power and reaction time.

p131 Activity

- False
- True
- True
- True
- False.

p131 Check my learning

1 Progressive overload is continuing to increase the intensity of exercise over time to make continued fitness gains.

2 You should use the principles of training to design a training programme because they allow the body to make physical adaptations

to the body, which will improve the component of fitness being trained.

p133 Check my learning

1 Exercise intensity means the amount of effort or work it takes to complete a task.

2 Exercise intensity can be measured by calculating maximum heart rate (MHR), by using the Borg RPE scale and by calculating 1RM and 15RM.

3 Training zones are given as the range of heart rate values you should work within for training intensity to result in effective fitness improvement.

p135 Check my learning

1 The Borg Rating Scale of Perceived Exertion measures exercise intensity that runs from 6 to 20.

2 1RM can be used to identify muscular strength. 15RM can be used to identify muscular endurance.

3 Technology used to monitor exercise intensity can provide you with quick and easy measurements, it can calculate exercise intensity for you – you do not need to carry out any calculations or record heart rate.

p139 Check my learning

1 Reasons for carrying out fitness tests include:

- It gives baseline data for monitoring/ improving performance.
- Useful to determine if training programmes are working.

The results can give a performer something to aim for.
- It can design training programmes based on test results.

2 The term 'informed consent' means a person formally agrees, this is usually done by signing a contract.

p141 Check my learning

1 Calibrating equipment means you need to check that it is working correctly and measuring what it is designed to. For example, a stopwatch should accurately record seconds and minutes. You could start two stopwatches at the same time to check that they record the same amount of time.

2 To ensure fitness test results are valid you should record the results accurately in a table and make sure you use the correct units of measurement.

p142 Activity

Advantages: a lot of people can take part at the same time, it doesn't require any expensive or difficult to set up equipment.

Disadvantages: it might not be related to the type of activity you take part in, for example swimming or rowing don't involve running.

p143 Check my learning

The main advantage of having different tests to measure a sports person's aerobic endurance is to help ensure the reliability and validity of the results.

p145 Activity

1 Learner's own results.

2 Learner's own results.

p145 Check my learning

The mult-istage fitness test (MSFT), Yo-Yo test and Harvard step test can all be used to measure aerobic endurance. The MSFT and Yo-Yo test can be completed in a relatively small space, only 20 m is needed and lots of people can participate at the same time. They are both maximal tests, the participants continue until they are exhausted. The Harvard step test requires benches, a metronome and stopwatch. The height of the benches is different for males and females. This test is sub-maximal.

p146 Activity

A high level of muscular endurance is the ability to contract a muscle or group of muscles against resistance, for example bodyweight or weights, for a period of time. These muscular contractions allow the performer to work for long periods of time at a steady intensity. Muscular endurance is needed for those performers who take part in rugby basketball and netball, martial arts, gymnastics, boxing, kayaking and rowing.

p147 Activity

The conditions of the testing environment for muscular endurance using the one-minute sit-up test need to be the same each time the test is undertaken. The performer should be fully warmed up and motivated and the equipment (stopwatch) should be calibrated. The test should be carried out on a flat surface, with a mat, and ideally inside so that rain and wind do not affect the performer's ability to complete the test.

p147 Check my learning

1 It is important to carry out a thorough warm-up before a muscle endurance test to reduce the chance of injury and ensure the muscles are ready to carry out endurance exercises.

2 The term 'RPM' means reps per minute. It measures a performer's speed. For instance, the number of sit-ups they can complete for one minute.

p148 Activity

1 Motivation can affect the reliability of the sit and reach test because if the performer is not

motivated and not interested in carrying out the test they will not try their hardest. If the test is repeated and on this next occasion the performer tries their best, the results cannot be compared.

2 The performer should be fully warmed up and highly motivated before taking the test.

p149 Check my learning

1 Gymnastics, javelin and hurdling.

2 By making sure that the test is appropriate for the sports performer and the sport or activity they participate in. You should check the equipment is calibrated and follow the standard procedure for the test.

p150 Activity

1 Validity is an accurate reflection of something.

2 Validity of a speed fitness test can be ensured by making sure that the results are measured and recorded correctly, the standard procedures are followed, and all equipment (stopwatches, gate timers) is calibrated.

p151 Check my learning

1 Normative data is information which is characteristic for a specific group which is used as a point of reference. Using normative data provides a reliable way to compare the athlete's fitness test results against the 'norms' for their age range.

2 Using normative data when referring to fitness test results allows you to compare, analyse and evaluate results.

3 One strength of a speed fitness test for measuring speed of a rower is that it can be done easily, without much equipment and with several people at once.

One weakness of a speed fitness test for measuring speed of a rower is that the skills used in the test do not replicate those used in rowing.

p153 Activity

The One Rep Maximum is a good test to measure muscular strength in a wide range of sports performers because you can select different muscles to test, for example biceps or quadriceps.

p153 Check my learning

1 So that they can ensure validity and reliability of the test. The test administrator needs to know how to perform the test so that the performer does not get injured.

2 The performer needs to know the technique for weightlifting before carrying out the 1RM test for muscular strength to make sure that they do not get injured.

p155 Activity

BMI testing might not be the best way to measure body composition for a performer with low levels of muscle, such as a jockey, because it doesn't take into account the amount of muscle in the calculation. So, the result might not be a true reflection of their BMI.

p155 Check my learning

1 Body composition is what your body is made of: bone, muscle and fat.

2 BMI, BIA and waist to hip ratio can be used to test body composition.

3 The performer needs to be properly hydrated as dehydration can result in a higher body fat reading in BIA testing.

p156 Activity

1 Motivation can affect the reliability of the Illinois agility run test because the performer is not motivated and not interested in carrying out the test they will not try their hardest. If the test is repeated and on this next occasion the performer tries their best the results cannot be compared. The performer should be fully warmed up and highly motivated before taking the test.

2 The environmental conditions should be the same each time testing is carried out to make sure that the results can be compared and are valid. You could not compare the results from an agility test completed on a dry day to one on a wet surface on a rainy day.

p157 Check my learning

1 To ensure that agility tests are reliable you should make sure that everyone follows the test protocols, and the equipment is calibrated.

2 An advantage of using the T-test to measure agility of a netball team is that it does not require much space, any expensive equipment or a large area. A disadvantage is that there is a risk of injury if the participants are not warmed up and are rushing to get the whole team through testing.

P159 Activity

Challenge

Someone who has longer limbs will be able to score higher than someone with shorter limbs, but this does not mean that they have a higher level of balance.

p159 Check my learning

Balance is important for a sports performer because it allows them to perform skills without falling over.

p160 Activity

For three selected sports or activities that require a high level of coordination, describe how coordination is used in that sport.

p161 Activity

Support

Tennis, netball and cricket.

Challenge

The stick flip test might not be suitable to measure coordination for all sport participants because not all sports require as much coordination of the arms, such as football, cycling and sprinting.

p161 Check my learning

1 You could use the stick flip test to test coordination for a large group of people if you had lots of sticks needed for the test. The test doesn't need much time, space or expensive equipment and there is a low risk of injury.

2 Football, sprinting and cycling.

p162 Activity

It is important for the person carrying out the ruler drop test to accurately line up the ruler before dropping it to make sure that the test is valid, and the results can be compared. It makes sure that the test is carried out exactly the same way every time.

p163 Activity

The benefits of carrying out an online reaction time test are that it is a reliable method of testing because the test is the same every time, it is also easy to setup and doesn't require much equipment or time.

The weaknesses of carrying out an online reaction time test are they are limited to using a keyboard which means the test is only assessing a sports performer's hands and fingers reaction to a response on the screen, this does not reflect the way most sports performers use reaction time in their sport, such as a sprinter leaving the blocks when they hear the starting gun.

Sports performers who could benefit from using online reaction time tests to measure their reaction time include sprinters, netball players and swimmers.

p163 Check my learning

1 The term 'reaction time' means the quickness of a response.

2 The benefit of high levels of reaction time for a performer who takes part in a racket sport such as tennis is that they can react quickly to the ball coming towards them. They need to get their body and racket into position quickly or they risk missing the ball.

3 Pre-test procedures that need to be followed before administering a reaction time test include calibrating equipment and collecting informed consent.

p164 Activity

Different types of sports performers would select the vertical jump or standing long/broad jump test to measure power because it is more suited to the types of movements used in their sport, for example a netball player needs to be able to jump upwards whilst standing still, so they might select the vertical jump. Sports performers might also choose to use both tests to measure power because both tests are relevant for their sport, for example a rock climber or basketball player.

p165 Activity

Motivation can affect the reliability of the Margaria-Kalamen test because if the performer is not motivated and not interested in carrying out the test, they will not try their hardest. If the test is repeated and on this next occasion the performer tries their best, the results cannot be compared. The performer should be fully warmed up and highly motivated before taking the test.

p165 Check my learning

1 Power is a combination of strength and speed.

2 Sports activities which require power are often short bursts, explosive and speedy.

3 An advantage is that the test requires no expensive equipment. A disadvantage of the vertical jump test to measure power for a boxer is that the test is not relevant to the boxer's sport because they do not jump vertically in their sport.

p167 Activity

1 Aerobic endurance.

2 Speed.

3 Flexibility and speed.

4 Aerobic endurance and speed.

Name:	William Arthur (male)		Height (m):		1.71		
Age:	15		Weight (kg):		75		
Fitness component	Fitness test	Test 1	Test 2	Test 3	Average result	Unit	Rating
Aerobic endurance	12-minute Cooper run	2450	2810	2650	2637	m	Very good
Muscular endurance	One-minute press-up test	36	38	33	35.7	No. of reps	Good
Flexibility	Sit and reach test	8.9	10.11	9.2	9.40	cm	Average
Speed	30 m sprint test	4.4	4.3	4.4	4.37	secs	Below average
Muscular strength	Grip dynamometer	48	50	53	50.3	kg	Good

p167 Check my learning

1 Normative data is information which is characteristic for a specific group which is used as a point of reference.

2 A fitness test result is a measurement collected from a test, normative data is information from a large group of people who have completed the test previously. Normative data allows you to interpret the test result and make comparisons to 'average' results.

3 It is important to interpret data so that you can make comparisons with other people of a similar age and gender.

p171 Check my learning

1 The two components or parts that make up a warm-up include a pulse raiser and mobility/stretch.

2 A thorough warm-up should be performed before training to minimise the risk of injury and increase the performer's alertness.

p173 Check my learning

1 You identify exercise intensity by working out MHR or maximum heart rate. MHR is calculated by using the equation 220 minus your age.

2 A performer should work at 60–80 per cent MHR intensity to improve aerobic endurance.

p175 Check my learning

1 Continuous, circuit, Fartlek and interval training.

2 a Swimming endurance training drills to develop a strong aerobic base so they can swim greater distances with less muscle fatigue.

   b It is best to focus on aerobic training or jogging to develop the aerobic power and strength of the muscles.

p177 Check my learning

1 Flexibility is the range of movement at a joint.

2 The purpose of stretching muscles is to increase their elasticity, length, to prevent injuries and to increase blood flow (and oxygen delivery) to the muscle.

3 Types of stretching are proprioceptive neuromuscular facilitation (PNF), static active and static passive.

p179 Activity

Suggestions for a muscular endurance circuit training class of 10 people could include activities with 45 seconds of work, such as press-ups and different types of squats, and 15 seconds of rest.

A successful circuit for muscular endurance should use body resistance exercises or low-load weights with high repetitions.

p179 Check my learning

Appropriate muscular strength training for a rugby team with access to a sports field could include free weights. These could be used as part of a circuit or players could work in pairs with the weights. Equipment such as tyres or a player's own body weight could be used to replicate movements they use in the game, including scrums (pushing against another player or a stationary object) and flipping tyres to replicate tackling players.

p180 Activity

Strength is the amount of force a person can produce. To perform well in strength sports and activities the sports participants need muscles which can carry high loads and perform a low number of repetitions.

p181 Activity

1 Advantages: can increase the strength of targeted muscles and muscle groups for particular sports, safer than free weights – there is less chance of injury from not being able to lift the weight, participants can train alone.

   Disadvanages: The equipment is expensive, you might need to join a gym or leisure centre to use the equipment, each machine exercises only one muscle or muscle group, so many different pieces of equipment are required.

2 A thorough warm-up must be completed to prevent injury and it can become boring.

3 A beginner would benefit from using fixed resistance machines to train muscular strength, this would reduce the risk of injury and allow them to learn the correct technique before they use free weights.

p181 Check my learning

1 Weightlifting, basketball and rugby.

2 Use exercises which have a low number of repetitions and use high loads.

p182 Activity

Acceleration sprint training can benefit the performance of a 100 m sprinter because it will enable them to get out of the blocks quicker and improve their sprinting performance, especially their sprint start.

p183 Activity

A suitable method of training to develop speed for a 100m sprinter is interval training because it will allow the sprinter to work anaerobically and increase their speed on the track.

p183 Check my learning

1 Acceleration is an increase in the rate of velocity with time. Something that has velocity is moving with speed and direction.

2 For speed training you would increase the number of rest periods and increase your work intensity.

3 Hill runs, parachutes, sleds or using bungee ropes could help a hockey player improve their speed.

p184 Activity

1 SAQ stands for speed, agility and quickness.

2 To develop their physical ability and motor skills. This will improve their ability to perform skills such as balances, somersaults and jumps.

3 Sprinting and then changing direction over a set course, lunges and jumps.

p185 Check my learning

1 Agility is the ability to change direction quickly.

2 Advantages: you can make the drills specific to the tennis player's needs, for example catching a tennis ball, throwing the ball at a target, hitting the ball, running pyramids or shuttles.

Disadvantages: injury can occur if the performer is not properly warmed up, the drills need to be set up before the training session, which takes time and preparation.

p187 Activity

Jumping onto a high box or vault, lunging, two-footed kangaroo jumps.

p187 Check my learning

1 Plyometrics are exercises which involve the use of explosive movements which cause rapid muscle contractions.

2 Advantages: it doesn't require expensive equipment, it can be set up easily and quickly, it can mimic movements used in sports.

Disadvantages: it can lead to injury if the performer does not use the correct technique and it can be boring to repeat the same exercise over and over.

3 Beginners or anyone with an injury should not use plyometric training.

p188 Activity

1 They would be more stable and less likely to fall over when performing skills such as balances and tumbles.

2 A 16-year-old gymnast needs to be able to balance whilst they hold a position for a period of time (static balance), for example a handstand. They also need to be able to balance whilst moving (dynamic balance), for example during a floor routine they need to maintain their balance as they move from one part of the routine to another. A balance training programme for a 16-year-old gymnast should include both static and dynamic balance. For example they could include balances that require holding a position for longer periods of time and balances that require movement from one position to another without falling.

A 45-year-old weightlifter would require balance whilst they hold the weight, but also as they get into position, so they do not fall or drop the weight. The main type of balance required by a weightlifter is static balance. A balance training programme for a 45-year-old weightlifter could include balances which require the performer to remain still and hold positions for longer periods of time.

3 It is important to complete a suitable warm-up in order to avoid injury. The muscles and ligaments should be warm enough to allow them to stretch to complete the activity.

p189 Check my learning

1 Static balance is the ability to remain upright when stationary and dynamic balance is the ability to remain upright whilst moving.

2 A netball player could practise shooting into the goal or practise passing to improve their coordination.

3 A stimulus is something that produces a reaction. For example, a loud bang will make you look to see what made the noise. The noise is the stimulus.

4 By using a machine to pass balls to the player at different heights, speeds and directions, which they have to return.

p191 Activity

The advantages of using circuit training to improve aerobic endurance for a netball team are that they can all take part at the same time and there is no need for expensive equipment.

p191 Check my learning

1 Additional requirements for training methods are factors which allow a coach or athlete to select the most appropriate methods of training for an individual or group, their sport

or activity and the provision of facilities and equipment available to them.

2 The ease of set up could affect the selection of a training method for an individual athlete because it makes the method easy or difficult to use. If the method has little or no equipment and can be set-up quickly and easily by someone on their own, it is more likely to be used regularly by an athlete.

p193 Activity

Two other disadvantages of using fixed resistance machines as a training method to improve muscular strength include the risk of injury if the performer has not carried out a thorough warm-up. Even with fixed resistance machines there is a need for a partner or spotter to help them with the exercises and to make sure they are safe when lifting weights. Disadvantages can also include the availability of the machines and the cost. If the machines are kept in a sports centre or gym, sports performers can only access them when the facility is open. The machines are often very expensive, and this can limit the number of machines a sports performer has access to.

p193 Check my learning

1 Access to venue/location of training when referring to a training method means that the sports performer cannot carry out the training method without access to a specific venue or location. For example, if they need to use an athletics track and it is only open in the evenings the sports performer will not be able to train in the day.

2 Access to venue/location of training affects a training method's suitability for training an individual or a team because if the venue or location are far away the sports performer or team may not be able to get to there without requiring transport.

p195 Check my learning

1 The additional requirements for fitness training methods include: the number of people that can take part, cost of equipment, ease of set up, access to venue/location of training, risk of injury to the performer if performed incorrectly, effectiveness of training for given sports performer, specificity to component of fitness, replicating demands of the sport.

2 Cost is an additional requirement for fitness training methods because if the equipment is expensive, it will limit the ability to buy it and use the training method related to the equipment.

p197 Check my learning

The additional requirements for using fixed resistance machines and free weights to improve muscular strength include cost; if the cost is too much, the performer will not be able to afford to buy or use it. If the equipment is difficult to set up, it may not be used frequently or it might take a long time to set up, which means that training time is lost.

p199 Check my learning

1 Provision is something that has been provided or supplied, for example if a football pitch has been supplied, it is available to use.

2 Public provision.

3 Private provision.

4 If there are no facilities or equipment access, the performer will not be able to participate in their training method.

5 Learner's choice.

p201 Activity

When you take part in exercise your breathing rate increases; this is so that the body can breathe in more oxygen and deliver it to the working muscles. It also lets the body exhale more air and more waste product, carbon dioxide.

p201 Check my learning

1 Adaptation is a process of change which has made the body function better in its environment.

2 Cardiovascular and respiratory systems make up the cardiorespiratory system.

3 Long-term aerobic endurance adaptations to the cardiorespiratory system would be beneficial to an international triathlete because they include cardiac hypertrophy, a decreased resting heart rate, increased respiratory muscle strength and increased capillarisation around the alveoli. These four adaptations allow the heart to function more effectively, to pump more blood during each beat and to collect more oxygen from each breath, in which it can be delivered more effectively to the working muscles.

p202 Activity

The breathing rate of an Olympic marathon runner at rest is lower than that of a rugby player because a marathon runner's body has adapted to their cardiovascular endurance training and a result of this is a decreased resting heart rate. A rugby player needs cardiovascular endurance, but also speed, so they will train both components of fitness to be able to keep up with the pace of the game, their training will not decrease their resting heart rate as much as a marathon runner because they also need the ability to sprint.

p203 Check my learning

1 The main function of the respiratory system is to help you breathe. The respiratory system's main job is to move fresh air into your body while removing waste gases.

2 Long-term aerobic adaptations to the respiratory system would benefit an international triathlete by helping them to adapt to different climates and environments for competition.

p205 Check my learning

1 The main function of the muscular system is to produce movements.

2 The function of the skeletal system is to allow movement, support the body, protect internal organs and store minerals.

3 An increased range of movement permitted at a joint, increased flexibility of ligament and tendons, and increased muscle length.

4 They will have more movement at their joints, this would allow them to reach further forward with their arms to block a pass or shot at goal and they will be less likely to have an injury.

p206 Activity

1 Capillaries deliver and remove oxygenated and deoxygenated blood to and from the muscle tissue.

2 An increase in the number of capillaries surrounding muscle tissue means that more blood and nutrients can be delivered, and more waste products can be removed. This will allow the muscle to use oxygen more quickly, this means the rower's muscles will be able to contract for longer without fatigue.

p207 Check my learning

1 Swimming, rowing, long-distance running, boxing and cycling.

2 Muscular endurance training helps to increase muscle tone, this improves posture and the muscles which stabilise joints during movement. Joint stability helps to reduce the risk of injury to muscles and joints and also allows the correct technique to be used, which will better improve muscular endurance.

p209 Activity

It can help to increase their power, strength and muscular endurance due to an increase in muscle size.

p209 Check my learning

1 Ligaments and tendons allow movements by pulling on muscles and bones. Ligaments attach bones to bones, and tendons attach muscles to bone.

2 Bone density is the consistency or how compact the bone is.

3 By increasing their strength and power so that they can put more force behind a punch or jab and are able to block their opponent with more strength.

p211 Activity

1 Lactic acid is a waste product that builds up during activity.

2 Because it will allow your muscles to work more efficiently for longer and allow them to recover faster after exercise.

p211 Check my learning

1 Learner's own response. Examples include: Sprinting, football, hurdles.

2 Learner's own response. For example, benefits include an increased tolerance to lactic acid and the ability for muscles to work more efficiently for longer, and also allowing them to recover faster after exercise.

p214 Activity

1 The aim could be to increase their ability to perform somersaults in gymnastics, the objective could be to improve agility by carrying out SAQ training.

2 The aim could be to improve their aerobic endurance and the objective could be to complete a training programme for aerobic endurance, which contains Fartlek training.

3 Aims and objectives give a clear indication of the purpose of the training programme.

p215 Check my learning

1 One aim could be to improve their aerobic endurance.

2 One objective could be to improve their aerobic endurance by following an aerobic training programme that includes interval training.

3 Collecting personal information allows you to design a programme to meet the specific needs of the performer.

4 The cyclist's attitude and motivation can impact a training programme negatively or positively. If they have a positive attitude, they will be highly motivated to train and follow their training programme. If they are not motivated and have a poor attitude, they will not train regularly and may not follow the training programme regularly.

p216 Activity

1 Olivia has a contraindication to exercise, surgery to her knee. But it was over a year ago and she is now ok to train.

2 You should make sure that they are fit to exercise, this might mean asking the participant to check with their doctor to get

a signed letter that states that they are fit enough to take part in a training programme.

p217 Activity

1 Smoking, stress and time spent training/taking part in physical activity.

2 Stress could make Olivia lose motivation and not maintain regular training. It could also cause her to lose sleep and overeat or undereat.

3 Knowing someone's occupation is a good indication of their physical activity level.

p217 Check my learning

1 Contraindications are factors that could be harmful to health.

2 Questionnaires and interviews.

p218 Activity

1 Hugo.

2 Muscular endurance.

3 Muscular strength and power.

4 Power or aerobic endurance.

5 Power or aerobic endurance.

p219 Check my learning

1 Frequency, Intensity, Time, Type.

2 To make sure that it is tailored to the sports performer. The frequency identifies how often the performer trains, intensity means how hard they train, time shows how long they should work or train for and type allows the training method to be specific to their needs.

p220 Activity

1 Intrinsic motivation is when a sports performer takes part in sports and activities because they want to.

Extrinsic motivation comes from external rewards, such as prize money, a trophy, status or celebrity status.

2

Reason for participating in sports activities	Intrinsic or extrinsic motivation
Takes part in cricket because they love the sport	Intrinsic
They train to improve their skills so they can be the best 100 m sprinter in their club	Extrinsic
They enjoy being part of a team, working together with others and winning as a team	Intrinsic
They want to win the prize money	Extrinsic

p221 Check my learning

1 Enjoyment, improved performance and meeting their fitness goals.

2 To increase a sports performer's motivation and keep them interested in training and performing.

p223 Activity

Measurable – the fitness tests can be repeated once a month to check progress.

Achievable – she should aim to move her ratings for power and aerobic endurance in two months.

Realistic – the programme needs to be set at a level of intensity which is appropriate.

Time related – there should be short, medium and long-term goals.

Exciting – the programme can include activities and training methods which she prefers and enjoys, she can work with a partner and the rugby team.

Recorded – she can use a log or diary to record her progress.

p223 Check my learning

1 Motivation is the reason for behaving in a certain way.

2 SMARTER goals can be used to help design a training programme to be specific for an individual performer. They can make the programme interesting, relevant and something the performer will want to complete.

3 SMARTER goals can help maintain motivation because they are achievable, the performer will want to complete the programme and meet the goals. Motivation can be kept high by having activities which the performer enjoys completing.

Index